ROME

FROM

THE

GROUND

UP

ROME
FROM
THE
GROUND
UP

JAMES H. S. McGREGOR

THE BELKNAP PRESS OF

HARVARD UNIVERSITY PRESS

Cambridge, Massachusetts

London, England

Library of Congress Cataloging-in-Publication Data

McGregor, James H. (James Harvey), 1946–

Rome from the ground up / James H. S. McGregor

   p. cm.

Includes bibliographical references and index.

ISBN-13: 978-0-674-02263-8 (alk. paper)

ISBN-10: 0-674-02263-7 (alk. paper)

1. Rome (Italy)—Description and travel.

2. Rome (Italy)—History.

3. City planning—Italy—Rome—History.

I. Title.

DG806.2.M4   2005

711'4'094563—dc22   2005048213

For Sallie, Ned, and Raphael

CONTENTS

ROME

FROM

THE

GROUND

UP

INTRODUCTION

Rome has been designed and redesigned many times, but it is not a planned city. Unlike Haussmann's Paris, Rome has never been subdued to a single overarching vision or plan of organization. This is not to say that Rome is "decentered," as postmodern theory would suggest. Rome is an agglomeration of historical cities, each with its own powerful focus, which have shared a common territory and now are merged into a single capital. This book explores these many contiguous Romes that have succeeded one another in the Tiber floodplain. Each of its chapters describes the changing engines that have powered the city's growth in successive periods and provided it with distinct centers and novel topographies.

Freud, the inventor of psychology, and the great German writer Goethe both saw Rome as a palimpsest—a manuscript page that had been erased and written over many times. Archaeologists have turned that metaphor into a methodology, with remarkable results. Anyone who looks at modern Rome, which now spreads far beyond the limits of the ancient walls, would probably take that metaphor as a reliable guide to the city's complex past. Despite its widespread appeal, though, the palimpsest metaphor is a key of limited usefulness in this place. Unlike Babylon or Troy—at least Troy as Schliemann pictured it—Rome is not a series of concentric cities piled one on top of another. It is instead a series of generally small cities that grew up here and there along the Tiber at various times to suit various purposes. In some parts of the vast territory embraced by modern Rome, these cities have overlapped repeatedly. In other areas, significant development has been largely confined to a single era. As a consequence, some parts of Rome are complexly overlapping—as the palimpsest metaphor suggests—but many are not. Rather than sorting through the city layer by layer, vertically, this book explores an ideal journey through times and places that for the most part lie side by side. That ideal journey is at the same time an itinerary through the present-day city of Rome.

This organizational concept makes *Rome from the Ground Up* different from most histories. This difference is especially marked and especially important in the book's presentation of the modern city. In describing the present, the palimpsest metaphor is at its most misleading. What archaeology values is necessarily *underneath* the modern city, which may appear to veil or hide the "authentic," the "essential," the "historical" Rome. In its most influential and destructive epoch—the Fascist era— Roman archaeology actualized the palimpsest metaphor through the brutal razing of neighborhoods near the Forum and the Capitoline hill and forced the displacement of thousands of people. Mussolini was very clear that the monumental past must be framed by "a tranquil zone of silence" that was to be carved out of what he could see only as the vulgar fabric of the modern workaday town. In discarding the metaphor of the palimpsest, this book, like contemporary Roman archaeology, reconnects the modern city with its ancient counterparts.

Ideas and ideologies come and go, and both the city and its past change to reflect them. The key to the various Romes that have succeeded, continue to succeed, and will succeed one another is their particular sources and centers of power. Power in Rome has always included the ability to shape the city, or at the very least to direct the city's attention toward one or another key site. The ideal center of the earliest city was the Tiber Island, a ford in the river and the intersection of two major trade paths. Power in Republican Rome centered on the Senate house at the end of the Forum nearest the Capitoline hill. The Empire drew power away from that center, at first toward the opposite end of the Forum, once associated with Rome's kings, and then to the Palatine hill. The power center of Rome in the seventh century shifted to the papal palace at the Lateran. When the popes returned from Avignon in the mid-fifteenth century, they chose St. Peter's as their stronghold. One hundred and fifty years later they abandoned the Vatican for a palace on the Quirinal hill. When national troops entered the city in 1870, Pope Pius IX lost the Quirinal Palace and reestablished his court at the Vatican. Since that time, spiritual power has been rooted in the Vatican, while secular power holds the Quirinal, a division that makes the modern city bipolar.

All of those centers in one form or another exist today in the modern city. The successive Romes that responded to the magnetic pull of each of these ideological poles are still there side by side, complexly interlaced and overlaid at their boundaries but largely distinct in the zones nearest their centers. Though this book is historical and discusses the city in chronological sequence, it presents that history concretely through descriptions of monuments that still exist today. In each chapter these monuments are described, for the most part, in the order that readers would encounter them as they walked through the city.

While the book is concerned with architecture and planning, it also looks at the city's history in more intimate terms. As a long-term project, Rome has offered great scope to the imagination, and many creative and talented people have had a hand in shaping the city. Some have created streets and plazas, vast public buildings and great monuments. Others have created beautiful and inspiring works on a smaller scale—the Roman Curia, the Pantheon, and Michelangelo's Sistine ceiling. These works prompt not only admiration but also curiosity about the ideals that they, like the city itself, expressed for their sponsors and creators.

Chapter One

TIBER ISLAND AND
THE ANCIENT PORT

A southwest wind blew out of Africa. Behind it, at a slower pace, came Africa itself. The breeze cooled as it crossed the ancestral Mediterranean and picked up moisture. Slipping over the Apennines, which the African plate in its slow northeastward drift was heaving up, the clouds opened. Heavy rain drenched the bare slopes, eroding and channeling, crafting a system of west-flowing streams. Not far from the base of these raw mountains, some forty miles inland from the present coast of Italy, these new rivers—the Tiber among them—after a steep flight down mountain rock, flowed into a shallow bay of their natal sea.

About two million years ago the steady thrust from Africa cracked the sea floor beneath these shallow bays to open long parallel gashes. Molten rock from deep within the earth channeled to the surface through these fissures, and a string of volcanoes was born. The first erupted in Tuscany; then in a general southeastward trend, they burst from the ocean floor in a loose chain of conical mounds. The impulse went through the territory that would become Latium—the province of Rome—then angled in historic time toward Naples and Sicily. Vesuvius and Mount Etna are its latest offspring.

Spewing out lava, ashy dust, and rock, the volcanoes raised themselves above the water. Outflow measured in cubic miles gradually filled in the shallow coastal bays and made them plains of rock. The sea where the river once ended was driven south and west, and the Tiber followed. Charged with fresh waters from the volcanic slopes, it carved a new course through solidified ash and lava. For the most part it was an easy job. Water was abundant, and the newly minted rock proved soft and soluble. Working its way across the gently sloping plain in wide loops and meanders, the river carved a deep and spacious bed for itself. In time, the flat volcanic plain became a deeply etched, eroded canyon land. (1)

At a spot now some thirteen miles from the sea, the river came upon

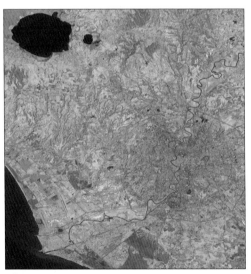

1

a hard tongue of rock it could not scrape or melt away. At what would become Rome, the Tiber split, leaving a rocky island in midstream while it coursed through shallow rapids on either side. A little south of this island a marshy side canyon opened to the east. The Romans named it the Velabrum. Another canyon intersected further downstream, striking a north-south line.

Having left behind this one irreducible island, the Tiber continued on its way toward the sea, fully mature, broad, deep, and impassable. Nearing the coast, it slowed, spawning dense mosquito-breeding marshlands that stretched for miles in every direction. For settlers who began moving into the region in large numbers some 3,500 years ago, the deep river and the hostile marshes along its edge formed a potent natural barrier. On its eastern margin

Latin civilization took root. Latin
towns dotted the Alban hills, the
long-stilled volcanic cluster that
had given birth to the region.
Latin settlers occupied Rome as a
frontier outpost sometime in the
eighth or ninth century BC.

2

   Across the Tiber from this Latin
bridgehead, people known as
Etruscans inhabited a wide swath
of central Italy that extended from the sea inland to the Apennines and
as far north as the Arno River, which flows through present-day Florence.
The Etruscans, who gave their name to Tuscany, were more numerous,
wealthier, and more powerful than the Latins. They were also more cosmo-
politan, trading goods, techniques, and ideas with Greek colonists who
had settled in Sicily and southern Italy.

   The main point of contact between the Etruscans and the Latins was
the first place up the Tiber from the Mediterranean where the river could
be forded. The shallow rapids flanking Tiber Island made a rough but
manageable passage for men and animals in all but the highest water. All
contact and all commerce between the principal civilizations of central
Italy funneled through this ford. The great peninsular footpath that linked
the peoples of northern Italy with those in the south also crossed the
Tiber here. And just here it intersected a path from the coast which took
its name—Salaria—from the sea salt traded inland. Around this shallow
ford and the wooden bridges that soon replaced it, the city of Rome
found its source of life and wealth. (2)

"So much then, for the blessings with which nature supplies the city; but the Romans have added still others, which are the result of their good judgment. If the Greeks are to be honored for their achievements as builders of cities that are renowned for their wealth, beauty, security, and good harbors, the Romans must be counted superior in matters to which the Greeks gave little thought: the construction of roads, aqueducts, and sewers that wash out the filth of the city. They have so constructed the roads that run throughout their country by cutting through hills and building up valleys, that their wagons can carry boatloads of goods. Water comes to the city in such quantities that veritable rivers flow through the city and the sewers; almost every house has cisterns and water pipes and abundant fountains. The sewers themselves, vaulted with close-fitting stones, have room in some places for wagons piled with hay to pass through them" (Strabo, *Geography* 5.3.8).

Standing today at the river's edge, you would never imagine yourself to be in the bottom of a wide canyon at its point of intersection with narrower side canyons. You seem to be standing on level ground and looking up at modest hills that rise above the wide river plain. All the same, the celebrated Seven Hills of Rome are really the uneroded remnants of a volcanic plain seen from the prospect of the river that dissected it. A matter of perspective, but since the river and this island within it are the city's nucleus and its most ancient rationale for being, it is wise to adopt the river's point of view.

Empathy with the Tiber in other matters is more difficult. Like all too many urban rivers, it lies far below street level in a deep and narrow chasm, visible from above but almost out of reach. Steps lead down to

3

broad pathways at the river's edge, but until recently almost no one strolled along them, even on those rare occasions when they had been cleaned of silt and weeds. (3) In an effort to draw Romans back to their river, the city has attempted to spruce up the sidewalks, adding artwork and even an artificial beach near the Vatican. Sightseeing boats, loaded with tourists, now travel through the center of the Eternal City.

This radical containment of the Tiber is tribute of a sort, a measure of the river's power and a veiled testimony to its role in carving the ground on which the city stands. Most of Rome still lies in the Tiber's natural floodplain. Throughout the city's long life, the unrestrained river repeatedly submerged it. Plaques on the façade of the church of Santa Maria sopra Minerva and in other places around the city record the high-water marks of past floods. More than 130 major floods have been recorded in the city's 2,700-year history. In 1870, the year Italy became a nation with Rome as its capital, an especially devastating flood led to a long-range plan, which was completed in 1900. Today, the river that shaped Rome and gave it life is contained behind barriers bigger than those the ancient Romans built to keep the barbarians out. Romans call these Tiber embankments I Muraglioni, The Great Walls. The river was channeled and contained within these steep confines. Levees were built along both banks, some as high as twenty feet above street level. River life ended, and a Berlin Wall divided ancient neighborhoods. Tree-lined avenues were designed at the levee tops, but they were too remote from the river to serve as the greenways their designers imagined. Now these wide roads are mobbed with traffic that further isolates the river.

The one spot in Rome where people and the river still seem to be on friendly terms is Tiber Island. The river is at its widest there, and its confining walls are far apart. The point of the island that breaks the current has been streamlined and merges with the piers of the modern Ponte Garibaldi, but the downstream end is welcoming. The pavement at the river's downstream edge has grown to the scale of an urban beach. There are even a few straggling plane trees. People sun themselves here; they walk along or sit and listen to the river. It is the one spot in Rome—a city of fountains—where the sound of rushing water completely drowns out the noise of traffic.

Ochre-painted walls and oddments of brick and stonework support the buildings above; a solitary square tower guards them. Moated by the river, the densely built-up island has the look of a romantic medieval town. Of the island's substance—the stolid lava core with its sand and silt accretions—nothing at all can be seen. Both the medieval walls and modern flood control cover the island like a synthetic crown over an ancient tooth. The most prominent surviving features of the island the Romans knew are the two ancient bridges that connect it to the mainland, a third ruined bridge below, and a sculpted ship's stern at its downstream end.

The Pons Fabricius, one of Rome's most celebrated and picturesque

bridges, carries on the work of
the prehistoric river ford as it
links the island to the Latin
shore. (4) Built in 59 BC as part
of a general restoration of Tiber
Island, the bridge is Roman in
every way. The stone from
which it was built was created
by the same volcanic eruptions

4

that laid the groundwork of the city itself. The bridge's structure embodies the most characteristic Roman architectural technique, the keystone
arch. Despite surface differences, the companion Pons Cestius, which
links the island to Trastevere, shares these characteristics. Though one is
faced with brick and the other with a marble-like stone called travertine,
the muscle and bone of the two are the same. On the underside of either
bridge the vaults, which are made of large, close-fitting blocks of a gray
volcanic stone called peperino, are identical. Travertine blocks carefully
tied into the stonework of the central span rim and reinforce each vault.

The volcanic eruptions that put the ground under Rome's feet made
the Roman countryside a supply yard of building materials. For much of
the city's history it has subsisted entirely on this domestic store. The earliest Roman buildings were made with materials quarried inside the city
itself, and much of the soft rock beneath Rome is warrened with caves,
pits, and tunnels. As the political and military power of the city expanded,
higher-quality building materials from an ever-widening area were substituted. The peperino in these bridges, the product of a late volcanic erup-

tion, was quarried in the Alban hills. The marble-like travertine, formed by mineral-rich secretions from volcanic hot springs, came from Tivoli, where it is still quarried today. Both stones are easily worked, strong, and durable. Travertine stands up especially well under compression, and it is often used at points of stress where load-bearing is essential. As Rome's power expanded, the city gained access to building materials from the whole Mediterranean basin. In its most powerful periods, exotic imports like marble, granite, and porphyry supplanted the local stone.

Like all Roman monuments, these bridges embodied the three characteristics that the Roman architect and theoretician Vitruvius, in *De Architectura,* identified as essentials of Roman building. All structures, he declared, both private and public, built simply for pleasure or dedicated either to the common welfare or the cult of the gods, needed to manifest firmitas (stability and endurance), utilitas (usefulness), and venustas (beauty of materials and proportion). The bridges show how much Roman engineers knew about firmitas in the face of the river's power. The central support is pointed on its up-river side into a chisel-like cutwater that breaks the force of the current and shears off floating objects. The gentler curve of the downstream edge counteracts undercutting by backward swirling eddies. The arched opening in the central support of Pons Fabricius reduces the lateral thrust of floodwaters. It is the arches of the bridges, though, which are their most impressive and most characteristic feature. Though the stones forming them are not cemented together (their surfaces have been pointed up with mortar in modern times), each semicircular arch spans nearly seventy-five feet. This wide span lifts the roadway well above flood level and reduces the number of piers in the water. Temples and monuments might be more eye-catching, but they lack the harmony and balanced tension of these bridges.

Architectural historians are uncertain whether the Romans invented the arch on which these bridges, like so many Roman structures, are based. It may be that they learned to build and use it from the Etruscans. Roman mastery of its principles and devotion to its use are undisputed. As gravity pulls down, the flared upper end of each wedge-shaped block in the arch squeezes the stones to either side. This redirected force travels sideways along the curve of the arch and into the supporting piers. The central keystone works in the same way as all the other stones in the arch.

The island "between the bridges," as an ancient Roman map described it, has a curious history of its own. In the third century BC a new myth transformed the ancient crossroads. The story of how the healing god Aesculapius came to Italy and chose Tiber Island for his sanctuary was a favorite one, and it was repeated many times. This is a short version of the story as an unknown Roman writer told it: "Once when Rome was stricken with a plague, the Romans, following the advice of an oracle, sent ten men headed by Quintus Ogulnius to the shrine of the healing god Aesculapius in Epidauros. While the men stood admiring the enormous statue of the god there, a serpent more awe-inspiring than horrible glided from its lair in the temple. To the wonder of all, it passed through the center of town and directly onto the Roman ship, where it settled in the cabin of Ogulnius himself. Bearing the god, the legates sailed to Antium where their ship was becalmed. The serpent left the ship there and entered a nearby temple of Aesculapius, but after a few days it returned. While the ship was working its way upstream against the current of the Tiber, the serpent again left it and swam to the nearby island where a temple was consecrated to him; after that the plague abated in a miraculously short time" (*De viris illustribus* 22.1, cited in *Breviarium*, p 563).

This myth transformed Tiber Island in the popular mind from an ancient river crossing into a sacred ship grounded in midstream. In time, Roman architects and engineers brought that vision to life, and faint marks of the island's transformation can still be seen. On its downstream end above the wide modern walkways are remains of the sculpted stern of a Roman warship—a trireme of the type that brought the god to the city. The ship's stern is decorated with a now-faceless bust of the god and the mythical serpent, which curls around his staff. Ancient sources refer to more stonework around the island, and it may be that the upstream end of the island was fitted with a travertine ship's prow. Some scholars believe that the entire island may have been reshaped by Roman engineers into a representation of the mythical ship of the god of healing. Renaissance reconstructions of the city often show it that way. But whatever the extent of this ancient project may originally have been, time and the river have reduced it to one small fragment of ship-shaped rock.

The Temple of Aesculapius was long ago absorbed into the fabric of the church of San Bartolomeo. Nothing remains except the sacred well of the god, which breaks through the steps leading to the central altar. The less tangible but more remarkable recollection of the healing god is the Hospital of the Fatebenefratelli, founded in 1548 on the site of earlier medieval hospices that carried on the healing work of the classical centers. The tradition of Aesculapius continues in this working hospital, which has made a specialty of the treatment of AIDS.

The fragmentary bridge below the Tiber Island is similar in structure to those that moor the island to the mainland. Though its façade is newer, the bridge itself is older than the island bridges. Its ruined state shows that the Tiber at its worst was more than a match for even Roman engineers. The Romans called this bridge the Pons Aemilius in honor of Scipio Africanus in whose consulship (142 BC) it was transformed from a wooden bridge on stone piers into one made entirely of stone. This re-

modeling, which used the same techniques as those employed in the Tiber Island bridges some eighty years later, lasted only into the third century AD. Repairs carried out at that time lasted about a thousand years, but the bridge was again severely damaged by flood-waters in the thirteenth cen-tury. It was evident by the

5

fifteenth century that major repairs would be required to save it. Papal architects, including Michelangelo, were drawn to the project, but they could do nothing to prevent disaster. About 3:00 p.m. on Christmas Eve, 1598, during the worst flood in the city's history, the bridge collapsed, never to be repaired. Since then it has been known as the Ponte Rotto, the broken bridge. (5)

Framed by a modern arch in the Tiber embankment just below the

6

Ponte Rotto and the modern Palatine Bridge is the opening of one of Rome's most famous ancient monuments, the Cloaca Maxima. (6) Dwarfed by its modern frame, only the top of its triple arch of volcanic stone is visible—that and the surprisingly clear stream of water it discharges into the river. The great sewer of the Romans was originally a stonewalled channel some five feet wide—a Tiber embankment in miniature—designed to catch runoff from the hills and drain the low-lying marshlands of the Forum and the Velabrum. The ditch was later vaulted and buried underground; eventually sewage from public latrines in these areas was channeled into it, to the great detriment of the river.

The Roman natural historian Pliny, who found the Egyptian pyramids extravagant and pointless, was very proud of Rome's useful and efficient public works. Though built in the reign of one of Rome's Etruscan kings, the system still ranked as a singular Roman achievement. Pliny called the Cloaca Maxima "the most praiseworthy work of all" and boasted that "it made Rome a city suspended in air that men could travel underneath in boats. Seven rivers flow through it united in a single channel. Their swift current like a mountain stream sweeps away everything in its path. Swollen by rains, they batter their channel; sometimes the River in flood backs up and the two currents collide, but still the structure holds. Immense building blocks are washed through the streets, but the sewer stands. Buildings above fall to the ground spontaneously or brought down by fire; tremors shake the earth, but the sewer that has lasted now some seven hundred years since the time of Tarquinius Priscus seems virtually indestructible" (Pliny, *Naturalis historia* 36.106).

Along the left bank of the river downstream from the Ponte Rotto, from prehistoric times until the nineteenth century, stood the port of Rome. At first it was just a river port serving the hundred navigable miles of the Tiber and linking the water trade with the land routes that crossed the river. As Rome's influence expanded in the imperial period, ships from every Mediterranean port docked here; a rare few sailed in from beyond the Pillars of Hercules, from western Gaul or Britain. At the edge of the river, the Romans built embankments with stairways and ramps down to the water. Ships, which had been towed up the Tiber against the current, were moored to great iron rings, some supported by lion-head bosses. Beyond the docks were small private warehouses and huge imperial complexes where goods were sorted and stored. All the riverside remains of the Roman port were obliterated by the Tiber embankments, but the area inland preserves substantial traces of the commercial life of the port, the great roads, and the foreign communities that settled nearby.

The neighborhood of the port was confined to the narrow low floodplain between the Tiber banks and the steeply rising flanks of the Capitoline, Palatine, and Aventine hills. In this small area, the dominant features were two great open marketplaces, one for cattle and the other for produce. Private houses and public buildings of all sorts surrounded these squares, serving and staffing the markets and also drawing support from them. Through a combination of forces that have themselves been part of the life processes of Rome, a handful of these buildings have survived. The most significant of these survivors preserve the architectural taste and scale of the Roman Republican era (509–44 BC). In much later eras, themselves widely separated in time, the preservation of these monuments reflects entirely different processes. After a series of barbarian invasions and the fall of the Roman Empire in the sixth century, both the poverty and the conservatism of Roman Christianity led to the reuse of abandoned structures. In the early twentieth century, the prevailing style of archaeological preservation, coupled with Mussolini's desire to create a monumental center in Rome, forced a new style of preservation.

The Forum Holitorium, the produce market of ancient Rome, stood between the warehouses of the port and the base of the Capitoline hill. Produce was sold in bulk in the market and retailed throughout Rome. The Forum Holitorium today is nothing but a treacherous intersection in one of Rome's busiest streets. Its travertine pavement, brought to light in excavations of the last century, has been reburied. Somewhere under the street, too, stand the remains of a monument called the Columna Lactaria—the milky column. Romans left unwanted infants at its base to die or be adopted or enslaved. A short distance away, where the traffic-choked Via Petroselli meets the equally congested Via della Greca, is an open area that has been known for centuries as Piazza Bocca della Verità. In ancient Rome, this same area was known as the Forum Boarium, or cattle market.

The word forum, common to these market squares and to the government center of the Romans on the other side of the Palatine hill, means an open area, a simple square or piazza. Originally these markets, like the Roman Forum itself, were wide spots on the great road where busi-

ness—both public and commercial—went on. Until the beginning of the
third century BC the lumping together of commercial and government
business was fixed by law. Markets were held every eight days, and on
market day those Roman citizens who lived on farms outside the walls
would come into town both to trade and to handle city business. By
requiring that government issues be decided on non-market days, the Lex
Hortensia (297 BC) separated the two activities legally. In time, physical
separation followed. Commercial activity concentrated along the river,
while governmental activity took place inland. Eventually both the commercial and governmental fora were transformed from vacant lots without
pretensions and ready for any kind of business into monumental architectural complexes.

The cattle market was served by the converging roads and the port.
Live cattle brought downriver by barge or driven along the road were mar-
keted here, then driven off to be butchered in other parts of the city. Salt
useful for the preservation of meat and hides came upriver from the
coast. The god Hercules, borrowed from the Greek settlers of southern
Italy, perhaps in imitation of the Etruscans, became a divine model for
the activities of the market. "After killing Geryon, Hercules drove his cattle, which were of extraordinary beauty, to this area. Near the Tiber, which
he had forded while driving the herd ahead of him, he paused to rest and
eat while his cattle grazed on the thick grass in a quiet meadow. When
he fell asleep, a man-eating monster of that region by the name of Cacus
was overcome by the beauty of the cattle and decided to steal them.
Hercules soon tracked the thief and killed him, winning back his cattle
and liberating the region from a savage predator. In thanks an altar was

7

built and dedicated in his name" (Livy, *Ab urbe condita* 1.7, 3–4).

Like the Aesculapius myth attached to Tiber Island, this story records the importation of a foreign god onto Roman soil. The Aesculapius myth reshaped the island and gave it a new place in the Roman mind, but this story of Hercules celebrated the Tiber crossing and the cattle market for what it was. The divine legend promoted the mundane activities of trade and travel to the mythic level.

Of the many buildings which grew up around the Forum Boarium, only a few have survived. In the church of Santa Maria in Cosmedin, however, bits and pieces of adjacent structures—some in ruins—were grouped under a single roof. (7) The crypt of the church was dug into a mass of square-cut blocks of volcanic tufa, remains of the Ara Maxima, or Great Altar, of Hercules, a site so ancient it preceded the founding of the city of Rome. The core of the church, the area immediately inside its porch, was made by filling in the open arcades of a Roman building that may originally have been a statio annonae where grain was distributed to the poor. While some prominent archaeologists dispute this suggestion, it would make sense for this office to be located close to the port where grain ships unloaded. It would also fit with the early history of the church itself.

Santa Maria in Cosmedin, like other churches in this area, was a diaconia rather than a place of worship. A diaconia, from which the church office of deacon takes its name, is a building for storing and distributing grain to the needy. When the Roman bureaucracy that fed the poor ceased to function, a papal bureaucracy grew in its place. Historically, the diaconia took over from the statio annonae, as it may have done physically in this building.

The church porch shelters a curious monument that is often reproduced in earrings and pendants. Called the Bocca della Verità, it has given its name to the square and the region of town itself. A marble disk some five feet in diameter with the mask of a streaming haired river god at its center, it probably served as a Roman sewer lid; it may once have covered a drain that fed into the Cloaca Maxima. The Italian name means "mouth of truth," and legend has it that if you tell a lie with your hand in the god's open mouth, his jaws will snap it off.

On the side of the Piazza Bocca della Verità away from the river, near the start of the Via del Velabro, stand two more monuments closely associated with the Forum Boarium. The Arch of Janus is a marble-faced double archway with prominent niches in its outside walls intended to hold sculptures of some sort. It was probably built to commemorate a triumphant general, but traders in the Forum Boarium almost certainly used it for shelter and as an informal place of business.

A flight of steps to the left leads via a short street to a diminutive arch just beyond. Called the Arcus Argentarius, this small structure was a gateway to the open marketplace. The inscription says that it was built in 204 AD by the "cattle merchants and bankers of this place" and dedicated to the reigning emperor Septimius Severus, his wife, Julia Domna, and his son, the future emperor Caracalla. Soon after the arch was dedicated, the inscription had to be rewritten to keep pace with a rapid swerve in imperial political correctness—an expense the sponsors of the arch would have been wise to anticipate. The name of a second son, Geta, was erased from the stone when Caracalla murdered him. The name of Caracalla's father-in-law was removed when he was liquidated; after the murder of his daughter, her face was chiseled away. Scenes inside the little arch show Caracalla piously performing sacrifice.

The arch adjoins an ancient church with a vexed history called San Giorgio in Velabro. Like Santa Maria in Cosmedin, the church was originally a diaconia where grain off-loaded from ships on the Tiber was stored and distributed to the poor. And like many Roman churches in the archaeological zone, and many center-city churches in the United States, San Giorgio has lost its congregation. It survives as one of Rome's most popular "wedding churches" and is usually dressed in white. The price of this sentimental popularity was paid when the Mafia, trying to pressure the government, bombed the church in 1993. The merchants of the old Forum Boarium probably knew what political risks they were running when they dedicated their little monument to the imperial family. In contemporary Italian politics, where celebrity itself can be a political force, a prominent church can become the target of programmed violence.

Restored again since the bombing, the church had already suffered a radical form of renovation early in the twentieth century that the Italians called repristinization. Its purpose was to return a historical structure to its original or pristine condition by stripping away everything that had been added to it in the centuries after its completion. Restoration of this kind turned buildings rich in accumulated history into austere shells more faithful to twentieth-century tastes than to those of their creators. The brutal process was carried on wholesale in this region of the city. A crowded working-class neighborhood a century ago, its buildings were seized by the Fascist government. In a pattern repeated through much of central Rome, the population was dispersed, with many people forced to live in shantytowns at the city's edge. Their houses were torn down and their churches were desanctified, all in an effort to uncover the Roman past.

8

In an address to Rome's governor in 1925, Mussolini laid out his ideal of archaeological recovery: "In five years time," Il Duce decreed, "Rome must astonish the peoples of the world: it must appear vast, orderly, and powerful as it was in the days of Augustus . . . All that has weighed her down in the centuries of decadence must disappear. You must also liberate the majestic temples of Christian Rome from the parasitic and profane structures that cluster around them. The monuments of our two-thousand-year history must loom up like giants out of an ample void" (*Archeologia e citta* 38).

The best preserved and most precious remnant of the complex life of Rome's port is the square Temple of Portunus (widely though incorrectly identified as the Temple of Fortuna Virilis). Portunus, as the name suggests, was the god of ports, and his temple was suitably located between the port and the marketplaces inshore. It is a small and delicate temple set close to the ground and modestly proportioned. (8) The style is Greek;

and with a few changes the temple could be converted to a house in the Greek Revival style of nineteenth-century America. Like the nearby bridges, the temple, which dates in its present form from sometime in the first century BC, was built of native materials. The walls of the sanctuary (or cella) and the half-columns set into it are volcanic tufa from a quarry on the Anio River. The freestanding columns are travertine. A layer

9

of ornamental plaster once covered the stone; traces of it are still visible on the frieze below the temple's roofline. (9)

The round temple slightly to the south was dedicated to Hercules the Victor, as are several other monuments in this area. It was built sometime in the second century BC and paid for by one Marcus Octavius Herrenus, an oil merchant whose business centered around the port. Above a stepped circular platform of volcanic tufa stands a cylindrical cella surrounded by twenty marble columns, all but one of them intact. The interior is paneled with travertine. The original dome of this remarkable building fell down long ago and was replaced with an incongruous tile roof in the shape of a Chinese rain hat. (10)

The church of San Nicola in Carcere was built into the ruins of three Roman temples. Both inside the church and on the outside walls, substantial remains of these older structures can be seen. As the city's population shrank and its ancient deities were outlawed, the Christian Church

took over abandoned buildings and
reused them. Most of the surviving
Roman structures in this area owe
their preservation to such imaginative
recycling, followed by repristinization
in the twentieth century. The temples
were rectangular gabled buildings on
low platforms with a short flight of
stairs leading up to them. Greek in

10

style and built of volcanic materials, they resembled the Temple of Portunus. The major difference, and the reason why parts of three temples
came to be included in one church, is that each of these three temples
had a small cella flanked by a freestanding colonnade. The church

builders knocked down the cella of
the central temple, because the sanctuary was too small to serve Christian
worship. They then reached beyond to
include the near colonnades of the
temples to either side. Filled in with
rubble, these colonnades formed the
side walls of the new church. The
incorporated columns and the fill
between them are now exposed on the
outer side walls of the church. (11)

While there is general agreement
about the gods to whom the temples

11

were dedicated—Janus, Spes, and Juno Sospita—it remains unclear
which god was worshipped in which temple. Janus, the god of entries
and beginnings, was a deity of the port. Spes, or Hope, was a god that
travelers, sailors, and merchants often invoked. Only Juno, wife of the
chief god, Jupiter, seems out of place here.

Across the street from the three temples and against the base of the
Capitoline hill are the few remaining arches of a portico that once
extended through the region. One section of the double arcade is built of
peperino, the adjacent one of travertine. Porticos, which sheltered pedestrians from traffic and weather, were another adaptation of the Roman
arch. The arches in each section, or bay, gave access to the street. They
also distributed the weight of a vaulted roof—an elongated version of the
vault that supports the Tiber bridges—onto the supporting pillars. The
attached columns strengthened the pillars but were mostly ornamental.
They helped create a stylistic harmony between the many Greek-style
colonnaded buildings in the area and the arched structures that did not
require columns for support.

This portico may have been part of a long arcaded shelter that lined
the Via Triumphalis, the route followed by honored generals, their armies, and the captured spoils of war. (The triumph, which the Romans
regarded as so characteristic of their culture, may originally have been
an Etruscan ritual.) When the portico was not serving its ceremonial purpose, it must have been a useful adjunct to the market. A retreat in bad
weather—the market square itself was open to the sky—it may also
have served as the unofficial address of particular merchants and
traders.

In broader terms, the portico was a piecemeal attempt not only to ornament but to organize and open up this crowded workaday neighborhood. The Via Triumphalis served symbolic needs, but it also speeded the flow of traffic and gave the sprawling web of streets in this densely settled area a defining axis. By the Late Republic, Rome's long-term and completely unplanned growth had made the city a spider web of twisting alleys crammed with shops and high-rise tenements. The difficulty of finding one's way around was something characters in Roman plays could joke about.

> *Syrus:* Do you know the portico down there near the market?
>
> *Demea:* Sure I do.
>
> *Syrus:* Go up the street past it. When the road turns uphill go right down it. Keep going straight until you see a shrine with an alley just beyond it.
>
> *Demea:* Which one?
>
> *Syrus:* The one with the big fig tree.
>
> *Demea:* I know that one.
>
> *Syrus:* Go on through there.
>
> *Demea:* That alley's a dead end.
>
> *Syrus:* You're right. My mistake. Go back to the portico . . . Do you know that rich guy Cratinus' house? Go past it, turn left, then straight up the street to the temple of Diana; turn right there and just before you come to the city gate there's a flour mill with a pond; across from it there's a workshop. That's the place (Terence, *Adelphi* 573–584).

Across the Vico Jugario is the Area Sacra di San Omobono, a site of great interest to archaeologists but one that is very difficult for nonprofes-

12

sionals to understand. Some of the excitement stems from the traces uncovered here of very early occupation of the area. Otherwise, the focus of the excavation is two temples founded in the sixth century BC and rebuilt many times afterward. The temples are dedicated to the goddess Fortuna and the Mater Matuta. Fortuna, the goddess of luck, was a favorite deity of people in risky businesses like transport and trade. Roman historical sources connected the temple with the Etruscan king Servius Tullius, who invoked the goddess's protection over the activities of the port. Mater Matuta was an ancient Italic goddess. Her cult, linked to that of Cybele and the Great Mother, may have attracted foreign worshippers from the port and the established émigré communities nearby.

The greatest monument bordering the Forum Holitorium was the Theater of Marcellus. Julius Caesar began it, and like most of his construction projects, it served a sly political purpose. It established the dictator's presence in a part of the city that had been dominated by the Circus Flaminius, an important meeting place of his opponents. Augustus, Caesar's nephew and heir, completed the theater and dedicated it in 13 BC to the memory of his own son-in-law, Marcellus, who had died a decade before.

Roman theaters were D-shaped. The stage stood at the flat end, and spectators—as many as 15,000—were packed on banked seats in wedge-shaped sections at the curved end. The outer wall of the curve was made up of three tiers of open arcades flanked by partially attached columns. The lowest tier was decorated with Doric columns, the middle tier with columns of the Ionic order, and the top, which has largely disappeared, with Corinthian columns. (12) The superposition of Greek orders on a Roman arcade undoubtedly strengthened its fabric, but the main effect was stylistic. It created a composite that retained the strength and flexibility of Roman architecture but spoke the international language of Greek style. This fusion remained a touchstone of Roman architecture through the Augustan period. Vitruvius canonized it in his *De Architectura*, and it remained vital into the Late Empire. Renaissance architects made it the basis of their revivalist style.

13

Theatrical masks decorated the keystones of the arches. The curved massive outer wall of the theater, which has recently been cleaned, is made of travertine, as are the arched tunnels leading to the seats, at least for the first ten feet or so where the heaviest load was concentrated; after that they are made of brick. The surviving section of the arched wall is beautifully proportioned; and despite its battle scars, the travertine has stood up well under two millennia of abuse. (13)

The Greeks invented theaters, and any comparison of the violent spectacles of the Roman theater with the masterpieces of Greek drama makes the Romans look crude and second-rate. Roman theater buildings like this one, however, are anything but crude. In structure the Theater of Marcellus takes a long step beyond the Greeks—a step that is particularly striking in comparison to the conservative Greek-revival temples in this part of the city. While the builders of the Temple of Portunus recreated Greek fashions in local materials, the builders of the Theater of Marcellus asserted their independence from Greek models. Like Greek theaters in general, the celebrated Theater of Dionysos in Athens was built into the side of the Acropolis. The stage is freestanding, but the sweeping tiers of seats are supported by the hill. The foundations of the Theater of Marcellus, by contrast, are rooted in the same tongue of volcanic rock that formed Tiber Island. Its curved travertine wall—an arch on its side—sustains the massive pull of the seats.

That freestanding wall, built of Roman materials, also incorporates and articulates the Roman arch. The penetrating archways that carry the weight of the building and give access to the seats are vaulted. Those archways are pictured in the open arcades of the façade, but even these representations are functional, lighting the interior, reducing the mass of the wall, and evenly distributing the weight of the building. The curved façade of the theater is similar in structure to the porticos that flanked the Forum Holitorium. Romans superimposed such arcades for workaday purposes like carrying aqueducts over rivers and deep valleys. The Theater of Marcellus uses the same practical form in a very dignified and beautiful way. The builders of the Colosseum a hundred years later were content to imitate it; the architects of the Renaissance regarded it as an ideal model of classical form.

The Theater of Marcellus survives because it was taken over by a powerful family in the Middle Ages. While the rounded wall has been restored, the front of the building, which houses the Orsini family, shows no trace of the original structure. Excavations at the foundations of the Theater of Marcellus also uncovered remains of the Temple of Apollo. Dedicated as early as the fifth century BC, this temple was rebuilt many times; the three standing columns and other remains now visible date from the Augustan period. While the building served religious purposes primarily, the Roman Senate sometimes met here and in the nearby Temple of Bellona, especially when a triumph was to be voted.

The Vicus Jugarius was the main Roman street between the river and the Roman Forum. It passed through the Velabrum, the once marshy canyon between the Capitoline and Palatine hills drained by the Cloaca Maxima. That Roman street paralleled an even earlier pathway that had avoided the marshy bottomland by climbing part way up the slopes of the Capitoline hill.

 # THE ROMAN FORUM

"Proca, king of the Latins, had two sons, Numitor and Amulius; at his death he passed on the crown to the older son, Numitor. Violence, however, overwhelmed the father's will and the morality of the era when Amulius deposed his brother Numitor and usurped his throne. The usurper compounded his crimes by killing his brother's sons and condemning Rhea Silvia, Numitor's daughter, to a life of perpetual chastity as a Vestal Virgin. While he pretended to honor her in this way, his real aim was to keep her from producing an heir. The founding of a City and empire whose greatness is second only to the divine must have been determined by fate, however, for Rhea Silvia gave birth to twins. She named the god Mars as the father of her sons, either because it was the truth or in an effort to excuse her crime. Still neither god nor man could shield her or her children from the cruelty of the usurper."

"The priestess was bound and imprisoned; Amulius ordered her sons to be drowned in the Tiber. By the will of some god the river had spread beyond its banks and flooded the marshes so that the men assigned to kill the twins were unable to reach its main channel. And so as if by decree of the deposed Numitor, these men placed the twins in a wooden trough and set them adrift in a pool where the Riminal fig tree—anciently called the fig tree of Romulus—still stands. They were confident that the floodwaters would soon carry the boys to the swollen river, but they were mistaken."

"The forum was an empty wilderness then. They say that when the pool where the boys were floating dried out and they rested on land again, a woodpecker brought them bits of food. A thirsty wolf coming down from the nearby mountains saw the boys and ran toward them. Later when a shepherd named Faustulus happened on them, the wolf was nursing the boys and gently licking them with her tongue" (Livy, *Ab urbe condita* 1.4, 1–7).

The shepherd adopted the boys, who were, of course, Romulus and Remus, and took them to live with him in his hut on the nearby Palatine hill. In time Romulus, repeating the violence of his grandfather's generation, killed his brother and founded the city of Rome; he assumed power as its first king. Other Latin kings succeeded him; then for two hundred years Etruscan kings ruled the city. For centuries a fig tree stood in the

 Roman Forum, as a remote descendant does today, recalling how nature—in the form of the river, the tree, the woodpecker, and the wolf—preserved the city's founder when his own family tried

to destroy him. So important was the task and so great the effort of founding this city "second only to the divine."

The Roman Forum begins in the shade of the fig tree. (14) Originally nothing more than a marshy meadow up a side canyon from the Tiber, the Forum grew so extravagantly during Rome's rise to power and was ruined so completely after the fall that its essential simplicity is hard to grasp. The petrified forest of columns towering above frenzied swarms of tourists makes it next to impossible to imagine that there is anything simple or natural about the place, or that its origins and the rationale for its development could possibly still be evident. Imagine this overgrown cemetery empty of men and monuments. Unleash the river, undam the springs, tear the covering earth from the Cloaca Maxima. The sound of rushing water replaces traffic noise; the ground turns green and spongy under foot. People come down from the hills and congregate near the fig tree; travelers pass through; there is conversation, buying and selling, arguments.

For a century or so after the date the Romans celebrated as the beginning of their city (April 21, 754/753 BC, by our reckoning), the scene around the tree stayed much the same. Sometime around 600 BC, things started to change. To overcome the marshiness of the soil, the Romans under their Etruscan kings channeled the springs at the base of the adjacent hills and dug a drainage ditch. At about the same time, the area around the fig tree was paved with stone to make an all-weather meeting place. That area has been repaved many times—now it is covered in travertine blocks—but it has always remained open to the sky. The Italians call this "the central area of the Forum," to distinguish it from the complex of monuments included in the "archaeological zone of the

Roman Forum" surrounding it. In the strictest sense, though, the open area *is* the Forum. Like the courthouse square in an American town, the empty space of the Forum could be put to almost any use. Day in and day out, trials were held and public business debated; politicians shouted speeches, candidates for public office—their togas whitened (candidatus) with chalk—schmoozed and pressed the flesh; mobs collected and dispersed. Before the Colosseum was built, gladiators fought in the Forum; freaks of nature were exhibited; festivals and banquets were held; public and private art was displayed.

It is typical of the Romans' respect for the important things of their past—a respect tinged with superstitious fear—that the open area around the fig tree was repeatedly repaved, but as long as the Roman Republic lasted it was never built over, though monuments were placed on its fringes and periodically removed. Even in the Empire, when the democratic ideal the Forum symbolized came under attack, the monumental development of the area was, with one great exception, generally cautious. When Julius Caesar was assassinated, his body was burnt on a pyre in the Forum. A temple was built on the spot and dedicated to the deified dictator, and for the first time in its long history the area of the Forum was abruptly reduced. Finally, after the capital of the Empire had moved to Byzantium and the political life of Rome had been destroyed, monuments like the upstart Column of Phocas (604 AD) were placed within the bounds of the Forum.

It was clear from the start that the Forum was not the perfect setting for everything that went on there. Wooden pedestals and benches were set up to create outdoor courtrooms. Overflow crowds sat on the steps of nearby temples. The climate posed a problem, and so did the increasing complexity and formalization of Roman government. When all decisions were made in public assemblies, the open space of the Forum was ideal. When power was distributed among the citizens at large, the Senate, and various government bureaucracies, it made more sense to create separate places for each to meet. Religion was also an essential part of civic life, and many buildings in the Forum area were dedicated to the cults of the state. Over the long course of Roman history things happened that seemed to demand some form of public commemoration, on every scale. All these forces combined to create the complex of monuments that pressed against the open field around the fig tree. Their purpose was always the same: to isolate some facet of civic life and to give it emphasis. Their cumulative effect, however, is bewildering. A clamor of structures compete for attention and overshadow the very area from which they all draw power and meaning.

Rome is rainy and cold in the winter—it snows every third or fourth year—and stifling in summer. Julius Caesar reputedly paid to have awnings put up over the Forum in the summer to make the heat more bearable. A more permanent response to the problem posed by the weather had already been created. Across the street from the Forum (directly to the right of the main entrance from the Via de' Fori Imperiali) stand the ruins of the Basilica Aemilia. It was the fourth such building in the area, but the earlier ones have disappeared without a trace. A distinctly Roman type of building, the vast basilica combined a large indoor meeting space (a forum with a roof) and outside porticoes (ready temporary shelter from rain and sun). Without its roof, the wide marble floor, spiked with stubs of columns, looks exactly like the Forum itself. The scant remains of its portico—little more than a double line of column bases—flanks the street.

Between the portico and the basilica stands a wall of rough-cut orange volcanic tufa with three large openings to let the crowd from the Forum into the building. Flanking these entrances and connecting the portico with the building are a series of small shops. These shallow rooms held the offices of moneychangers who made the Forum area the Wall Street of ancient Rome. While the association between government business and banking was unofficial, it was permanent and real, and the bankers were as much in demand as the lawyers who waited for business near the speaker's platform just down the street.

The Rostra, where speeches were made and lawyers clustered, was a raised platform decorated on its front with the bronze prows of captured warships. Posted on the narrow end of the Forum, this functional monument, which originated in the beginning years of the Roman Republic, was rebuilt and repositioned by Julius Caesar and extended by Augustus. A much-restored version stands in the same position today. Called the Rostra Veteres—the old rostra—to distinguish it from a newer platform on the opposite end of the Forum, it served a simple but important purpose: to elevate a speaker above the heads of the crowd so he could be seen and heard. It was the Forum's sound system, but it also summed up the political ideal of the Roman Republic: persuasion rather than force. So strong is the association between speech-making and this place that in English we use the word "rostrum" to mean a speaker's podium or platform, unaware that the Latin word refers to the ships' prows that decorated this monument rather than the platform itself.

An obscure but very significant monument once stood near the Rostra; nothing survives but its location. Called the Miliarium Aureum—the Golden Milepost—the monument, erected by Augustus, was the ideal beginning point of all Roman roads. Distances to the great cities of the Empire were measured from this point. Tiber Island was a real crossroads, and in the earliest period of the city's life the Forum was a wide spot in the road a little removed from that crossing. As Rome's symbolic power prevailed over her real economic power, Rome's center shifted both ideally and physically. At the end of the Republic, a conservative and wily politician, the emperor Augustus, paid homage to the traditional political center of Rome—the Senate end of the Forum near the base of the Capitoline hill. He marked this symbolic location as the place where all those roads that lead to Rome converge. At the same time, however, Augustus was carrying on a rival subversive policy that would lead in a few years to a displacement of the very center his monument celebrated.

To the right of the Rostra stands one of the best preserved monuments of the Forum, the Senate chamber or Curia Julia. (15) It should come as no surprise that Julius Caesar, who put his hand to that symbol of popular power, the Rostra, also exerted his might in both real and symbolic ways over the Senate. After a fire destroyed the old Senate chamber, Caesar took it upon himself to create a new Curia in a slightly different position, which was named in his honor. The surviving structure was rebuilt several times

15

during the Empire and transformed into a church in the seventh century; it is nevertheless faithful to Caesar's vision.

Visitors now cluster at the building's open door, as the sons of senators did in antiquity. A central aisle inside with its original mosaic floor intact separates three ranks of low platforms to either side. The senators sat on benches on these platforms, the most powerful men nearest the center. When the Senate was especially crowded, the newest members stood behind the last row on either side. The presiding officer sat directly ahead on a raised dais, with a statue of the goddess Victory on his left; the statue of an emperor now stands in its place. Niches for additional statues punctuate the walls, which were originally paneled with marble.

Light came from the high windows and from the front door, which was always left open during debate so that citizens and senators could keep an eye on each other. The building had a roof—the present one is a restoration—which made it more congenial than the weather-swept Forum, but it was unheated, and the windows were probably unglazed. Cicero describes a day so cold that the Senate was forced to adjourn; the tougher Forum crowd mocked the senators as they fled the frigid building.

Traditional Roman government was split between the mass of citizens—the plebeians—and the noble families or patricians. The plebeians met and deliberated in the Forum. The patricians' deliberative body was called the senatus not in reference to its patrician makeup but because of the older men—seniores—who were supposed to fill it. These men, some three hundred in number, met regularly in the Curia and temples around the city. Rome's dual assemblies served as the model for bicameral legislatures throughout the world. Most such systems, like that of the

United States, are calculated to maintain a balance of power between their distinct constituencies; but in Rome, the power and wealth of the patrician families far outweighed the political might of the plebs. In all but name, the Roman Republic was an oligarchy ruled by the strongest senators.

As the first century BC progressed, the boldest and most ambitious of these men realized that the enormous power wielded by the Senate could be seized. Several men made this attempt, with varying success, before Julius Caesar captured the full power of the Senate for himself. To put a stop to what seemed an attempt to reinstate the monarchy, Brutus, whose ancestor had expelled the last Etruscan king, assassinated Caesar. As everyone knows, of course, Caesar's assassins were pursued and defeated by Julius' adopted son, Octavian. Octavian formed a three-man government with Marc Antony and Lepidus, but then made war on his partners until only he (with his new name, Augustus) was left to rule. The Republic and its institutions—the Senate among them—persisted, but they were a powerless relic of the past in the Roman Empire that Augustus inaugurated.

Two marble reliefs on display in the Curia show the Roman emperor Trajan distributing grain to the poor and burning the records of debts. The real focus of interest, however, is the background of the two scenes, which shows important monuments of the Forum as they looked in the first century AD. Romulus' all-important fig tree anchors each scene. They also show the columned façades of two nearby temples (Temple of Saturn; Temple of Titus and Vespasian) and the arcaded openings of a basilica on the far side of the Forum (Basilica Julia). The opening of the

16

Vicus Tuscus, which led through the Velabrum to the port, comes next, then the new Rostra at the opposite end of the Forum with a temple (Castor and Pollux) and the Arch of Augustus in the background. (16)

A bureaucracy supported the activities of the Senate. Across an open courtyard from the Curia, where the modern Via della Curia now runs, was the Secretariat, long ago incorporated into the church of Santi Luca e Martina. Senate records along with those of the state were stored in a building called the Tabularium, which is still visible as the lowest story of the Palazzo Senatore on the Capitoline hill. The three open arches of the Tabularium (the rest are closed in) serve as backstop to the ruined temples that occupy the narrow end of the Forum complex. (17) Like the Theater of Marcellus, the Tabularium combines Roman arches with an overlay of Greek architectural detail (some architectural historians refer to this combination as the Tabularium motif). An engaged column in front of each pillar supports an entablature. A modest cornice accentuates the springing point of each arch. This treatment adds some strength to the arcade, but its main purpose is to create a visual harmony with the Hellenistic buildings nearby.

The newest feature of the Capitoline museums is an underground gallery which leads to the Tabularium and the Temple of Veiovis. The Tabularium served in antiquity as a repository for the laws of Rome. These laws were inscribed on bronze sheets—tabulae—and archived in the Late Republican structure. Closed to the public for generations and used as a repository for Roman artifacts, the Tabularium offers a prime vista over the Roman Forum. The Temple of Veiovis, rediscovered in 1939 during the creation of a subterranean passage between the two Capitoline museums, was dedicated in 192 BC. The dedicatee is an avatar of the god Jove represented as a young man and associated with the underworld. The cult statue discovered nearby is exhibited in the gallery, as are the remains of a Roman house of the Republican period.

The Arch of Septimius Severus, erected in 203 AD, celebrated an imperial triumph over the Parthians. The square panels above the side arches display a pictorial history of the bloody campaign; Parthian captives, like those who marched in chains behind the victor, decorate the bases of the applied columns. When the procession ended at the Temple of Jupiter on the Capitoline hill just beyond this arch, these captives were led away to be strangled in the Mamertine Prison; then their corpses were exposed on the roadway above the arch. Like the small arch dedicated a year later by the bankers of the Forum Boarium, this arch too has been revised to stay abreast of political developments. Markings around the fourth line of the large inscription at the monument's top show that the lettering was changed to obliterate the name of the dedicatee's unfortunate son, Geta,

17

murdered by his brother Caracalla. A name on display in the Forum was the highest tribute any Roman could hope for, but the process was reversible. Romans called this official forgetting damnatio memoriae.

Most Romans, even powerful emperors like Augustus and the autocrats who succeeded him, were unable to make their mark so close to the ideal center of Roman public life as Julius Caesar. Moving and rebuilding the Rostra and the Curia, entombed on a piece of the Forum itself, Julius made his legacy an inseparable part of Rome's heart. While many men shared his ambition, their ability to realize their dreams was limited by space and tradition rather than their own means and imagination. The Arch of Septimius Severus and the temple dedicated to Titus and Vespasian nearby are more commonplace entries in the historical hall of fame the Forum represented for Romans. That even powerful men acceded to these pressures is demonstrated again and again by the restoration rather than replacement of these prominent buildings in the Forum area.

Uphill from the Arch of Septimius Severus, the Roman road called the Clivus Capitolinus passes below a square terrace that marks the boundaries of the Temple of Concord. It may have been dedicated in the fourth century BC to celebrate an important political accord between patricians and plebeians. Then again it may not. With an uncertain history and no standing columns to single it out, the temple is undistinguished in every sense. Directly to the right, more or less centered under the Tabularium, is the Temple of Titus and Vespasian. This temple, dedicated by the latter emperor to his predecessor, the conqueror of Jerusalem, was rededicated after Vespasian's death to both emperors. Massive statues of the two "deities" were enshrined inside it. The temple, which faced the

Forum, has three standing Corinthian columns almost fifty feet high; they support one last angle of the building's architrave.

Tucked back in the corner at an odd angle to the Tabularium stands the Portico of the Dei Consentes. According to historical tradition, this building, which dates from the first century AD, housed gilded bronze images of twelve gods—the Greek pantheon perhaps. The building is more interesting for its style than its contents. Rather than an arched arcade in the Roman tradition, the portico features a rank of modest Corinthian columns supporting a marble beam. Like the Temple of Titus and Vespasian next door, it reflects the international Greek or Hellenistic style rather than any Italian tradition.

The Roman architect Vitruvius believed that Greek architects first developed their techniques by working in wood. When they replaced wood with stone very early in their history, they continued to treat stone as if it were a heavier, stronger, and more durable species of wood. Contemporary architectural historians think that Vitruvius overestimated the importance of wooden architecture to the Greeks. Still, his ideas highlight a difference between the Greeks and the Romans. The Greeks did not imagine stone as a substance that required or permitted a dynamic architecture, and they continued to carve it into columns and beams and to stack pieces of it on top of one another like blocks. Indigenous Roman architecture based on the arch used stone in a more complex way. But as the temples of the Forum show, Roman architects slighted their own tradition for nearly two centuries while they worked instead in the international Greek style.

That Greek style is evident in the largest, best-preserved, and most significant monument at this end of the Forum, the Temple of Saturn. Much restored as all Forum monuments were, the temple was founded in the earliest days of the Roman Republic. Though the Romans thought of Saturn as Roman rather than Greek and adapted his myth to celebrate their own form of government, when this temple was rebuilt in the third century BC it took the form of a Hellenistic monument. An overblown

Ionic temple on a high platform, it turned its side to the Forum. The eight standing columns, which supported the pediment of the building, face the Curia. (18) Arched openings in the massive foundations are the building's most curious feature. These subterranean vaults housed the Erarium or treasury of the Roman government. Adaptations of this kind made it possible to piece together a world government center out of the materials of the Forum.

18

According to Mediterranean legend, the god Saturn ruled an innocent and perfect golden age before men were tempted to violence or corrupted by greed. Roman legend located his kingdom on the Capitoline hill. In time, Saturn was driven from power by his son, Jupiter, the god whose temple crowned the Capitoline in historic time. The new god ruled a world like our own in which human nature leaves much to be desired. By celebrating the god of the golden age after their expulsion of the Etruscan kings, the early Republicans may have been setting up the mythical time before Jupiter as a model for their own era.

The southwestern side of the Forum is dominated by a single structure, the Basilica Julia. (19) Julius Caesar bought the land at Manhattan prices, then had the shops and private buildings on it torn down to make way for this structure, which he donated to the state. Augustus completed it. Three steps lead to a broad marble platform originally divided into a two story portico and roofed meeting hall. Colonnades divided the hall into a central aisle and four side aisles. Several courts held session here simultaneously, partitioned off from one another behind huge curtains. The stairs, floor, and column stubs are original. The brick arcades on the Capitoline end of the building are modern restorations.

Along the edge of the Forum that faces the basilica are a series of honorary columns and column bases somewhat earlier in date than the more central Column of Phocas. Guaranteed eternal fame by being memorialized in the Forum, the dedicatees of these monuments cannot be identified because the inscriptions have disappeared.

The Temple of Castor and Pollux (Dioscuri), like the Temple of Saturn, was a powerful symbol of the Roman Republic. Saturn's temple expressed the hope that by expelling the Etruscan kings, Rome could bring back a golden age of peace and justice. The Temple of the Dioscuri honored two Greek gods who fought alongside the Romans to realize that dream. It commemorated the gods' help in battle and their miraculous appearance in the Forum. When King Tarquin was expelled from Rome in 507

19

BC, allied Etruscans cities attempted to reinstate him and the monarchy by force. In the Battle of Lake Regillus in about 496 BC the Roman army routed the Etruscans and cancelled that threat. Late in the afternoon when Roman victory was certain, two men were seen leaving the battlefield. A few minutes later these same men were seen in the Roman Forum watering their horses in the spring of Juturna at the base of the Palatine hill. They announced the Roman victory and then disappeared. The Senate often met in this temple, and the courts of the Forum clustered around it. Bankers had their offices in the security of its thick foundations, a private version of the state banking carried on in the basement of Saturn's temple. Three standing columns identify the temple's location.

The northwestern end of the Forum at the base of the Capitoline hill radiated with the power of the Senate and the dreams of the Roman Republic. At its opposite end the Forum reflected both the power of the ancient kings and the prominence in public life of the descendants of Julius Caesar, who held the office of pontifex maximus (now a title of the Pope). That may be why his body was brought to this end of the Forum for cremation. In 29 BC Augustus dedicated a temple to the deified emperor that became a symbol of the imperial family and its power. By placing the shrine of the dynasty's founder in the symbolic orbit of the royal household, Augustus may have hoped to transfer the king's sacred power to the imperial family.

In the second of his great odes, the Roman poet Horace compared the death of Julius Caesar to the Tiber in flood. In his poem, the water "flowing inland from the sea" backs up through the Velabrum, overwhelms the Forum, and lies "dejected at the monument of kings and temple of the

Vestals." While the flood, like the bloody struggles after Caesar's death, brought chaos and devastation, it was also a repetition of the flood that bore up Romulus. The poem goes on to suggest that Augustus, Julius' successor and avenger, will be the founder of a new Rome, whose symbolic center will shift from the fig tree at the Senate end of the Forum to the Temple of the Deified Julius opposite.

Almost nothing remains of the Temple of the Deified Julius. There are remnants of the brick and rubble core of the foundations and a more substantial block of the porch surrounding a circular altar built on the site of his cremation. The monument survived nearly intact into the Renaissance, when it was dismantled in a period of months and its materials used in papal buildings, St. Peter's among them. The speaker's platform that Augustus built in front of the temple and facing the older rostra at the far end of the Forum has disappeared almost completely.

The ruins of the king's household, the Regia, stand in a small triangle of land in front of the columned façade of the Temple of Antoninus and Faustina. The building, which housed the chief priests of the Roman state, contained two sanctuaries: one devoted to Mars, the god of war, and the other to Ops, the goddess of abundance. Together, these two deities represented the king's twin concerns, warfare and the resources of the community. While the Romans thought of the Regia as the home of all their kings, both legendary and real, they remembered it chiefly in their histories, and probably in their political mythology as well, as the home of the Etruscan kings. Later Romans were very ambivalent about these rulers. Historians were quick to attribute many of early Rome's most important achievements, like the building of the Cloaca Maxima and the codification of law and ritual, to Etruscan kings. At the same time, they regarded the expulsion of the kings as a triumph over tyranny. In both cases, they may have understated the truth about the Etruscan contribution and the persistence of their influence.

Archaeologists now speak of Rome under the Etruscans as "la grande Roma dei Tarquini," the great Rome of the Tarquins, the dynasty of Etruscan kings. These rulers did indeed preside over the draining and paving of the Forum, the codification of law and ritual, probably the development of trade, and the foundation of civic order. Great houses at the edges of the Forum and on several of Rome's heights testify to their wealth, taste, and power. Their temples shaped Roman worship, and their rituals, like the triumph, became defining features of Roman public life. Many archaeologists see a period of rigid class warfare between plebs and patricians as the greatest legacy of their expulsion. But others point to that very expulsion as an illusion. Brutus' mother was a Tarquin, and the ruling families of Rome in the following centuries included many of Etruscan origin. Even Rome's conquest of the Etruscans themselves—an important part of their eventual domination of the entire Italian peninsula—may have been directed by and carried on in alliance with Etruscan families and Etruscan cities.

The Etruscan kings were spiritual as well as political leaders. Rites performed in the king's household ensured the well-being of the country. When the founders of the Republic expelled the kings, their sacred duties were passed on to priests appointed by the state. The rex sacrorum and the pontifex maximus took over the king's ritual duties and performed sacrifices for the nation. They also preserved records of important historical events in the life of the Roman city and state, as well as prodigies that marked each year and called for special sacrifices or other ritual acts. On the outer walls of the Regia, inscriptions preserved the memory of singular achievements by the rulers of Rome. Records preserved inside the complex told of lightning strikes and comets, earthquakes and two-headed calves which the Romans believed were signs of the gods' attitudes or intentions.

After the dissolution of the monarchy, the sacred fire on the king's hearth, which had been maintained by the women of the royal household, became the responsibility of the Vestal Virgins. The holy women of the king's spiritual household lived in the Vestal complex next to the Regia. Representatives of one of the most ancient and sacred priesthoods of Rome, these six women, who were chosen at age five or six and dedicated to thirty years of chastity and service, maintained the fire on the city's ideal and sacred hearth. The Vestal complex includes the Shrine of Vesta and the House of the Vestal Virgins. The shrine, where the sacred fire always burned, was a round temple with a cylindrical cella and attached columns surrounded by a curved Corinthian colonnade. The marble building was similar in many ways to the Round Temple in the Forum Boarium. In its present form the temple is a much-restored version of an extensive remodeling carried out in the second century AD.

The Vestal Virgins themselves lived in the spacious and pleasant house called the Atrium Vestae beside and slightly to the rear of the shrine. The atrium from which the vestal complex takes its name is a large area in the center of the house that is open to the sky and surrounded by a portico. There are basins for fountains and an octagonal garden in the center. The complex may seem like a medieval cloister shut off from the world and focused on its enclosed garden, but the majority of Roman houses were built in the same way. The city homes of wealthy Romans typically had such areas, though they were almost always smaller than this. Some of these houses had fountains, too, but the atrium was more commonly used to collect rainwater for storage and reuse.

The vestal's house was a two-story residence, as many Roman town houses were. The ground floor held public rooms for receiving guests and for dining, as well as service rooms for cooking, storing, and milling grain: in addition to maintaining the sacred fire, the Vestals prepared a special ritual bread called mola salsa. The bedrooms, which were upstairs, opened onto a second portico above the first. The distinctive feature of the house is the row of statues dedicated to the memory of the

20

most dutiful and pious chief vestals. The vestal complex stands at the limit of the sacred boundaries of the Forum.

While there had always been private houses in the Forum area, the Regia and the Atrium Vestae are the only public buildings based on the form of a house rather than a temple or forum. (The Curia Julia is an enlarged temple sanctuary or cella.) Since the Republican Regia and Vestals' house are both symbols of the king's residence, it makes historical sense that they would take this form. During the Empire the emperor's household—that ever-expanding residence on the adjacent Palatine hill—embodied the same symbolism. Just as the emperors

moved the center of national life away from
the Senate end of the Forum, they also tried to
fix it symbolically on the household rather than
the Forum or Curia.

The largest and best-preserved monument
in this area is also among the least important
historically. The Temple of Antoninus and
Faustina was built in 141 AD by the emperor
Antoninus Pius to commemorate his beloved
wife. The temple walls, which rise above the
entrance ramp to the Forum, are made of

21

peperino, originally paneled in marble. (20) The crude gaps at nearly
every joint were cut by men of the Middle Ages and Renaissance as they
salvaged the bronze clips that held the paneling in place. Deep rope
burns high on the columns reflect an unsuccessful attempt to pull them
down for reuse.

The nearby Temple of Romulus is an unusual and well-preserved
structure, which was dedicated to a son of the emperor Maxentius rather
than the founder of Rome. The cylindrical inner chamber of the temple,
which was completed early in the fourth century AD, is embraced by a
convex porch. Part of the building's foundations are now exposed, and its
entryway—including the original bronze doors—which was then at ground
level, is now a few feet in the air. (21) When archaeologists decided to
excavate the Forum to first-century BC ground level, they left this building perched a little above ground. As a commemorative building, the
temple is like many other imperial dedications. What distinguishes it is

its style—it is not a Hellenistic temple—and the materials from which it was built. The Temple of Romulus was once covered with a veneer of marble; with the marble gone, it appears to be a brick building. In reality, it is a one-piece concrete structure; the brick facing was added to smooth over the joints in the concrete and make a uniform subsurface for the marble facing.

Early in the first century BC the Romans began to explore the creative possibilities of building with concrete. They had been using mortar to bind stone and brick together for centuries. It was only in the first century, however, that they discovered the way to make this mixture of sand and lime hard and durable enough to stand alone as a building material. By adding a granular volcanic stone called pozzolano to their mortar along with stone or rubble, they invented a material that could be molded into virtually any shape and only grew stronger with age. As they mastered the new material, they found that they could make structures that would have been impossible using Hellenistic techniques. Late in the first century AD they began to elaborate on the plastic forms of their own architectural tradition in magnificent concrete buildings.

The Sacra Via which passes in front of the Temple of Romulus was an important ceremonial route, but it was also the best address in Republican Rome. All its residents, the so-called Sacravienses, were supposed to be patrician families with deep pockets. Excavations along the road have exposed portions of their houses. Looking into the excavations at the small cubicles with their mosaic floors, it is hard to imagine that these are indeed remains of the houses of the very rich. Wealthy Roman houses, while often quite large overall, devoted much more of their space to public than to private rooms.

A typical house of the late first century BC had a street-level entrance, sometimes flanked by shops under the same roof but walled off from the house itself. A narrow entryway led to the first public area of the house, the atrium with its roof at least partially open to the sky. Beyond the atrium stood the tablinum, a reception area for guests and an all-purpose room for family use. This was usually flanked by a dining room. The tablinum often led into the peristyle, a formal ornamental garden (the kitchen garden was behind the house) usually surrounded by a portico for shade and shelter but open to the sky in the middle. Bedrooms and summer dining rooms surrounded this garden, as they did in the atrium of the Vestals. Bedrooms, like many of the rooms exposed here, were small and windowless; the only light and air came from the door. Frescoes in predictable styles and colors covered the walls; mosaics—of which some fragments survive here—decorated the floors. A small but richly ornamented bed and a chest for clothes might be the only furnishings.

Further up the Sacra Via, just past the ruins of a medieval cloister, stands the Basilica of Maxentius. It was begun by the emperor whose son is memorialized in the Temple of Romulus and completed, in a slightly altered form, by the next emperor, Constantine. It is sometimes referred to as the Basilica of Constantine. The tremendous scale of the building and the preservation of three vaulted rooms show the power and plasticity of Roman concrete architecture. Supported on six enormous piers, the building's central vault rose more than a hundred feet above a floor roughly twice the size of the Roman Forum. (22) To roof an area half the size, the Basilica Julia required some fifty closely spaced columns. Among Roman buildings the Basilica of Maxentius best compares to the great imperial public baths—vast open spaces that accommodated thou-

22

sands of people at a time in a setting that was both opulent and comfortable. Great train stations like Grand Central in New York or Union Station in Washington, D.C., are its American cousins.

While the Basilica of Maxentius could certainly have handled the Forum crowd more efficiently than the Republican basilicas, it was too far from the Forum to be useful. It was instead the headquarters of administrators and judges who challenged the authority of the older government centers. Constantine abandoned Rome to build a new capital at Byzantium in the east. This move abruptly shifted power away from the older centers in the Forum and the imperial residence on the Palatine hill and focused it on the office of the urban prefect in the Basilica of Maxentius. The emperor was not completely absent. A colossal statue of Constantine stood in an apse—a massive semicylindrical niche—at one end of the basilica. Parts of it are now visible in the Capitoline Museum. (23)

There were colossal statues of the emperors Titus, Vespasian, and Antoninus in other temples in the Forum, but none of these buildings combined devotion to the cult of the deified emperor with civic administration as the Basilica of Maxentius did. Nor had anyone ever used a basilica as an imperial temple before. This curious innovation might have been an architectural dead end; instead it helped to direct the use of the basilica away from legal matters toward religious ones. It was Constantine

who made Christianity the semi-official religion of the Roman Empire. To
provide for mass participation in the worship of the newly accepted deity,
he sponsored the construction of temples on imperial lands around the
perimeter of the city. Old St. Peter's was one of
them. Since Christian worship, unlike Roman sacrifice, took place inside the sanctuary, traditional
temples were unsuitable. The basilica was the only
building style in the Roman architect's repertory
that could accommodate large numbers of people,
and this became the Christian standard. Curiously, all the basilicas
Constantine sponsored were built in the style of the multi-columned
Republican buildings rather than the soaring Basilica of Maxentius.

   When Constantine made the Basilica of Maxentius the local administrative center of a distant government, he wrote the final chapter in the
political history of the Forum. Until the first of the barbarian conquests
in 400 AD, the Forum remained a kind of Williamsburg or Plimouth
Plantation—an interesting site, full of buildings rich in historical associations, but powerless and remote. Constantine abandoned a city that was
still near the height of its powers, though its population had dropped
from its peak of over a million residents. An urban survey of the late third
century recorded more than 46,000 apartment buildings, 1,800 large-
scale private houses, and more than a thousand public buildings, including baths, temples, basilicas, theaters, and circuses. What can be seen
in the Forum today, aside from the foundations turned up by modern
archaeology, survives primarily because the Church, the only Roman institution to weather the city's fall, reused it.
   The Sacra Via turns left at the corner of the basilica and skirts the

podium of the Temple of Venus and Rome. Designed by the emperor Hadrian, the temple was dedicated in 121 AD on the anniversary of Romulus' founding of Rome. Its massive scale, which probably influenced the size of the basilica next door, was a response to the dimensions of the Colosseum. (24) Except for the enormous platform on which it was raised, little remains of the building except a curious concrete structure in the shape of two half-cylinders—Roman vaults on their sides—which join at their arcs. From the outside, unbroken colonnades made the building look like a single massive temple. In reality, the two gods of

its dedication—Venus and the personification of Rome—were worshipped in separate temples set back to back. The linked half-cylinders are the twin apses of the two temples, and one of the many innovations of Rome's most inventive architect. Like Constantine two centuries later, Hadrian was born outside Rome and seemed to hate the capital. For years at a time he toured the provinces, making life hell for negligent administrators. When he was in

24

Italy, he preferred his villa in Tivoli. Despite his distaste for Rome, Hadrian restored older monuments and designed new ones, including the Pantheon, the city's greatest building.

The Arch of Titus is the final monument in the archaeological zone of the Forum. Like the Arch of Septimius Severus, it depicts a Roman triumph—the brutal testimony of victory and subjugation that extended the

Empire and delighted the hometown crowd. Dedicated sometime after
81 AD, this arch commemorated the conquest of Israel and the destruction of the Temple in Jerusalem. One of the bas-reliefs on the inner walls
of the single-arched monument shows the victorious emperor in his four-
horse chariot. The opposite scene shows Roman soldiers displaying treasures looted from the city, including the sacred seven-branched Menorah.

Chapter Three

THE IMPERIAL CITY

After threading its way past the Basilica of Maxentius
and the foundations of Hadrian's Temple of Venus and
Rome, the Sacra Via turns sharply right. Beyond the
Arch of Titus it begins to climb the Palatine hill, which
overshadows the Roman Forum on the southeast. A
short way up the slope, just past the site of the Arch of Domitian, the black
volcanic Roman pavers disappear and a modern path continues upward into
a ruin-strewn green and tree-shaded park. Umbrella pines crown the hillside;
cypresses tower like living obelisks over thickets of oleander and hibiscus;
olive trees with silver-green willowy leaves shiver in the wind. Before excavations began in the Forum more than a century ago, the whole ancient center
of Rome was covered with trees, shrubs, and flowers like this.

In the Late Republic, the Palatine's cool pastoral landscape, close to the
city's business center and the simple monuments of the remote past, began
to draw patrician Romans. In the Renaissance, that pastoral sentiment was
felt again, and the hill became the site of rural villas. Lost to imagination in
the rigorous excavations of the late nineteenth and early twentieth century, a
similar ideal is coming to the fore in contemporary Rome. The city's archaeological centerpiece, which long served nationalist and imperial ends, is now
being reconceived as a traffic-free urban green space.

In the Republican era, the Palatine was a luxurious enclave in the center of a sordid town, a short walk away from the Forum in the morning and an easy climb back home at night. Cicero and Marc Antony both owned houses here. Cicero spent 3.5 million sesterces for his (perhaps as much as five million dollars in today's U.S. currency); the land alone was valued at two million sesterces. The future emperor Augustus was born on the Palatine, and his decision to govern from there transformed the hill from a wealthy community into a new center for Rome. Ancient tradition gave the high-priced neighborhood symbolic appeal. Establishing the imperial household on this hill staked a claim to antiquity rivaling that of the Forum below.

Legend, celebrated by the official Augustan poets and historians, located the earliest Roman settlements on the Palatine. The shepherd who rescued Romulus and Remus, the city's legendary founders, lived on the Palatine, it was said. After Romulus performed the divination that made him, rather than his brother, Remus, the founder of Rome, he laid out city walls that embraced the hill and extended both into the Forum area and toward the river. The Romans identified one ancient structure near the House of Augustus, which they continually maintained and repaired, as the hut of Romulus. Modern archaeology is less romantic and less specific, but it has confirmed the presence of early settlements on the hill.

Octavian (born 63 BC), the nephew and adopted son of Julius Caesar who would become the emperor Augustus (reigned 27 BC–14 AD), was born on the lower slope of the Palatine hill just above the site of the Arch of Titus. After defeating Sextus Pompey in 36 BC, he bought a house on the far slope of the hill from the orator Hortensius. Over the years, he purchased adjacent houses and linked them with the first to create an informal compound. In a move that parallels his strategy of cobbling imperial supremacy out of bits and pieces of existing political offices, he dedicated a part of his private house to the public. After his death, this house became the ideal foundation and in part the physical core of successive, increasingly grandiose imperial residences.

The portions of the House of Augustus that modern archaeology has uncovered are probably the private areas. The rooms exposed include a peristyle, a fish pond, and several rooms ornamented with painted decoration in the style of the first century BC. Both the physical scale of the house and its spareness contrast very strongly with the glorious imperial palaces that followed. Augustus' biographer, Suetonius, writing a century later about the house he knew only by reputation, described it as "without extravagance in its little colonnades of peperino columns; its rooms without marble decoration and floors without pictorial mosaics" (Suetonius, *Augustus* 72.1).

Near Augustus' house stands the House of Livia. Named for Augustus' wife, this house is probably one of the buildings the emperor added to his original purchase. Its association with Livia is based on a short piece of lead water-pipe stamped with her name. The house is now entered through a courtyard with simple mosaic pavement; the original entrance was probably in the eastern end of the house, which is still buried in the hillside. A series of painted rooms opens from here, and a narrow corridor leads toward the atrium, which is surrounded by small bedrooms. The painted decorations of these rooms are among the very few examples sur-

viving in Rome; some of the paintings have been detached from the walls
and are now on exhibit in the Palazzo Massimo.

Near the House of Augustus are several ruined structures and areas
still under archaeological excavation. These include a famous library and
a Temple of Apollo which played an important role in Augustan political
propaganda, and archaic structures which the emperor also exploited in
his drive to establish (like Mussolini, Augustus would have said "reestab-
lish") the Palatine hill as the point of origin and symbolic center of
Rome.

Augustus lived in what official histories agreed to call a simple house,
but the ceremonial demands of the Empire, the luxurious tastes of successive emperors, and the widespread use of concrete in architecture all
combined to expand the imperial residence to a massive scale. Around
the core of Augustus' simple house, the emperor Domitian (81–96 AD)
and his architect Rabirius created a palace which was to become the official Roman residence of the emperors until the fourth-century displacement of the capital to Constantinople.

Rabirius began by reshaping the hillside. On the side toward the
Forum (and on the opposite flank, facing the Circus Maximus) he shored
up the slope and built into it, creating a series of ramps, buttresses, and
chambers that overlooked and dominated the Forum below. Today, these
eroded structures with their roofs broken in and their outer walls fallen
away are like a raided hive or a broken stump mined by termites. Having
shored up its flanks, Rabirius flattened the hilltop to create a platform for
the palace. A plaza fronting the building offered an unobstructed view of
its soaring façade, which contemporary poets compared to a second

mountain set on top of the Palatine. There probably were trees and gardens surrounding the palace, as they now surround its ruins. The Roman
architect Vitruvius thought a palace should have "groves of trees and
wide walkways appropriate to the dignity of the sovereign" (*De Architectura* 6.5.2). Refined versions of this landscape found their place inside
the palace as well, where they refreshed and delighted the emperor and
his family.

From what remains today it is very difficult to get an adequate sense
of what must have been a building of overpowering magnificence, or to
find a sumptuous palace among the dirt paths, shattered walls, and column stubs on the Palatine. By comparison with the maze of broken corners and reconstructed gardens on the hilltop, the Forum below seems
remarkably clear and straightforward. Some few structures do stand out
against the horizon of broken spires and brick mesas, however, and
they make it possible to become oriented in the confusing remains of
Rabirius' palace and to get some sense of its layout and function.

An official visit to the imperial palace would have begun in one of two
large chambers opening on to the great plaza. The larger of these was the
aula regia, or imperial audience chamber. Here visiting dignitaries would
see the emperor seated on an elevated throne under the half-dome of an
apse in a space of unparalleled luxury. A smaller basilica stood beside
the audience hall. In this hall the emperor, again enthroned in an apse,
received the more important members of his government. (The living
presence of the emperor in these great halls was monumentalized by
Constantine in the Basilica of Maxentius.) A third front chamber may
have been used by the imperial guard. The audience chambers framed

25

the emperor in opulence in rooms of enormous dimensions. Selected visitors moved beyond this overwhelming theater of power to a seemingly more intimate environment.

An open square marked with column stubs on its inner border and a sunken octagonal maze at its center stands directly behind the imperial audience hall. This structure, always open to the sky, was the peristyle or colonnaded courtyard of the public wing of the palace. Carefully screened visitors passed into this more welcoming and more informal setting. Beyond the peristyle is the third public area of the palace, the triclinium or state dining room. This complex included an apsed and roofed chamber and two adjacent roofless ones. One of these open-air rooms is today still buried underneath the Antiquarium; the other is represented by an elongated, boat-shaped fountain.

At dinner the emperor would recline in the apse, surrounded by his many guests in an elegant room where ducts in the floor provided heat in the winter. Through the large windows of the room, the diners could see this fountain and the one opposite framed by gardens to either side. Here the emperor could appear in a different, though still ceremonial and politicized, role. The figure of austere majesty became a generous host.

Behind the triclinium and the other public areas of the palace, an

extensive private residence served as the comfortably luxurious and sheltered home of the emperor and his family. Here, the role that he played
in public as he awed dignitaries or displayed the hospitality of the Roman
state could be abandoned in fact and not just in appearance.

The private apartments of the complex are grouped around a sunken
courtyard marked by a four-sided fountain with four D-shaped channels
at its center. (25) The domed and alcoved rooms that open off this small
courtyard are arranged around one another in complex and appealing
rhythms. Each is a subtle triumph of imagination and continued testimony
to the remarkable flexibility of imperial concrete architecture. In antiquity
this suite could be reached only by a single narrow staircase that was
closely monitored and defended. Domitian (who was assassinated in 96
AD) was obsessed with security, and so were most of his successors.

The largest and most conspicuous area of the private palace is the
elongated sunken lawn that stretched the full length of the palace on its
left flank. (26) Known as the Stadium of Domitian, it is shaped like a
Roman circus or horse-racing track,
with a flat end where the starting
gates stood and a rounded end where
the charioteers turned their teams to
head into the home stretch. There is
a similar structure at Hadrian's villa
in Tivoli. Unlike the real race course,
the Circus Maximus, which stands in
the valley just beyond the curved end
of this structure, Domitian's stadium

26

was probably not meant for competition. The large oval outlined in the grass toward the curved end and a smaller D-shaped one at the near, flat end were probably fountains. Pillars against the outer walls supported a one- or two-story vaulted portico. Palace rooms on two levels opened onto it and received light and air from this expanded version of the peristyle at the center of the public palace.

No one is quite sure what to make of this so-called stadium. It is too compact for real chariot racing, though large enough for pleasure riding. It was probably a sheltered green space within the palace where carefully tended trees and flowers as well as potted plants that varied with the seasons surrounded cool fountains. The hippodrome shape may have been an architectural fantasy, a deliberate contrast of the heat, danger, and excitement of the race course with the cool green retreat of the palace garden.

While the imperial palace can no longer overwhelm us by its scale, it offers eloquent testimony to the Roman ability to shape space for private as well as political purposes. It also documents the Roman love of gardens, nature, and the outdoors. Even though the Palatine hill had been urbanized for centuries, the imperial palace still reflected a desire within the most rarefied and politicized setting to preserve intimate contact with the green world outside.

The real race course which Domitian's garden imitated, the Circus Maximus, stretched just beyond the palace in the low ground between the Palatine and Aventine hills. This depression drained a wide area in the southeastern parts of the city. A stream flowing through the site was buried and vaulted, and like the Cloaca Maxima it discharged into the Tiber. Historical sources record the circus's use for games dedicated to the Etruscan kings. Improvements to the course and permanent seating are most clearly documented in the Augustan period, however. Augustus himself added an imperial box—the pulvinar—to the circus seating and placed a very notable, trend-setting monument on the infield or spina of the circus. This monument, erected in 10 BC, was an obelisk some eighty feet high brought on specially constructed ships from the Egyptian city of Heliopolis, where it had stood before the Temple of the Sun. Its hieroglyphs record a dedication to the Sun God Ra by the pharoah Ramses II, who reigned from 1290 to 1224 BC. Augustus' placement of it within the circus, which had symbolic associations with the sun, may have reflected the fact that in Egyptian religion the obelisk was dedicated to the sun. His predominant motive, however, was political. Public display of the obelisk reminded Romans of the emperor's triumph at the Battle of Actium over the Egyptian queen Cleopatra. Tacitly, though just as clearly, it also reminded them of his triumph over Cleopatra's ally and Augustus' former partner in rule, Marc Antony.

At the same time that Augustus imported this obelisk (which was re-erected in 1589 by Domenico Fontana in the Piazza del Popolo), he brought another to be erected in the Campus Martius. Like the obelisk in the Circus Maximus, this monument also came from Heliopolis, where it was erected in the sixth century BC. Historians have argued, though not without dissent, that Augustus made it serve an unusual, seemingly practical purpose, though one plainly linked to the sun. He made it the gnomon—the shadow-producing central spire—of a giant sundial that spread across an entire plaza. This obelisk was re-erected in front of the Palazzo di Montecitorio in 1792 not far from its original site. A metal sphere pierced with a hole through which sunlight shines now tops the monument. The small spot of light, projected onto a calibrated band set into the pavement of the piazza, imitates, though with little accuracy, Augustus' original. Augustus decorated his imperial mausoleum with two small obelisks. One now stands in front of the Quirinal Palace and the other behind the church of Santa Maria Maggiore.

In imitation of Augustus, subsequent emperors also brought obelisks to the city. Caligula placed one near the spina of what later became known as the Circus of Nero in the Vatican. Old St. Peter's was built next to it. In the sixteenth century, Domenico Fontana, the architect of Sixtus V, placed it in its present location in front of the new basilica. Sallust placed an obelisk in the garden of his villa. The allure of the objects was so great that some emperors took the easier and less costly route of commissioning copies. Constantius, the grandson of the emperor Constantine, brought a second Egyptian obelisk to the spina of the Circus Maximus almost four centuries after Augustus placed the first one. The Byzantine emperors were great patrons of horse racing, and though they had little interest in Rome in general, they may have valued its sporting heritage. In the long decay of the circus during Late Antiquity, this obelisk and that of Augustus collapsed and were buried by debris. Sixtus V sponsored their excavation and used them in entirely new ways as landmarks in his reorganization of Rome in the late sixteenth century.

An inscription above the door of the Palatine Antiquarium shows the continuing political power of the Palatine hill in the Italian imagination. The building, a convent expropriated by the national government after 1870, was dedicated when "Victor Emmanuel III was King and Emperor, Benito Mussolini was leader [Il Duce], 2691 years after the founding

of the city; 1938 years after the birth of Christ and 16 years after the reintroduction of Fascism." Despite the political energies reflected in this
inscription, the collection itself has no evident political tendency. Most of
the objects on exhibit were collected during the long series of excavations
on the Palatine hill, some of which continue today. They come from every
epoch in the history of the site.

Among the most important are the remains and especially the reconstructions of the earliest settlements on the hill (basement level). On the
main floor are painted fragments of reliefs from two Augustan temples
and three striking figures in
black marble that have been
identified recently as statues
from the portico of Augustus'
Temple of Apollo. Art in the
imperial period, based for
political reasons on Greek

27

models, could be used for decoration or propaganda, or simply to overwhelm and impress the viewer. This small collection represents some of
these historical realities, but while the objects are arranged chronologically, they are presented in the stark isolation that modern museology
dictates. This presentation, which answers our notions of beauty, frames
the objects in a way that is alien to the experience of a Roman viewer.

The Belvedere and the modest plots surrounding it are the remains of
the once extensive Farnese Gardens, which at the time of their creation
in 1625 could claim to be the first botanical gardens in the world. (27)
The gardens have been reduced and reconfigured as excavations over the

past two centuries have exposed remains of the imperial residence. What survives now mainly serves as an overlook (bel-vedere means "good view") on the city and especially the Forum below, but they represent, as the green spaces within Domitian's palace also did, the continuing attempt to make the city more livable by bringing the natural world inside. (28)

28

In the late Republican period and well into the first century AD, Rome beyond the narrow confines of the Palatine hill was a very unpleasant place to live. When the Romans laid out a town in open country, they followed a well-established plan. Wide streets, one running north-south, the other east-west, crossed at the town center. Land at this principal intersection was set aside for the Forum, with its combination of legal and economic services, and the capitolium, or temple area, where sacrifices could be performed to the trio of chief state gods. A series of parallel streets running off in both directions completed the town grid. Each city's administrative center made it a little Rome, but the resemblance ended there. Rome itself had grown up helter-skelter, spreading its streets in tangles from the historic arteries that gave it birth. Traffic in this labyrinth was so dangerous that Julius Caesar enacted a law forbidding all but emergency use of vehicles during the day.

When night fell on this maze, it gave up every claim to decency and order. Carters and robbers ruled. Gangs, some of them made up of the

sons of important men, roamed the streets looking for trouble. Beleaguered citizens barred their doors and windows, whatever the weather. To
go outside after dark without torch-bearers and armed guards—protection
only the richest could afford—was foolhardy. Julius and Augustus Caesar
tried to organize this chaos by buying buildings, then demolishing and
replacing them. Augustus reorganized the city administration and created
both an urban police force and a fire brigade, but the intractable fabric
of the old city stymied his efforts and those of his immediate successors.

   During the night of July 18, 64 AD, an event began which changed
both the shape of the city and the conditions of its future growth. The
historian Tacitus described the eruption and rapid spread of a fire "that
began in the area between the Palatine and Celian hills. There in shops
packed with flammable materials a conflagration broke out and gathered
strength; high winds drove it through the valley of the Circus Maximus
where there were no mansions with extensive grounds or walled temples
that might have slowed its onrush. Now at full strength, the flames over-
ran the low-lying districts along the river before sweeping up and over the
hills. The huge fire outpaced all attempts to fight or contain it. With its
narrow, twisting alleys and chaotic streets, the town fell an easy victim.
No one knew where to find safety . . . After burning out of control for six
days, the fire was stopped at the foot of the Esquiline hill where buildings had been pulled down and the rubble cleared away to create a fire
break. Still the fire erupted again in a less crowded part of the city where
fewer lives were lost but the destruction of temples and public buildings
was more devastating" (Tacitus, *Annales* 15.38–40).

   The emperor Nero seized on the vast areas of the city that had been

cleared by the fire to carry out two building projects. One of these was
his architecturally inventive but much-hated palace, the Domus Aurea, or
Golden House. The other was a reorganized city of Rome with a rational
street plan and a building code that made the ancient capital conform
to the orderly pattern of new Roman towns throughout the Empire. "The
districts untouched by the new palace were not rebuilt as they had been
after the Gallic fire [of 390 BC] indiscriminately and piecemeal, but in
measured lines of streets, with broad thoroughfares, buildings of restricted
height, and open spaces, while porticoes were added as a protection to
the front of each apartment building . . . New buildings were to be solid,
untimbered structures of peperino and travertine. There was to be a
guard to insure that the water supply, which in the past had been illegally
diverted by individuals, would be available for public use, in greater
quantities and in more locations" (Tacitus, *Annales* 15.43).

From this point forward, as long as the Empire remained viable, the
pattern established by Nero's response to the great fire of 64 remained in
effect. Nero's immediate successors, the Flavian emperors Vespasian,
Titus, and Domitian, continued his policies, and so did their successors,
the Antonines. Despite the horrors of the fire and its wholesale destruction of Rome's cultural past, the city that emerged from the ashes was a
better place to live for people of every rank. Many believe that the second
century AD was Rome's true golden age. The emperors improved the
architectural fabric and added to the amenities available to every inhabi-
tant through vast public works. They also followed Nero's lead (though
they were very careful to avoid and even decry his example) in creating
luxurious palaces and villas for themselves and their families both within
the heart of the city and on its fringes.

This imperial rebuilding, however, set an ominous pattern for urban development. The Rome of the Tiber crossing was a trading center, economically self-sustaining. During much of the Republic, Rome was supported by the wealth of the many senatorial families. Imperial Rome existed to manifest the power of the emperor alone. In Nero's vision it served as his extended court—the public wing of his symbolic palace. And from his reign onward, the emperor became the engine of the city's growth. When the emperor's power waned or his attention turned elsewhere, the city would inevitably falter.

Nero's Domus Aurea—a city in itself that was probably designed by Severus and Celer, the architects of his urban renewal—stood on three of Rome's seven hills and filled the valley between them. More than a vast building, it was a country estate laid out on once-urban land that had been swept clear by the great fire. Given Nero's exploitation of the fire and his eagerness to place blame for it on the city's small Christian community, it is easy to accept the Roman view that he started the fire himself. Whatever its origin, he took full advantage of the opportunity it presented him to live, as he said, "like a human being."

"The size and splendor of the house will be sufficiently indicated by the following details. Its vestibule was large enough to hold a colossal statue of the emperor a hundred twenty feet high; and it was so extensive that it had a triple portico a mile long. There was a pond, too, as big as a sea, surrounded with buildings to represent cities. There were tracts of open country with plowed fields, vineyards, pastures and woods, with great numbers of wild and domestic animals. Throughout the palace every surface was plated with gold inset with gems and mother of pearl. There were dining rooms with ceilings of carved ivory, where panels could

be turned to shower down flowers and pipes sprinkled guests with per-
fume. The main banquet hall was circular and constantly revolved day
and night like the heavens" (Suetonius, *Nero* 31.1–2).

After Nero's forced abdication and death, the palace was briefly occupied by his short-lived successors. When Vespasian became emperor in
69 AD, he opened the hated palace to the public, as populist dictators
have continued to do through the centuries—though only after Nero's
magnificent art collection had been removed to the safety of the Forum
of Peace. Fires damaged the palace in 80 AD and again in 104. After
that second fire, one wing that was partially dug into the Esquiline hill,
and perhaps the only portion then standing, was filled in with dirt and
rubble to form a secure foundation for the Baths of Trajan. During the
Renaissance these buried ruins were rediscovered. Painters like Raphael,
Pinturicchio, and Ghirlandaio imitated the decorative styles they found
within and created a vogue for what became known as "cave" or "grotto"
art—the grotesque.

After years in which the Domus Aurea was closed to visitors, some 30
of the 150 known rooms of the complex were reopened in the late twentieth century. Among these are the rooms most celebrated for their painted
decoration, including the nymphaeum of Ulysses and Polyphemus, the
Room of the Gilded Vault, the room of Hector and Andromache, that of
Achilles and Scyrus, and the Octagonal Chamber. Little is known of the
role these rooms played in the life of the palace, though they are
assumed to be parts of the private residence. The paintings of country
scenes and famous lovers rather than political figures support this view.
No service corridors, latrines, or in-floor heating, however—features that

mark the imperial suite in the Palace of Domitian—have come to light. Perhaps this part of Nero's palace was used only in mild weather when sunlight streaming into its open courtyards and south-facing windows kept it light and relatively warm.

Despite uncertainties about its original use and the burial which transformed it from a sunny pavilion into a blind cavern, the house offers a remarkable inside view of a Roman imperial building. The entire structure is built of brick-faced concrete. Paintings, decorative stuccos, marble, or other precious materials were used only to enrich the surfaces. Colonnades along the south façade were purely ornamental. While the decoration of the palace was uncommonly rich and the scale monumental, the core forms of the building—its vaulted rectangular rooms and corridors—appear in structures of every kind in the period. Vaulted rectangular rooms set side by side in long rows formed warehouses. With a square window above the front door to provide light for a mezzanine floor, the same structures made a row of shops, as they do in the Market of Trajan. Stacked on top of each other and set around light-gathering courtyards, they formed the apartment buildings in which most Romans lived. Despite the new materials that composed them and the range of purposes they could serve, these vaulted chambers were direct descendants of the arches supporting the Tiber bridges or the vault of the Cloaca Maxima.

The most distinctive and forward-looking structures in the palace are not its standard rectangular rooms but those spaces that are formed by the intersection of vaults. The Octagonal Chamber is one such complex. A domed room with south-facing windows and an oculus—a circular window in the roof—is surrounded by an embracing passageway that opens onto more traditional rooms set at oblique angles. The play of light would have been particularly interesting. The bright central chamber is lit in an obvious way by its oculus, but its dome hides secondary openings that light the ambulatory and side chambers. This invisible light source would have created an eerie glow in the surrounding corridor and complex shadows in the recessed chambers all around. The effect was created purely to delight, to make this an interesting and diverting space, which is surely the purpose of an imperial pleasure palace.

Circular and annular ground plans became a hallmark of the late Empire. At the moment of the official conversion to Christianity, such structures, along with the imperial basilica, became staples of Christian building design. It is somewhat uncanny to stand in this complex of rooms in Nero's pleasure palace and discover in them the architectural ancestry of the martyrium and indeed the very sepulcher of Christ as it was reinterpreted for millennia in Christian baptisteries throughout the world.

After an interval of nearly seventy years, excavations of the imperial fora were resumed in the 1990s. The first campaign of excavations in this area adjacent to the Roman Forum was Mussolini's most controversial archaeological project. Il Duce wanted to write his name and the name of Fascism across the center of the national capital. For his purposes the imperial fora were ideal. His instructions to the excavators were very clear: "Everything that can be conserved should be brought to light and offered for the admiration of citizens and tourists. The Roman subsoil is an inexhaustible mine of precious objects, the rare indeed unique remains of a superhuman civilization. They are not just to be disinterred but restored to their precise function as living documents of a civilization that was buried but not dead, of an art once interred that is still alive and vital" (quoted in *Archeologia e Citta,* pp. 109–112).

Begun by Julius Caesar and completed by Trajan, the imperial fora expanded Rome's government center beyond the confines of the Roman Forum. This expansion both supplemented the Forum and rivaled it, in vast and impressive structures that were associated historically with Roman autocracy rather than republicanism. Even the location of these imperial structures was apt: they began where the Corso, Rome's nineteenth-century parade route, ended. Mussolini envisaged these historical sites as the launch pad for imperialist forays throughout the Mediterranean. Here, as elsewhere, he excavated with a heavy hand. He began by destroying a working-class neighborhood—first evicting its thousands of residents and then demolishing their homes to get at the archaeological materials underneath. Eager for results, Mussolini forced the pace of the work; objects were lost, and record-keeping was spotty.

Worst of all for the preservation of the site, Fascist planners laid out a major roadway—the infamous Via del Impero—through the center of the site. After hasty excavations that laid the sites completely bare, gangs of workers heaped rubble on the centerline of the newly opened site to form a roadbed. This broad avenue at modern street level split the archaeological area down the middle and repositioned it below ground level. Eviscerated and seen only from above, the imperial fora have for most of the past century been truly visible only in the imaginations of a handful of architectural historians.

Current excavations, which have already uncovered most of the Forum of Nerva, the Forum of Caesar, and the Forum of Trajan, envisage the clearing of an additional 15,000 square meters in three simultaneous excavations. The areas to be uncovered, when combined with previous excavations, will create an archaeological park spanning the area from the Capitoline hill to the Colosseum. The Roman Forum and the imperial fora will be reunited in an unbroken archaeological zone from the Palatine hill to the slope of the Esquiline. The ideal was first enunciated by a royal commission in the nineteenth century.

For both historical and pragmatic reasons this is an extraordinarily bold step for the modern city to take. It was generally assumed that the excavators would remove Mussolini's Via del Impero. Instead, they have acknowledged its historical importance, however dark, and the street is now scheduled to be preserved as a pedestrian walkway over the site. Closing this road to traffic, however, would cost the city a major artery through its highly congested center. The simultaneous creation of a central archaeological zone, which, if not positively green, would at least be nonpolluting, would be an important expression of the modern city's ecological vision. Whether the plan's advocates have sufficient energy and finesse to win approval for this ambitious plan remains uncertain.

The Forum Julium (Forum of Caesar) was planned by Julius Caesar both as a monumental approach to the Senate he had rebuilt and as a symbolic competitor with that key Republican institution. While it served the public, it also furthered Caesar's political ambitions. His forum was not laid out as an open market square after the pattern of the Roman Forum. It followed the form of a walled Hellenistic shrine: a deep portico

surrounded an open rectangular plaza. One narrow end of the complex
connected to the Senate by two doors in the back wall. Literally plugged
into the central political institution of Republican Rome at one end, the
complex spelled out the mythological foundation of Caesar's claim to pre-
eminent power at the other. The Temple of Venus Genetrix, a goddess
associated both with the founding of Rome and with the family of Julius
Caesar, stood at the opposite end on a raised platform. A statue of Julius
seated on Bucephalus, the horse of Alexander the Great and a symbol of
world domination, stood in front of the temple. The message of the forum
is easy to decode: Venus sponsors Julius and supports his drive to dominate the Senate.

In addition to the cult image of the goddess, the temple housed an
array of impressive objects that were on permanent public display. These
included paintings, a collection of engraved gems, and a golden statue of
Cleopatra. It was a peculiar kind of museum in which objects distinguished by their beauty, rarity, kitsch, and notoriety were displayed in a
setting that was both religious and political. Imperial museum practice
followed a similar pattern from that point forward. Under the guise of
pious benefaction, beautiful and curious objects became covert displays
of political muscle.

Excavations in this area have also uncovered a public latrine, the
largest so far discovered in the Roman Mediterranean. Low benches
with keyhole slots line the walls of a roofed structure with open sides;
channels beneath the building lead directly to the Cloaca Maxima.

The Forum of Augustus, which is set at right angles to the Forum of
Caesar, follows a similar ground plan. A portico surrounds an open plaza

29

in front of a temple on a raised platform. The temple here, dedicated to Mars the Avenger, is doubly linked to Caesar's Temple of Venus. In Roman mythology, Mars, the god of war, is Venus' husband. The epithet "avenger" added to Mars' name in the temple dedication ties the god to Augustus' pursuit of Julius' assassins and his vengeance for the death of his adoptive father. Despite the temple's name, cult statues of both Mars and Venus stood in its apse. The Senate sometimes met here, as it also did in Caesar's forum, but only on matters associated with the god of war.

In the open piazza in front of the temple, Augustus with a winged Victory beside him was represented driving a four-horse chariot. Though trophies of important victories were collected here, a disciplined sculptural program replaced the cabinet of curiosities on display in Julius' forum. The openings between columns in the portico sheltered statues of famous Romans, linking Augustus with the historical as well as the mythological past. The portico also served as the headquarters of the urban praetors (senior administrators) responsible for order and justice in Rome; their "offices" were located not by number but by reference to individual statues.

Two deep exedrae bulged out from porticoes on either side of the temple; Vitruvius described similar structures in Greek palaestrae and noted that they were set aside for teaching. One of these semicircular areas contained a colossal statue dedicated by Augustus' heirs to the emperor's genius, the personal directing god—a kind of guardian angel—who was also the source of his successor's power and legitimacy. A portion of the colossal hand and the oversized footprint of this personification turned up in recent excavations. Triumphal arches at each side of the temple formed monumental entrances to the complex.

The most conspicuous feature of the Forum of Augustus that still stands is the high retaining wall of peperino with bands of travertine reinforcement at the back end of the complex. The outline of the gabled roof of the Temple of Mars is traced on its surface, along with the opening to the right of the temple, the end wall of the portico, and a substantial portion of the outer drum of the two exedrae. There are a few standing columns remaining of the many which originally surrounded the temple. (29)

Augustus and Julius built their fora in the period before the great fire. To make space for their projects, they were obliged to purchase private properties in an area close to the Roman Forum at rates comparable to the Palatine. The Forum of Nerva (or Forum Transitorium) was begun by Domitian and completed by his successor in an area cleared by the fire. The purpose was to transform the Argiletum—an ancient street that connected the Forum with the popular Subura quarter up the Esquiline hill— into a monumental entranceway that would also link up with the existing imperial fora. Architecturally innovative on the Palatine, Domitian chose to work within the spatial constraints and prevailing Hellenistic style in this highly symbolic area. His forum opens in a majestic apse-shaped portico at the end toward the hillside. This ceremonial entrance feeds pedestrians past the Temple of Minerva into an elongated plaza with shallow porticoes on either side that open on to the other imperial fora. At its far end it delivers visitors into the Roman Forum between the Curia and the Basilica Aemelia.

While the excavators of the Forum of Nerva have set the recovery of this imperial structure of the late first century as their primary goal, they have also explored remains both above and beneath the first-century level. This allows them to present the forum as one historical moment among others, an approach that contrasts strongly with Mussolini's ideal of setting significant monuments free of the "encumbrances" of less favored periods. It not only sets the forum in the broadest historical context but also defuses the political force of privileging one historical period and its ideals over another. By the same token, preserving the Fascist artery over the site is intended to ease that period of its still powerful political burden. While most evident in the Forum of Nerva, this even-handed approach governs the excavations of all the imperial fora. This approach also characterizes the newest museum installations in Rome.

Excavating in this more inclusive fashion, archaeologists have uncovered private houses of the Late Republican period destroyed in the fire of 64 AD. Particularly striking is their recovery of an ergastulum, or slave dormitory, a series of tiny rooms with heavily barred windows and locked doors; planks wedged in niches in the walls were their only furniture. Roman slaves came from all the provinces at the edges of the Empire, including Spain, Africa, and France, but the majority were from the Near East. A relatively small percentage were the children of slaves; others had been abandoned or sold into slavery by their parents; some became slaves through criminal penalty. The nation and city owned slaves who served in the courts of magistrates, cleaned the sewers, and maintained the aqueducts. Work in the state-owned quarries and mines was the worst form of public servitude. The majority of privately owned slaves worked in agriculture—many hundreds on the greatest estates, but even modest farms might include a few slaves. Slaves in the city household shopped, tended the gardens, cooked, cleaned, and attended to the personal needs of children and adults. The kitchen was the center of their household— their rooms were usually near it—and they made offerings for the welfare of their masters at simple kitchen shrines.

In the largest households the slave force included doctors, painters, manuscript copyists, teachers, accountants, and business managers. The emperor's slaves included all the ranks of cooks, butlers, and maids, along with hundreds of additional imperial slaves who formed the state bureaucracy. Such high-ranking slaves were more intimately involved with government and considerably more powerful than all but the most favored patricians. The status of slaves in general reflected that of the family they belonged to. Slaves could be and frequently were freed. Some ex-slaves became extremely wealthy; some few held public office. However powerful he might become, though, a manumitted slave was expected to cultivate the patronage of his former master.

Urban slaves shared space in their master's household. The English word "family" comes from the Latin word familia, which includes both the free and slave populations of a household. This word did not imply a sentimental bond. While favorite slaves might be coddled and manumit-ted, most were exploited and abused. Even under the Republic, urban households with slave populations numbering in the hundreds were not

unheard of. The imperial palace may well have housed a thousand slaves
or more. People spoke casually about shopping for slaves. Slaves whose
job was to open doors in private houses were frequently chained near
them like dogs. Slaves were routinely tortured if they became involved in
legal cases. If they were accused of crimes, their penalties were even
more severe than the extremes of Roman justice inflicted on the free.
Public executioners could be hired to discipline slaves.

The Forum of Vespasian (also called the Forum of Peace) resembled
those of Julius and Augustus, but since it was built in the decade following the fire, its scale could be much grander. Ancient writers are unclear
about whether this was a forum at all, since there is no record of public
business being carried out in it. Nor is the temple a dynastic one:
Vespasian made no claim to divine origin. Instead, it was dedicated to a
personified abstraction, Peace, not a traditional god but one of the many
godlike ideas that captured the imagination of first-century Romans.
Sadly, the peace specifically referred to was the brutal pacification of the
Jews. Sacred objects from the Temple in Jerusalem, which are depicted
on the arch of Vespasian's son, Titus, were on display here.

In more general and more optimistic terms, the temple celebrated the
concept of peace and its singular importance as a political goal of the
Roman Empire. From the temple a vast portico reached out; art treasures
from areas throughout the Empire were displayed here and in a library
attached to the complex. Especially important among them were treasures that had decorated Nero's Golden House. Rather than embracing a
paved plaza, the portico enclosed some kind of garden—an urban park
evidently—where anyone could enjoy quiet, greenery, and great art within

the subtle embrace of Vespasian's imperial program. Still, it was not just
a monumental hot spot designed to intrigue and impress but a real effort
at amenity. It handed over to the public a recognizable version of the
pleasures, both natural and artistic, of the Golden House and converted
the former emperor's private domain into a civic resource. In 211 AD in
a large open hall next to the temple, an enormous marble map of the
ancient city—called the Forma Urbis—was put on display. Fragments of
this map, which is so minutely detailed that it shows the ground plan of
houses within the city, have been coming to light since the late sixteenth
century.

The Colosseum was dedicated in 80 AD by Vespasian and his son
Titus. Its structure, more complex than that of the Theater of Marcellus,
combines a series of concentric elliptical travertine supporting walls with
a radiating series of concrete tunnels. (30) Its continuous façade superimposed Greek architectural orders on three original arcaded bays. A fourth
bay, pierced by square windows, was added by Titus after his father's
death. This top story supported tall wooden masts that anchored a move-
able canvas sunshade which could
be extended over the arena; sailors
manned them on performance days.
There were eighty arcades on each
level; seats and sections were numbered, and ample entryways and
ramps made the amphitheater
quick to fill and to empty. Though
apparently uniform, each section

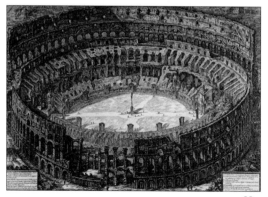

30

varies slightly with the curve of the ellipse. The applied columns on the lowest story are Tuscan; these are followed by Ionic orders, then Corinthian. This sequence of orders—from the simplest to the most ornate—became canonical in the Renaissance.

In the play of imperial politics the Colosseum, like the Forum of Peace, was a monumental repackaging and restoration to the people of some of the territory Nero had appropriated for his Golden House. The emperor in his private box and seventy thousand spectators arranged by social rank in the seats above watched grisly public executions, simulated hunts for exotic beasts, or fights among sometimes enormous troops of gladiators. The floor could be removed and the arena flooded for mock naval battles. The Christian empire abolished matches between gladiators in the early fifth century AD; staged hunts survived another hundred years.

Though it was a textbook example of the architectural orders, the building was mined for blocks of stone and bronze fittings well into the eighteenth century, when it was declared a Christian monument. Since it was mined most extensively during the Renaissance, the walls toward the Campus Martius suffered the greatest damage. A sixth-century AD earthquake that devastated many parts of the city may also have contributed to the destruction here. With little historical foundation, it was asserted that Christian martyrs had been among the many victims sacrificed in the Colosseum. In honor of that tradition, the Pope performs the Stations of the Cross there on Good Friday each year.

The last of the imperial fora to be built, the vast Forum of Trajan, was entered through a triumphal arch in the Forum of Augustus, an area which it imitated in various ways. Immediately inside this arch was an enormous plaza surrounded by the traditional portico and with deep exedrae bulging out on either side. An equestrian statue of the emperor, who ruled from 98 to 117 AD, stood in its center, and its buildings included a temple to the deified emperor. Behind this plaza stood the Basilica Ulpia, a five-aisled structure with twin apses, which, like the basilicas of the Roman Forum, carried its roof on parallel rows of marble columns, many of which are still visible. On the far side of the basilica two libraries flanked the Column of Trajan. General business was conducted in the basilica, where one atrium was dedicated entirely to ceremonies for the manumission of slaves. Its libraries held public records. Readings and lectures on literature were held in the exedrae. This forum, distinguished in scale from the others, is similar in its political symbolism. Like the Forum of Vespasian, it celebrates peace while it commemorates a significant victory. Much of the sculptural decoration referred to the emperor's war in Dacia (modern Romania), and the official history of that campaign scrolls up the emperor's column in bas-relief. The deified emperor was buried at its base.

The conservative architecture of Trajan's Forum had no place in the commercial buildings behind it. Instead, the creators of Trajan's Market were free to work in the materials and the style of the Roman architectural revolution. This wonderful and imaginative complex responds to structural and social problems created by the Forum of Trajan. It replaces commercial space that may have been eliminated and acts as a retaining wall to shore up the slopes of the Quirinal hill that were cut into as the forum was built. The rooms at its base are arranged in a semicircle

31

that responds to the exedra on the forum. (31) Their innovative forms and their extraordinary state of preservation make the markets unique. Moving through them is like being in the best preserved sections of Pompeii or Herculaneum; the site rises above and all around, visually and emotionally rather than just imaginatively impressive. Just inside the main entrance off Via Quattro Novembre is a large two-story vaulted hall with shops at floor level and galleries above. Each brick-faced shop has its broad doorway outlined with travertine and a square window above to light the mezzanine. (32) Architects of the Renaissance repeated this pattern of openings, and Fascist architects created whole complexes in brick with similar travertine moldings.

Descending the stairs to the sloping street, the overhead archways appear to have been turned on their sides. Doors, windows, walls, and pediments bend with the flow of hemicyclical walkways. With the exception of a few interior rooms used for secure storage, all these structures in their various shapes and orientations are both lit and heated by the sun. The exterior walkways of the labyrinth offer wonderful views across the Forum of Trajan toward the Capitoline hill.

32

Imperial monumental building was not limited to the Roman Forum and Palatine. The low-lying area embraced by the bend of the Tiber upstream from the island was an important area of development as well. Called the Campus Martius—the field of Mars—this zone lay outside the earliest walls of Rome; and as its name implies, it served traditionally as a training ground for war. During the Late Republic, monumental buildings began to appear in the area. The Porticus of Octavia near the Theater of Marcellus, the Theater of Pompey where Caesar was assassinated, the Mausoleum of Augustus, and Ara Pacis were all built in the zone before 64 AD. After the great fire, the pace of monumental development accelerated.

Over the centuries, however, the majority of those structures have disappeared. The outlines of a few—like the Theater of Pompey or the Stadium of Domitian—are impressed on the street plan of modern Rome; others, like the Hadrianeum, are incorporated in modern buildings. Most Roman buildings in the area were destroyed by a combination of assaults that included the barbarian sacks of the fifth century, a devastating earthquake in the sixth century, and recurrent floods. But the most significant force was the shift in Rome's population. Sparsely inhabited in the Roman period, the Campus Martius—along with Trastevere on the opposite side of the Tiber—became the population center of medieval and Renaissance Rome.

The most remarkable imperial building in the Campus Martius has been preserved through all these disasters. The Pantheon—a temple dedicated to multiple gods—is the triumph of the architectural genius of the emperor Hadrian. Trajan's successor, Hadrian ruled from 117 to 138 AD.

33

While the massive scale and the innovative double cella of the Temple of Venus and Rome spotlight the architect's bold imagination, the Pantheon's brilliant design subordinates that power to a serene harmony. Built on the scale of a Roman bath, the Pantheon fits the human frame, extending the imagination rather than overwhelming it. Originally preceded by a vast porticoed square like a Hellenistic shrine or an imperial forum, the Pantheon now stands at one end of a more intimate piazza. (33) The piazza's downward slope toward the temple and that of surrounding streets give dramatic evidence of the rise in ground level since antiquity. Some fifteen feet of Tiber mud and medieval refuse have buried the steps that once led up to the temple.

The deep porch of the building is supported on massive granite pillars and crowned by a travertine pediment. The famous inscription in the frieze records Agrippa—the builder, during Augustus' reign, of the first pantheon on this site—rather than Hadrian, the building's "restorer." Today, the curious drum shape of the building behind the porch is visible; the portico would originally have masked it. Deep within the porch a massive pair of bronze doors are flanked by twin niches which once contained statues of Agrippa and Augustus. The huge doors are among the very few Roman bronze doors remaining in their original site. Beyond them a completely unexpected vista opens up. Just as the monumental

inscription belies the true designer of the building, so the traditional rec-
tilinear temple porch completely fails to anticipate the building inside.

The floor of this unique structure, also original, is a vast mosaic made
up of sections of colored marble in patterns that inscribe squares within
squares alternating with circles inscribed in squares. The play between
these figures describes the geometry of the building at its most abstract
level. The floor swells gently toward the center of the building as if it
were the surface of the earth itself. The interior walls are marked off into
three zones. The lowest of the three is punctuated by seven recesses
fronted by columns. The wall space between each pair of recesses is decorated with a small raised aediculum—a miniature temple front with
columns, frieze, and pediment—that frames a niche. The seven large
bays, in which square and circular plans alternate, are like idealized temples and basilicas trimmed to the bare elements of colonnade, square
cella, and circular apse. Combined, they make this first zone into an idealized street of temple fronts, an image that is also recalled in the scenic
architecture of the Roman theater.

Each bay held a statue of a planetary deity: one of the five planets
known to the Romans—Mercury, Venus, Mars, Jupiter, and Saturn—plus
the Sun and Moon. The niches framed by the aedicula held statues of
other planetary deities, including deified emperors like Julius Caesar, who
at their deaths were said to be transformed into stars. These smaller figures have been replaced by Christian saints, while the large cult statues
have disappeared completely. None was in place after 609 AD, when the
Pantheon was converted to a church dedicated to the Virgin Mary.

Above a massive entablature with a bare porphyry frieze at its center, a second horizontal band begins. This area has been greatly restored, and its original use and configuration are in some doubt. The dome of the building, which springs from a spare cornice above this band, though stripped of the bronze stars once at the center of each coffer, otherwise reflects Hadrian's design. The dome is a true hemisphere, and if it were completed, it would touch the floor at its midpoint. Seen in cross section, that sphere would be inscribed in a square that is represented by the floor and wall lines. This abstraction is the source of one type of floor tile. The square-within-square tiles reflect the coffers that punctuate the dome.

Rather than a single square inscribed within another, however, the coffers appear to superimpose five layers of material. These represent the concentric spheres that the five planets were believed to trace as they orbited the earth. (The coffering is offset to accommodate the viewpoint from the floor of the building.) There are five rows of coffers, again representing the five planets, and twenty-eight coffers in each row, which correspond to the number of days in a lunar month. The center of the dome—some nine meters in diameter—is open to the sky and provides all the light in the building. (34) Through it, the sun's circular image travels across the dome and walls as the day passes. At night the stars are visible above.

When it rains in Rome, it also rains inside the Pantheon. The oculus transforms both the sun and the rain into mystical presences, divine personifications of their daily and unremarkable appearance in the real world outside. It also acts as a kind of heavenly atrium as it brings cosmic nature indoors. The coffers themselves become like shadow boxes, creating complex patterns of light and dark. The

effect is a subtle variant on traditional Roman

trompe l'oeil patterns in wall painting and

mosaic.

According to historical accounts, Hadrian

used the Pantheon to transform himself into a

divine emperor, the companion of the gods

and co-ruler of the heavens. This political use

of the space suggests another origin for its

shape, which links it to the emperor's other

great Roman project. If the centerpiece of the

34

Temple of Venus and Rome is two apses back to back, the interior of the

Pantheon can be seen as two apses face to face. Just as the apse at the

end of the basilica frames the living emperor or his image, here the dou-

ble apse of the Pantheon manifests his supreme power.

Perhaps as much as 99 percent of the art that decorated the

Pantheon, the imperial palaces, and the fora has been destroyed over the

centuries. The surviving objects dispersed throughout the world, though

few in comparison to the original wealth of the Romans, still amount to a

staggering number. An enormous quantity of Roman art has never left the

city. Two of the greatest collections—the Capitoline museums and the

Vatican museums—founded in the Renaissance, are discussed in later

chapters. Since its establishment in 1870, the Italian state has become

the possessor and caretaker of an enormous amount of Roman art as

well. For decades the state collection was housed in increasingly

deplorable conditions in the Baths of Diocletian. Finally, earthquake damage to that structure in recent times forced the government's hand. The massive collection was dispersed, and new quarters were found for it. After structural repairs, the baths were reopened to house a fraction of the original collection.

A substantial portion of the state's collection is now on display nearby, in Palazzo Massimo alle Terme, built late in the nineteenth century. A hospital during the Second World War, the building served for much of its life as a Jesuit boys' school. The basement, which has been transformed into a strong-room, contains a large collection of coins and gold work. The ground and first floors feature sculpture and other objects arranged in chronological sequence from the archaic period to the age of Constantine. On the third floor, frescoes and mosaics are exhibited. The museum, like all great Roman art collections, is overwhelming. Despite careful chronological grouping and excellent lighting, it is still the incredible mass of objects that impresses the viewer.

To best understand the imperial deployment of art, imagine this onslaught as a covert political message, a strong hint that all the beauty on display has been assembled for your pleasure through the wealth, power, and generosity of the emperor. Because Italian Fascists subscribed to this principle themselves, they had little difficulty in displaying the riches of the Empire. This museum, like most of the newest installations in Rome, tries to avoid a politically charged nostalgia and refuses to exalt one period and its worldview over another. By emphasizing the history of the uninteresting building that houses the collection, it hopes to demystify the Roman imperial era and present it as just another in an endless sequence of historical moments.

One of the central themes this collection illustrates is the triumph over a strong indigenous tradition of officially sponsored art in the Greek style. The collection begins with a display of Republican portrait busts and statues that shows the extraordinary strength of these private cere-monial objects. Prominent Roman families traditionally carried wax images of their distinguished ancestors in funerary processions. They shelved these ephemeral images along with others modeled in bronze, carved in stone, or molded in terracotta in a special shrine in their houses. There the busts served as memorials to remembered relatives as well as symbols of lineage and family connections.

Long lines of these portraits stand in the galleries that surround the courtyard, and there are especially fine ones in the first room. Here are strikingly realistic Roman heads of old and young, men and women. Almost photographic in their literalism, they aimed to preserve an exact physical image of individuals. Their characteristic variety and individuality contrast with the stylized coolness of the Hellenistic examples among them. Augustus, who favored Greek over Roman styles in the official art he sponsored, was responsible for the shift toward idealized portraits in the Greek style. His own image set the standard for the official portraits of his successors.

The statue of a general from Tivoli exemplifies the extreme contrast between Hellenistic idealism and Roman realism. A highly individual head surmounts a body that has sagged and thickened with age. At the opposite extreme, the headless emperor at the end of the gallery offers his commanding gesture and his military bearing in place of the individ-ual and human. Roman official art was not always so impersonal. Room 4 includes a number of marvelous imperial portraits, two in bronze, several of women and children. The delicate miniature bust of the monstrous

Caligula is especially appealing. Augustus hooded, as priests were when they performed sacrifice, is impressive both as a portrait but also as a study in the folds and thrusts of the Roman toga.

The Romans not only imitated Greek art, they also collected it. The Niobid group in Room 7 is one of the finest examples preserved in this way. The young woman stumbling to her knees and reaching back with both hands is pulling at an arrow Apollo has shot as a punishment for her mother's boast. Despite the terror and pain she must be feeling, decorum limits her muscular tension and facial expression. These strong emotions are expressed by her less refined guardian, whose limbs and clothes twist wildly.

This pattern offers an important clue to the use of Greek art in the imperial period. The emperor, like the stoical Niobid, conquers adversity through strength of character. Both have a philosophical depth of self-control that eludes her servant. Unfortunately it is all too easy for this message to be read superficially as a triumph of style or manner over the individual and human. (Think of Mussolini's signature scowl.) With many individual exceptions, especially in the portraits of women and young men, the triumph of official Greek taste over Roman traditions represented in the sculptural collection here shows a similar dehumanizing trend.

In its third floor galleries the museum presents the most widely cele-brated treasures of Roman painting. These remarkable works, which have not been on public display for decades in some cases, reemerge here superbly restored. While there are many isolated objects of great interest and beauty, wherever possible the exhibits recreate whole rooms or suites of rooms. The mainstays of the collection are rooms from two suburban

villas that may have belonged to the household of Augustus. One of these is a suite of
rooms from a villa along the river that was
discovered near the end of the nineteenth
century by the builders of the Tiber embankments. Perhaps nowhere else in Rome can
you get such a clear sense of the serene dignity of a great Roman house.

35

The absolute gem of the collection is the
beautiful garden room from Livia's Villa at Prima Porta. The room represents eternal spring in an open space fringed by low fences and a screen
of delicate fruit trees thick with birds. (35) The sky is bright and close.
Despite the realistic detail and color, the scene is so spare as to be
almost abstract. There is no architectural framing close-up, no town, tree,
or hill in the distance; still the boundaries of the room impose an architecture of their own. The room is like a peristyle garden without walls, a
sheltered, domestic green space with nothing beyond it but the sky. It is
enclosed and safe but also limitless, and suggests how a Roman might
have felt at home in the world. It is also a vision of the Empire, as a
safe domesticated space, green and productive, a utopia limited only by
the sky.

A modern museum has been built into the ruins of the Baths of
Diocletian. In a way that is not typical of contemporary Roman approaches
to old structures, this installation preserves no trace of the scale and
architectural style of the original. The structures and some of the sump-
tuousness of a Roman bath are best seen in three nearby buildings also

36

carved out of the bath complex. These are the church of Santa Maria degli Angeli, the Aula Ottagona, and the church of San Bernardo alle Terme. (36) The imperial forum was a monumental gift to the nation that certified the emperor's power and good will. Impressive as it may have been, a forum was not something the average citizen could appreciate day by day. To bring the message of power and benevolence to a more intimate level, imperial donors relied on public baths.

Every part of Rome was served by a multitude of such structures on every scale. Most citizens used them every day, not just for bathing, which the Romans thought of mainly as a hygienic necessity, but for recreation as well. Stretching over several acres, the imperial bath complexes included hot, warm, and cold water baths carefully arranged in sequence, as well as heated rooms for sweat-baths. Outside the bath building there were public gardens to stroll through and exercise grounds for running, wrestling, and other sports. Outbuildings in the complex housed public libraries, lecture halls, and rooms where anyone could sit and relax. No matter how poor or ill-housed, every Roman man, woman, or child could come home every day exercised, comforted, perhaps instructed, but certainly warmed and washed.

With its endless supply of fresh clean water, the bath pronounced a message in the clearest possible terms: the emperor is the bountiful source of the blessings that nourish life. This message was broadcast to select dignitaries privileged to share the emperor's hospitality in the tri-clinium of his palace on the Palatine. Crowd-pleasing shows in the Colosseum, theaters, and circus were similar and frequent treats. The daily gift of the bath, however, was a constant and widespread benefac-tion. It was one facet of the grander and more complex gift of water. Though the aqueduct system was begun under the Roman Republic, the emperors renovated and greatly expanded it. Under their sponsorship, a total of eleven aqueducts brought more than three thousand gallons of water per second to the city. The most important were the Aqua Claudia, the Anio Novus, Aqua Marcia, Aqua Tepula, Aqua Iulia, and the Anio Vetus. Water reached every region of the city through these aqueducts; it was distributed through channels and pipes to public fountains, where it was available to householders, to the baths, of course, and in some cases to private houses.

Pope Pius IV commissioned Michelangelo to convert a portion of the Baths of Diocletian into a basilica dedicated to Santa Maria degli Angeli. The plan called for an adaptive reuse of the structure rather than a dis-tinctive modification. As a result, it is possible to experience in this church something of the spaciousness and majesty of the imperial build-ing. A small vaulted room with wings to either side, originally a passage-way, opens into a monumental cross-vaulted space beyond. Now the nave of the church, this second chamber was once the tepidarium or warm-water bath. The soaring concrete dome springs from intact granite columns. The distinctive arched windows flood the rich interior with light. The art that fills the side chambers and the niches in the walls celebrates

Christian saints and martyrs, but the display itself carries on Roman traditions of presenting art to the public. (37) In the baths this majestic
room would have been only one stop along the bather's route, and it still
gives a sense of restless movement that interferes with the focus and
solemnity of ritual. In American architecture, Roman baths were imitated
to create great train stations, which connote movement rather than con-
templation. The enormous sundial that slants across the church floor,
though an invention of the eighteenth century, is something the Romans
might have admired.

The Aula Ottagona, another part of the extensive Baths of Diocletian,
is a brick-faced concrete cube, but its interior is octagonal in plan and

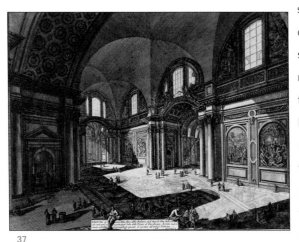

surmounted by an eight-faced
dome with an oculus at its
summit. The main floor is
raised above excavations on
the lower level. The building
has served a number of purposes over the years. For centuries it formed part of the
papal granaries, which, like
the Roman annona, distributed grain to the poor. In the

37

early twentieth century it was a movie theater. Then in 1928 it became
Rome's planetarium. The beautiful webwork inside the dome, which is
supported by a circular entablature and cast-iron pillars, held the small
screens on which the stars were projected. When the hall was later con-

verted to a museum, the spider web of the old planetarium was left
intact, and the effect was to create an alternative historical time from
which to view the collection of sculptures. Gathered from the great baths
of the city and representing the kind of imperial art on public display in
those multipurpose establishments, these sculptures, like the iron framing, belong to a moment of the past. Neither of those epochs, the installation asserts, is the unitary standard, the privileged ideal. Both are
moments in the flow of human time that happen to have left physical
traces in this place.

Among many undistinguished pieces in the collection, one object
(now undergoing restoration) stands out: the Seated Boxer, an extraordinary bronze found near the Baths of Constantine on the Quirinal hill. His
body slumps forward; his forearms rest on his thighs; his hands hang
limp, pulled down by the weight of studded leather wrappings. His
upturned face, cut and swollen, looks for a victory he does not expect.

The Romans were fascinated by suffering, its representations in art,
and its recreations in the theater and amphitheater. They admired professional fighters like this boxer and the gladiators in the Colosseum. The
writer Tertullian, who as a Christian was no stranger to the mystery of suffering, found the Roman fascination with such men paradoxical. "Men
give them their souls, women their bodies . . . On one and the same
account they glorify them and despise them, openly condemning them to
ignominy and the loss of civil rights. The perversity of it! Yet they love
those they punish and belittle those they admire" (*De spectaculis* 22).
Such strong feeling suggests a sense of identification with the gladiator
or the boxer, a feeling that apparently grew stronger as the Empire aged.

As the emperor monopolized power, individuals may have felt deprived of the same civil rights that gladiators were forced to abjure. And in the Seated Boxer's ability to endure pain, to survive or to die with equanimity and dignity, they may have found a terrible model of their own fate.

With the exception of the Baths of Trajan, which were built over a wing of Nero's Golden House, most imperial bath complexes were located away from Rome's center. This placement reflects the city's enormous growth in the imperial period. Not far from the Baths of Diocletian a substantial section of Rome's second city wall stands alone in a green island in front of the train station. The Servian wall, built of rough tufa blocks, was about twelve feet thick originally and stood nearly thirty feet high. Its name reflects a Roman belief that it was built in the time of the Etruscan king Servius Tullius. It actually dates from the time of the Gallic invasion of 392 BC. Some seven miles in length, it followed the contours of the land to form a defensive perimeter of the city from the fourth century BC to the age of Augustus.

From Augustus' time onward and lasting for about two centuries in a period known as the Pax Romana, the city had no need to defend herself against invaders. During this period the city began to grow, and urban neighborhoods filled in the entire area enclosed by the Servian wall. With no defensive purpose to serve, the wall's outline marked the limits of the heavily urbanized core of the city. Inside its perimeter, new neighborhoods housed the city's working population. These densely settled areas came in time to be served by one of the imperial baths. Small samples of these imperial neighborhoods have been uncovered in excavations beneath some of Rome's oldest churches, such as San Clemente and

Santi Giovanni e Paolo. In addition to the Baths of Diocletian, the Baths
of Caracalla on the Aventine hill survive.

Outside the Servian wall a different kind of development took place.
Wealthy Romans had for centuries divided their time between their town
houses and country villas, a trend that continued with a new twist during
the Empire. In the zone immediately outside Rome's Servian wall, a
hybrid dwelling came into fashion. In essence a country estate, it was
placed as close as possible to the city walls. The elite developed a
suburban outlook; they were close to the city but not quite of it. Their
architects laid out gardens that framed the distant cityscape in green.

The Romans called these new hybrids horti—a comical understatement meant to suggest that these luxurious homes were modest "market
gardens." By the end of the first century AD, horti ringed the city. Over
the centuries, the imperial family came to own a great number of them.
Beginning in the fourth century, when Christianity became the state religion, imperial properties in the same areas were donated to the Church.
Because of this pattern of imperial land ownership, Christian basilicas
came to be located outside the circuit of the Servian wall.

Built in the third century AD, almost six centuries after the earlier
walls, the Aurelian wall countered the first threat of alien invasion.
Following the broken contour of the land, the brick-faced concrete wall
forms an irregular circuit nearly eighteen miles long—the defensive
perimeter of Rome at the height of its power. Recognizing that the
Germanic tribes that had invaded the Italian peninsula would soon
threaten Rome itself, the emperors Aurelian and Probus commited vast
resources to this project, and it was finished in an incredible eight years.

Two centuries later the wall was finally breached and the city was sacked. In the millennium that followed, as Rome shrank to a fraction of its former size, the Aurelian wall, like the vestigial shoreline of a drained lake, traced the outline of the ancient city.

Chapter Four

EARLY CHRISTIAN CHURCHES

At first a minor cult that thrived in the Jewish and Syrian neighborhoods near the Tiber docks, Christianity became a major force during the reign of the emperor Constantine. While his motives and his commitment have been questioned, Constantine's own writings reflect a long acquaintance with the tenets of the religion and a continuing belief in its importance both to the emperor and to the Empire.

Constantine attributed his victory over his political rival Maxentius at the Milvian Bridge outside Rome in 313 to support by the Christian God. Among his first acts was a proclamation of religious toleration which restored confiscated property and civil rights to Christians. Soon after he endowed Rome's first public Christian church, San Giovanni in Laterano, and its baptistery. In 324 Constantine defeated his rival, Licinius, and became sole emperor of the East and the West. He immediately began work on a thoroughly Christian city, Constantinople, a new imperial center that would be unencumbered by pagan monuments. At this time he published a second edict urging his subjects to adopt Christianity but protecting the freedom of pagan worship and prohibiting the desecration or destruction of its traditional monuments and shrines. The emperor himself, however, deferred baptism until a few days before his death in 337.

By fostering Christianity and moving his court to Byzantium, Constantine set forces in motion that would, by the beginning of the sixth century, completely reshape and redefine the city. Rome was the traditional administrative center of a political conglomerate that stretched from Spain to Armenia and from the Sahara to Scotland. The celebrated network of Roman roads speeded communications between the provinces and the center; but distances were great, and travel even under the best conditions was often too slow to keep pace with events. Territories and provinces rebelled; Roman generals used their armies to gain control over the Empire itself. Invaders threatened. While some were repelled, others were allowed to settle within bounds. The Romans recruited these resident aliens as soldiers to defend their new homeland against the next wave of invaders.

Over the centuries, the administration of the Empire was reorganized, sometimes for reasons of political expediency but just as often for practical reasons: at various times there were teams of two or even four emperors; superior and subordinate emperors; an emperor of the East and one of the West. These divided administrations governed from cities in various parts of the Mediterranean world. Over centuries of improvisation and experiment, one clear trend emerged: the city of Rome lost its position at the center of the Empire, while Constantinople's stock as head of the Empire in the East generally rose.

With the ebbing of imperial power, the city lost its raison d'etre. Its wealth and population declined, but its fabric was still magnificent. Imperial donations maintained the enormous patrimony of public buildings—the temples, fora, baths, the palace itself. Visitors were still impressed; they could hardly separate what they saw before their eyes from the image of Roman supremacy in their minds.

Except for occasional pangs of nostalgia, the city's passage into political obsolescence was almost painless. But with the invasion of Alaric's Visigoths in 410 AD, the climate changed. Contemporaries were shocked that the seemingly invulnerable, proverbially eternal city could be violated. "The very head has been severed from the body of empire," St. Jerome wrote, "or to speak more truly, in one city the whole world has died" (*Commentary on Ezekiel* 1.3). St. Augustine, who cared much less for Rome, was just as strongly affected: "We hear terrible news of slaughter, fire, rape, torture, murder . . . We agonize over all of it and often weep" (Augustine, *De urbis excidio* 2.3).

The Visigothic sack, which lasted only three days, was just the first in a series of invasions. A natural disaster accelerated the damage. According to the historian Paolus Diaconus, a terrible earthquake in 442 brought down many temples and porticoes. Thirteen years later the Vandals sacked the city. The Goths attacked it repeatedly and occupied it during the early sixth century. When Byzantine forces tried to recapture the city in 536, one side or the other cut the aqueducts.

Administratively and technologically, Rome was in ruins by the mid-sixth century. A powerful and devastating earthquake in that same era accelerated the work of neglect and violent depredation. It was at this moment that Constantine's second innovation came to the city's rescue. The Christian Church under a powerful and patriotic leader, Pope St. Gregory the Great (590–604), stepped in to take command.

The city for which he and his clerical administration assumed responsibility had changed dramatically from the vast, powerful, and pleasant Rome of the second century. Reduced by invasion and disease, the population of Rome had shrunk to a quarter of its maximum. After the destruction of the aqueducts, this beleaguered population was forced to retreat to areas along the river, the only secure large-volume water supply. Once-crowded neighborhoods on the Esquiline and Quirinal hills were abandoned. Displaced Romans scavenged for living space among the deserted public buildings of the Campus Martius.

With the change of government came a change of government center. Power moved from the Forum and Palatine to the headquarters of the Roman clergy, which stood on the outskirts of the imperial city. For a millennium—from the sixth century until the sixteenth—Rome was structured like a ringed planet. Ordinary citizens clustered close to the Tiber; beyond them stretched an ever-widening zone where the imperial city was returning to wilderness. Still further out near the circuit of the walls stood a ring of great religious institutions where the government of Rome resided.

This peculiar and impractical organization had arisen because of conditions in effect two centuries earlier, when Constantine had established the first official Christian churches. In the crowded Rome of that epoch there was no central space available for the vast basilicas the new religion would require. The neighborhood churches already in use were too small to accommodate the mass of new converts. For land that was unoccupied and entirely under the control of the emperor, Constantine turned to the imperial horti, the suburban villas beyond the line of the old Servian wall on the fringes of the heavily settled city. On these suburban

estates a ring of monumental basilicas dedicated to Christianity was
built.

This decision was both expedient and politically astute. Rather than
confront Roman religion and tradition head-on, Constantine left the symbolic and religious core of the city—the Forum and Palatine—unmarked
by new monuments. Indeed, he and his successors provided for the
maintenance of structures dedicated to the now displaced former gods of
the city and the Empire. Unfortunately, when the city shrank in the inter-
vening two centuries, the new Christian monuments stood isolated from
the center of population.

The popes may have governed from the Lateran Palace on the outer
fringe of Rome, but without their power, wealth, and spiritual prestige the
workaday city that gripped both banks of the Tiber would have collapsed.
Pilgrimage and the trades that supported it, including church and secular
building and rebuilding, plus the goods and services required by a vast
clerical bureaucracy, fueled the Roman economy from Christian antiquity
until the sudden removal of the popes to Avignon a millennium later. As
long as the papacy remained powerful and in place, there was no source
or motive for dramatic change.

Within the repertoire of Roman building types, the basilica was the
most suitable for Christian worship. It could hold vast numbers of people—a necessity after the religion won official favor. The apse at its end,
which could be further emphasized by a decorated arch, focused attention
on the altar and the celebrant of the mass. At the time of Constantine's
conversion, churches of all shapes and sizes existed throughout Rome in
private houses and apartments, in disused shops and warehouses. The

emperor's sponsored structures and their successors, which at first supplemented these local congregations, soon replaced them with buildings
of uniform design, and in time the liturgy evolved into patterns adapted
to these spaces,

Though not dedicated by Constantine, the patriarchal basilica of
Santa Maria Maggiore followed the pattern he established. It was built in
the second quarter of the fifth century AD a short way outside the Servian
wall on a platform created by filling in an abandoned villa. The Council of
Ephesus in 431 had recognized Mary as the "Mother of God," and this
monumental church both commemorated and, in its mural program, illus-
trated this role.

Unlike such churches as San Giorgio in Velabro, Santa Maria
Maggiore has not been "repristinated"—stripped of accretions and ornaments and artificially returned to its "original" design. The church reveals
instead a long and complex history of preservation, restoration, and
sometimes dramatic rebuilding. Throughout its life, however, the core of
the basilica has preserved the character and spirit of Constantine's building program better than any other monument that survives in Rome
today.

The fifth-century church is completely invisible from the street. The
original entry would have led through an atrium—an open courtyard
surrounded by a colonnade—long since pulled down. In the far portico
of the atrium, doors in the same position as the present ones would
open onto the basilica itself. A monumental façade of the eighteenth
century with five doorways below and three in a loggia above now
leads into the church. In the loggia on the second floor of the entryway,

thirteenth-century mosaics tell a story that has long been identified with Santa Maria Maggiore. According to legend, on the night of August 5, 352, Pope Liberius had a dream in which the Virgin ordered him to build a church wherever it snowed in Rome the following day. The next morning a miraculous summer snow fell on the Esquiline hill and outlined the ground plan of the church.

Now as in the fifth century, the interior is dominated by a large nave that is flanked by smaller and lower aisles to right and left. (38) The structure of the basilica is typical and simple, as are the changes that the building has experienced. On each side of the nave a file of columns supports an ornamented marble beam or architrave. Each of the architraves carries a long wall with many windows that fill the nave with light. An elaborately paneled and

38

gilded Renaissance ceiling hides the wooden beams that rest on top of the nave walls and support the tiled roof. The side aisles of the original church were about half the height of the nave, and their pitched roofs met the nave wall below the level of the window openings. Light for the side aisles came from windows in the outer walls. At the altar end of the nave there is an arched opening. The original apse of the church, which was replaced in the thirteenth century, stood beyond that arch. Since no drawings of the earlier apse survive and the written record is ambiguous, no one knows exactly how it looked.

The thirteenth-century expansion of the apse is the most invasive of

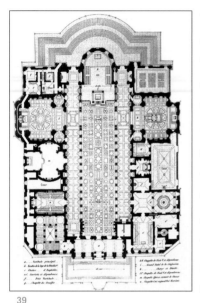

39

the many changes the church has undergone. Additions were also built against the outer walls of the original structure, where both side aisles now open on a succession of chapels. These chapels, which more than double the floor plan of the original building, block the light to the aisles and create shadow zones in a space that was at first uniformly bright. Two monumental chapels that open to either side of the high altar act like a transept, or crossing in the nave. (39) A buried shrine or confessio under the altar is another later addition. Two pairs of the original columns on axis with these additions have been moved and an arch built over them to further suggest that the building is cruciform in plan rather than rectangular. These features recall changes to Old St. Peter's, which were widely imitated.

Beneath the windows on both sides of the nave, a series of fifth-century mosaics illustrate scenes from the Old and New Testaments. Restored in 1593 and again in the last decade, the scenes are remarkable for their quality, number, and the state of their preservation. Scenes on the left side of the nave tell the stories of Abraham, Isaac, and Jacob. Those on the right illustrate the lives of Moses and of Christ. The mosaics of the nave are very difficult to see. Whether they could be used to instruct the faithful in biblical history and Marian theology is unclear. They do put her story on record, however, if only for an ideal observer.

In the mosaic program as in fifth-century theology, Mary gave birth to

Jesus in two orders of being. As a human mother, she joined her son physically to the generations that came before him, in the same way that all earthly generations, like those of Abraham, Isaac, and Jacob, are connected. In a mysterious way as Mother of God, she also linked Jesus spiritually with figures whose actions in the world anticipated his. When Jesus obeyed God's incomprehensible will, he was like a perfected Abraham; sacrificed on the cross, he was like Isaac; leading mankind out of captivity, he acted like Moses. Both literally and figuratively, Mary is the key to Jesus' connections with the divinely directed history of the Jews.

The historical narratives in the nave are linked both physically and symbolically by scenes on the triumphal arch in which Mary plays a key part. These well-known scenes include the Annunciation; the Adoration of the Magi; the Slaughter of the Innocents; Jesus' Presentation in the Temple; the Flight into Egypt; the Magi before Herod; plus idealized images of the cities of Jerusalem and Bethlehem. The inscription beneath reads "Sixtus III for the People of God."

The apse mosaics were created in the late thirteenth century by Jacopo Torriti when the fifth-century apse was drastically remodeled. The mosaics, in the Byzantine style, show Christ placing a crown on the head of Mary, who is enthroned beside him. Biblical figures and others from the thirteenth century, including St. Francis, Pope Nicholas IV, and Cardinal Jacopo Colonna, surround the two. Despite the nearly nine centuries that separate the arch and nave mosaics from those of the apse, the symbolic program of the church was preserved in them.

Though built in the ninth century, the nearby church of Santa

40

Prassede (the poet Robert Browning's "St. Praxed's") carefully imitated the form of Constantinian churches. In many ways it is a reduced-scale model of Old St. Peter's. The church is now entered from the side, but its original entrance was up a set of stairs and through an atrium surrounded by a portico. The nave, its upper walls supported by colonnades, is flanked by two side aisles. A triumphal arch opens onto a shallow elevated transept and apse. (40) The small windows that originally lit the nave have been replaced by four larger ones. Rounded archways on clumsy piers, which shore up the roof and walls, redefine the church as a dynamic succession of arches converging on the altar.

Like the structure of the church, the mosaics evoke the style of Early Christian Rome. The apse mosaic shows the Second Coming of Christ, who floats down from a dark blue sky among multicolored clouds. Peter and Paul with Saints Prassede and Pudentiana stand to either side; palm trees symbolizing faith, one with a phoenix—the symbol of rebirth—in its branches, flank the composition. A band of sheep below represents the Christian "flock." The arch mosaics, which date from the same period, are, like the biblical narratives in Santa Maria Maggiore, based on book illustrations. Though expanded in scale, little has been done to accommodate them to the space; their rectangular frames butt uncomfortably against the curve of the arch.

The Chapel of San Zeno, probably the resting place of the remains of St. Valentine, is an intact treasure of ninth-century architecture and decoration. Like the rest of the church, it recalls Early Christian monuments. The doorway to the chapel not only imitates such monuments, it assembles and reuses materials from earlier structures. Called spolia, such recycled materials were often used in Christian buildings. The columns and architraves in Santa Maria Maggiore came from earlier buildings, as did the nave columns in Santa Prassede. While Constantine and his successor prohibited the adoption of pagan temples for Christian purposes and outlawed the destruction of public buildings for any purpose, as imperial power waned and the city's fabric was damaged by sack and earthquake these prohibitions became impractical and unenforceable. People moved into abandoned structures and remodeled them to suit new purposes. Other buildings fell down or were pulled down, and builders scavenged their columns, capitals, beams, and moldings for reuse. Most Roman churches feature some reused antique materials.

41

Above the chapel doorway, stylized portraits in rondels surround a scavenged urn and an arched window. The interior of the chapel, designed to resemble an Early Christian mausoleum, incorporates reused columns in its corners. In a pattern that is typical of Byzantine play with architectural elements, these real columns lead upward to images of angels who in turn "support" a rondel enclosing an image of Christ. (41)

This passage from real to imaginary support mimics the metaphysical passage from the substantial earth of everyday experience to the realm of spirits beyond, where even the laws of physics (as Aristotle declared) were different. In one of the wall mosaics, Peter and Paul, dressed in stylized togas and standing on air, point to an empty throne which supports a cross. This image, like others in the church, refers not just to Christian antiquity in general but to specific mosaics in Santa Maria Maggiore.

In the late fourth century one of the larger rooms of a private bath was converted into a church dedicated to Santa Pudentiana. Frequently remodeled throughout the centuries and brutally repristinated in the

42

1920s, the church has little left of its original form. Far below modern street level, the remains of an atrium front a stripped-down façade. The intimate interior is dominated by a striking apse mosaic of the late fourth century, the earliest to survive. (42) In its center, Christ sits on an elaborate throne with an open book in his hand. Its inscription says, "God, Preserver of the Church of Pudentiana." He is surrounded by two ranks of apostles dressed in the togas of Roman senators and seated like spectators in a theater box. In their informal arrangement, their animation and individuality, these extraordinary figures retain the best qualities of Roman portraiture. The two standing women with crowns are probably allegorical figures; St. Pudentiana and her sister St. Prassede also offer crowns. An idealized arcade and cityscape surround

the figures. A symbolic cross and icons of the four evangelists—man,
lion, ox, and eagle—float in the sky above. St. Prassede and St.
Pudentiana were virgin sisters who dedicated their lives to comforting
and providing burial for those who suffered martyrdom for the faith. They
are usually shown with small bottles in their hands, with which they collected the blood of the slain.

Unlike Santa Maria Maggiore and the other churches that clustered
around it, the churches of Sant'Agnese Fuori le Mura and Santa Costanza
lie beyond the Aurelian wall on the Roman road called the Nomentana.
According to legend, St. Agnes, at the age of twelve, fell victim to the
persecution of Diocletian near the beginning of the fourth century. "The
son of Symphronius, the prefect of Rome, fell in love with Agnes; when
she rejected him outright, his father advised him to denounce her as a
Christian. The young man threatened, and when she again refused him,
he turned her over to his father, who, in revenge, had her exposed naked
in a brothel. Agnes's hair immediately grew and covered her; and the only
man who attempted to touch her immediately fell dead at her feet. Yet
not even this miracle—eloquent testimony of her purity and her faith in
God—could sway the enemy's hand. Agnes was decapitated with a sword
like a lamb offered in sacrifice, the very symbol of purity. Today in the
basilica that bears her name, on the morning of January 21, two lambs
are blessed and given to the Pope so that their wool may be woven into
vestments for the archbishops" (Acta Sanctorum).

St. Agnes was buried in one of several Christian catacombs on the
outskirts of Rome. Roman law and custom required burials to be outside
city boundaries, and Rome's vast population and long history meant an

ever-increasing demand for appropriate burial space. Outside Rome (and every other Roman city or town) the highways were lined with tombs of all sorts. Romans had traditionally cremated their dead; but in the early second century, customs shifted dramatically and burial became increasingly popular among those who could afford the larger tombs it required.

While Rome's Early Christian community was generally poor, belief in the resurrection of the body made inhumation a necessity for them. Around the turn of the second century, Christian communities began to bury their dead not with their extended families as pagans did but with co-religionists. They established cemeteries above ground and, underground, vast catacombs with extensive galleries lined with arched recesses for burials. The soft but sturdy volcanic tufa that underlies Rome made excavation of these labyrinthine galleries simple and safe.

According to popular legend, Christians fleeing persecution worshipped secretly in the catacombs. In reality, Christians were drawn to the catacombs not only by reverence for their own dead but because of their belief that many Christian martyrs were buried within them. The great basilicas linked to catacombs, like Sant'Agnese, served two purposes: to venerate the martyrs and to provide requiem services for believers who wished to be buried near them. When invaders threatened the city in the fifth and sixth centuries, the relics of many saints and martyrs were removed from their original burial sites in the catacombs and reinterred in churches inside the city walls.

The emperor Constantine's daughter, Constantia, was so devoted to the martyred St. Agnes that she sponsored the construction of a church on the site of her burial and had her own mausoleum built nearby. While ruins of Constantia's basilica remain, the present church was built in the sixth century AD. The Basilica of Sant'Agnese follows the familiar pattern of Early Christian basilicas, with one important difference. It was partially dug into the earth, so that its altar could be placed as close as possible to the grave of the sainted martyr.  A second story was added to part of the church at ground level. Wrongly described as a "women's gallery"—there was no separation of men and women in the early church—it is in fact an accessible space to accommodate overflow crowds. (43)

43

The entrance to the main floor of the church is down a long ramp. Its interior is divided into a nave and side aisles by a double arcade supported on reused columns. A second arcade opens onto the galleries above the side aisles and continues around the back of the church. The wall above the nave arcade extends above the gallery into a clerestory that lights the central space. In the apse vault there is a solemn and majestic Byzantine mosaic of St. Agnes with a phoenix on her robe to symbolize rebirth. To her left is Pope Symmachus and to her right is Pope Honorius, who holds a model of the church in his hands.

The mausoleum of Constantine's daughter, Constantia, has over the centuries been transposed into a church dedicated to St. Costanza. While most Constantinian buildings were architecturally conservative, a very few, like this one, display the refined taste and structural virtuosity of the

44

best imperial architecture. A central vaulted drum supported on a circular arcade above doubled columns is surrounded by a lower vaulted aisle. (44) The mausoleum might be visualized as the cross-section of a standard basilica rotated through 180 degrees: the central drum with its clerestory windows above is like a cylindrical nave enveloped by a continuous aisle. This aisle in turn was originally surrounded by a second ring with arched openings—a circular narthex or porch—now lost. Both less experimental and more successful, the mausoleum is a recognizable development of the octagonal room in Nero's Golden House.

The magnificent mosaics in the ring vault are among the oldest surviving. Scenes of putti (cherubs) harvesting grapes and making wine punctuate geometric and floral motifs set against a light ground. (45) While they are stylized to create a sense of onward movement in the annular vault, the scenes recall

45

the static green horizon punctuated with birds and flowers in the frescoes

of Livia's Villa at Prima Porta.

To the left and right of the entrance are mosaic portraits of Constan-

tia and her husband; niches in the outer walls hold other mosaics,

including one of a bearded Christ handing a scroll to St. Peter and the

figure of a youthful Christ in a landscape. Constantia's monumental por-

phyry sarcophagus is in the Vatican Museum; a copy stands in its original

place here. Porphyry, a blood red igneous stone, very hard and difficult to

work, was found only in Egypt. Its use was limited to the pharaohs;

because of its rarity and regal associations, Roman and especially

Byzantine emperors adopted it.

The church of San Lorenzo Fuori le Mura is similar in function and

origin to Sant'Agnese. Constantine built a large basilica near the site of

the catacomb where St. Lorenzo (St. Lawrence) was buried. One of the

most celebrated and beloved of Roman saints, St. Lorenzo was martyred

in 258. A deacon of the Roman Church, he was ordered to hand over its

assets to the emperor. He distributed them to the poor instead and

assured the imperial officers that these were the Church's true treasure.

He was ordered to be burned alive on an iron grill. According to tradition,

he told his persecutors, "I am cooked on this side; turn me over and

eat!"

By the sixth century Constantine's basilica no longer satisfied pil-

grims, who expected more direct contact with the treasured relics. Under

Pope Pelagius, the hillside was excavated and the grave of St. Lorenzo

was isolated, then surrounded by a small basilica. Galleries at ground

level formed a second-story arcade around the central shrine. Much later, a second church was built next to but not communicating with the earlier one. In the thirteenth century the two churches were combined into the present structure. Now entered through a low roofed porch, the later basilica, which has been stripped of its ornamentation, serves as nave to

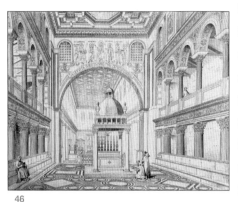

the earlier one. To unify these structures, the original floor of Pelagius' basilica was raised and its altar positioned above the martyr's tomb, which was in effect reburied. This raised floor struck the original columns at their midpoint. Eventually the hillside outside the earlier church was completely cut away. Despite all this backing and filling, the contemporary church,

46

which is now mainly used for funerals, is both curious and surprisingly harmonious. (46)

For sanitary reasons, the French, who occupied Rome in the early nineteenth century, reinstated the pre-Christian practice of burying the dead outside city limits. On the site of the abandoned Constantinian basilica, French designers laid out a new hygienic necropolis which was realized in mid-century under the direction of Virginio Vespignani. As urban in feeling and structure as Rome's nineteenth-century neighborhoods, the Campo Verano cemetery features blocks of free-standing mausoleums and multistoried tombs. Statuary, trees, and abundant flowers frame the well-tended graves. The square outside is lined with florist stalls. The Jewish Cemetery, which once overlooked the Circus Maximus and has since been replaced by the city rose garden, has been relocated here as well. Other non-Catholics, including such notables as Keats, are buried under the shadow of the Pyramid of Cestius near the Porta San Paolo in what is usually known as the Protestant Cemetery.

The core of Santa Croce in Gerusalemme was once a reception hall in the Sessorian Palace, an imperial property on the edge of the city where the emperor Constantine and his family lived in the early years of his reign. It takes its name from relics of the Holy Cross which Constantine's mother, Helen, is said to have brought from Jerusalem and deposited within it. The original space served only for private worship by the imperial family and retinue. To adapt it for public worship, the palace hall was divided into three aisles and an apse was added at one end. Although the palace walls are still visible on the outer sidewall of the church, the building has been remodeled and restored so often over the centuries that little of the original structure remains visible, inside or out. The monumental façade was added in the seventeenth century.

For half of its two-thousand-year history, the Catholic Church was governed from the cathedral of San Giovanni in Laterano (the Lateran). Constantine sponsored construction of the church as early as 313 in the immediate aftermath of his conversion. Built on an imperial hortus just inside the Aurelian wall, it took its name from the Plauti Laterani family who had owned the property in the time of Nero. To make room for the basilica, Constantine's builders leveled a compound of the imperial horse guards—punishment, some argue, for a unit that supported the emperor's defeated rival Maxentius.

As the Mother Church of Roman Christianity, the basilica was originally dedicated to Christ the Savior, but Pope St. Gregory the Great added dedications to both St. John the Baptist and St. John the Evangelist. The original building was a basilica not unlike Santa Maria Maggiore, though larger overall, and with two aisles of unequal height flanking each side of the central nave. An atrium fronted the building. While Constantine's basilica still forms the core of the contemporary building, little except the general plan of that church remains visible today. The Vandals sacked it in the fifth century; it was damaged by an earthquake in 896. Rebuilt in the early tenth century and richly decorated in the late thirteenth century, it burned to the ground in 1308. Despite the removal of the papacy to southern France in 1305, the basilica was rebuilt, only to burn again in 1361. Rebuilt yet again under Urban V and Gregory XI, it was radically refashioned in the Baroque style by Borromini. While he reused materials from the earlier phases of the building, only the apse remained substantially unchanged from its pre-Renaissance form.

As Christianity spread throughout the Empire, what visitors came to see in Rome gradually shifted away from traditional sites at the city's center and toward Christian shrines on its outer edge. The Lateran, like all the great basilicas that ringed Rome, was an object of devotion both for residents and for pilgrims, but because of the preeminence of the bishop of Rome, it attracted official as well as pious visitors. While these included foreign dignitaries and their ambassadors, the majority were clerics. Synods of bishops, official consultations, and appointments to clerical office required their presence in Rome. The need to consult authoritative texts of Church councils and scriptural commentaries brought them to the papal collections of manuscripts and documents. They were eager to learn and imitate the Roman liturgy and to adapt papal ceremonials to their own liturgies. They came to see the shrines, just as lay pilgrims did, but they were also on the lookout for relics they could transport to their churches back home.

Visitors ranged from the wealthy and powerful to the poor and infirm. Some few were guests in private houses; a smaller percentage stayed in the Patriarchal Palace itself. National communities with fluid populations grew up around St. Peter's outside the city limits. German visitors would find lodging in the area still known as the Borgo. The papacy provided free housing, food, and medical care for sick or impoverished pilgrims in its several hostels throughout the city.

The neoclassical façade of San Giovanni in Laterano, with five doors below and five arched openings in the loggia above, overlooks a vast piazza where the original atrium of Constantine's basilica stood. On the church's roofline, their partially carved backs visible from across the city, stand colossal images of both St. Johns and doctors of the Church who flank a central image of Christ holding the Cross. The overall effect is majestic, but the plaza, like the church itself, is usually deserted. The interior of the church, still divided into five sections in Borromini's baroque remodeling, glows with marble. Enormous statues of the Twelve Apostles peer from niches in the piers. Only the Pope can say mass at the altar under its fourteenth-century tabernacle. The transept is decorated with huge frescoes representing the Ascension, the Apostles, events from the life of Constantine, and the history of the basilica itself.

The scenes depicting Constantine form the core of his legend as the Church monumentalized it. These are Constantine's prophetic dream of the Cross which promises him victory over Maxentius; his triumph at the

Milvian Bridge; his messengers received by Pope St. Sylvester; the baptism of Constantine; and his gifts to the Lateran basilica. Juxtaposed with
portraits of saints and doctors of the Church, these scenes are a fairly
even-handed tracing of the secular thread that led to the foundation of
this singular basilica. Other retellings of Constantine's story, especially
that in the nearby church of Santi Quattro Coronati, used the legend very
aggressively to assert papal claims to secular as well as spiritual authority.

The restored and repositioned apse vault mosaic dates from the late
thirteenth century. Its roots in the Byzantine tradition and its theme connect it directly to the early Church. Christ appears in its upper center
surrounded by angels; beneath him a gem-encrusted Cross and a dove
symbolizing the Holy Spirit rest on a hill from which four rivers flow.
These are both the rivers that run out of Eden and also the life-giving
words of the four evangelists. The Virgin, a throng of saints, including
thirteenth-century figures, and Pope Nicholas IV surround the central figures. Symbolically, the mosaic depicts Christ, the original and ultimate
dedicatee of the basilica, as the source of spiritual life that flows through
Christian symbols, through the saints, and through the Church itself.
Though physically absent, Constantine is recalled by Christ's symbolic
gift of that most fundamental of imperial donations, water.

The Lateran Palace, which adjoins the basilica, was rebuilt in the late
sixteenth century. (47) Within its structure it incorporates remains of
papal residences that date from the fourth-century founding of the
Church. Like the basilica, the palace has endured enormous upheavals.
In addition to fires and earthquakes, the palace was repeatedly destroyed
by mob violence. In the Middle Ages it was customary for Romans to

sack the palace at the death of each pontiff. After continuous use as a papal residence for a thousand years, the palace was
abandoned completely during the removal
of the papacy to southern France—the so-
called Babylonian Captivity followed by the
Great Schism—which lasted from 1305
until the election of Martin V in 1417.
When Martin reestablished Rome as the
center of papal government, he and his
successors chose the Vatican rather than the Lateran as the site of their

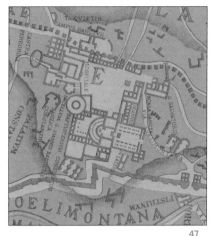

47

courts. Domenico Fontana, the architect of Pope Sixtus V, rebuilt the
Lateran Palace as a summer residence. It now contains the offices of
the Roman Vicar, who carries out the strictly local responsibilities of the
bishop of Rome.

The Scala Santa, venerated by pilgrims as the stairs Christ climbed on
his way to Pilate's court, survived the destruction of the medieval palace.
At their top stands the Sancta Sanctorum. Named for the Holy of Holies
of Solomon's Temple, it was the private chapel of the medieval popes.
Visible only through iron gratings, the chapel is richly decorated with
mosaics of the twelfth and thirteenth centuries. A gold-encased portrait
of Christ that was, according to legend, miraculously conceived and not
"painted by hands" stands above the altar. "It is the image of the Savior
at about the age of twelve encrusted with gold and gems and was (it is
believed) drawn by St. Luke and finished by an Angel. On the fourteenth
of August after Vespers in almost every year in the manner of an ancient

triumph it is carried on the shoulders of the most honored citizens to S. Maria Maggiore. Everyone in Rome and the neighboring towns goes there to see it; then after mass is sung on the following morning, it is carried back to the Chapel with equal ceremony" (Palladio, *Descritione de le chiese,* 1554).

Unlike the basilica and palace, the Baptistery, though somewhat enlarged and often repaired, remains much as it was in the time of Constantine. It stands on the foundations of a private bath structure of the Lateran hortus. Though smaller and octagonal rather than circular in plan, the building is similar in form to the mausoleum of Constantia. That resemblance goes beyond matters of period style or patronage. The architecture of the tomb strengthens the symbolism of baptism as spiritual rebirth. Like the eight notes of the octave, the eight sides of the building—the prototype for all baptisteries in the Western Christian tradition—also symbolize rebirth.

The outer aisle surrounds an inner colonnade. (48) Eight porphyry columns support an octagonal lintel; eight smaller columns rise above and support both the aisle roof and the drum of a small tile-roofed cupola. The original cupola may have been higher, which would have brought more light into the building, and it may have been domed. The rich paneling of the interior walls is

48

all work of the seventeenth century. Inside the colonnade stands the original font—a large urn of green basalt not unlike an imperial sarcophagus—chosen to accommodate baptism by immersion. Its curious copper
cover was added in the seventeenth century.

The two chapels that emerge from the side aisles were built between
the fifth and seventh centuries. The Chapel of the Baptism retains its
original bronze doors, a great rarity in Rome. When swung on their
hinges, the doors resonate with a sound halfway between that of a bell
and a gong. In the chapel on the opposite side, a mosaic of the mid-
seventh century shows a bust of Christ supported by angels and surrounded by saints, including Pope John IV. On the south side of the
Baptistery, there is a small narthex and the baptistery's original entrance.
One of its apse vaults contains rich floral mosaics of the fifth century
similar to those of a century before at Santa Costanza.

Santi Quattro Coronati, of very complex history, is one of the most
evocative churches in Rome. Its high, nearly windowless brick façade and
the single entrance under a massive square tower suggest a fortress
rather than a place of worship. The first church on the site was built into
a large hall in an imperial building and dedicated to four Roman soldiers
who had won the crown of martyrdom. These men were converts to
Christianity who were put to death when they refused to worship a statue
of Aesculapius. By the seventh century, the four soldiers had become
confused with four different martyrs, Severus, Victorinus, Carpohoros,
and Severianus, sculptors from Poland who because of their Christian
beliefs refused to sculpt an image of the healing god.

In the ninth century the earlier structure was replaced by a large basilica with an atrium, nave side aisles, and an apse. Sacked by the Normans at the end of the eleventh century, the partially ruined church was reconceived as a fortified monastery on the defensive perimeter of the Lateran. When invaders threatened, the Pope and Curia took refuge there. In form and in the symbolism of its most important chapel, it reflects that role today.

Inside the fortress gates, the central space of the original atrium remains open while its surrounding portico is enclosed. At its end stands the narthex of the original church, and beyond it a second atrium is open to the sky and, like the preceding one, walled off on its edges. This roofless area was the back of the nave; and the walls to either side follow the line of the colonnade that once separated the nave from the side aisles. Another elaborate entrance leads into the twelfth-century church proper— in appearance, a three-aisle basilica. Here in the front end of the nave a colonnade supporting a gallery has been added to right and left, and the side aisles have been completely walled off. The apse, which is too large for the nave, reflects the scale of the much larger original basilica.

The fortress mentality that conceived this defensive restructuring is represented symbolically in the frescoes of the twelfth-century chapel of San Silvestro. The chapel was designed not for the monastic community but for the use of the Pope and Curia. The fresco cycle here differs dramatically from the story of Constantine told in the transept frescoes of the Lateran. Rather than portraying Constantine as the divinely appointed victor over Maxentius, these frescoes replace that crucial event in the history of his conversion with another episode. The Constantine of this legend, afflicted by leprosy and inspired by a dream, sends messengers

to appeal for help from Pope St. Sylvester. The Pope, who with his followers is hiding from imperial persecution in the hill country outside
Rome, instructs Constantine to venerate images of the apostles Peter and
Paul, baptizes the emperor, and cures his leprosy. Constantine rewards
Sylvester with gifts symbolic of empire (the so-called Donation of
Constantine), and then leads his mule as the Pope triumphantly takes
possession of the city and the Empire for Christ. Constantine's sub-
servience in these wonderful scenes tells the story of papal politics at the
time of their creation. The very Normans who ravaged the Church are one
branch of a political dynasty that laid claim to imperial political authority
in Italy. These mosaics, which show the Pope taking precedence over the
emperor, make the counterclaim of papal superiority.

When the Normans pillaged the church of Santi Quattro, they also
burned the nearby church of San Clemente. The fact of that devastation,
however, completely vanished from memory until the mid-nineteenth
century. Workmen probing the foundations of the building in 1857 discovered the remains of an earlier church beneath, decorated with frescoes. One of them is inscribed with the earliest phrase in vernacular
Italian so far found. This discovery is a mixed blessing, however, since
the inscription reads fili dele pute, sons of whores. When the lower church
was excavated, it in its turn was found to rest on remains of a Roman
house and apartment building that had stood opposite each other separated by a small alley. The entire complex is now open, making it possible to survey the site in three distinct historical periods. (49)

St. Clement, ordained by St. Peter, is generally believed to have been
the fourth pope and to have ruled the Church in the last decade of the

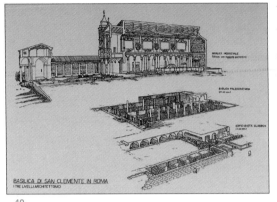

BASILICA DI SAN CLEMENTE IN ROMA
I TRE LIVELLI ARCHITETTONICI

49

first century. His Epistle to the Church at Corinth has an authority that is second only to that of the Apostles. The epistle is also valued because it offers the earliest testimony to the martyrdom of St. Peter during the Neronian persecutions. According to legend, Clement was exiled to the Crimea, where he was killed by being tied to an anchor and thrown into the Black Sea. A short while later, the sea opened up to expose the martyr's tomb, which had been built by angels at its bottom. The miracle repeated itself annually, permitting the faithful to pray at the martyr's tomb. His remains were brought back to Rome by saints Cyril and Methodius (who brought Christianity to Russia and invented its alphabet). They were deposited in the lower church of San Clemente; St. Cyril himself was also buried there in 869.

In a renovation that is unique among Roman churches, the medieval rebuilders of San Clemente duplicated the atrium of the earlier basilica. The covered entryway, open court, and columned portico preserved here have either vanished or been drastically modified in every other Roman basilica. The upper church, constructed sometime in the early twelfth century, is, like Santi Quattro, smaller than the one beneath, though built in the same style. The nave is separated from the side aisles by an arcade interrupted by two large piers at midpoint. This division marks the beginning of an enclosed choir with paschal candleholder and twin

lecterns. (50) At the far end of the church the triumphal arch and vault
mosaic, which date from the twelfth century, also revive decorative
schemes from an earlier period. The arch features a portrait of Christ sur-

rounded by symbols of the Evangelists.
Flanking these are large figures of saints Paul
and Peter, Lawrence and Clement. Below them
the prophets Isaiah and Jeremiah stand over
idealized cityscapes of Bethlehem and
Jerusalem.

While the symbolism of the arch mosaic is
familiar from the many Early Christian examples in Rome, the apse vault mosaic is unique.
An image of Christ on the Cross, flanked by the

50

Virgin and St. John, springs from a huge acanthus plant. Viny tendrils in
stylized curls spring from the same source and cover the entire vault.
Birds and putti, tiny animals, vintners, shepherds, and harvesters play
among the vines. The rainbow dome of heaven shines like a kaleidoscope
image above. Doves on the cross represent the disciples, as do the twelve
sheep below who surround the lamb of God
ringed with a halo. (51)

The many little scenes among the vines
may recall the comical figures in the margins
of Gothic manuscripts who go about their
business without a thought for the serious
text they surround. The vine motif and the
acanthus, which are both classical symbols,

51

suggest that the image actually reaches far back toward the few surviving examples of the earliest Christian mosaic decoration, like those in the vault at Santa Costanza and in the apse of the narthex at the Lateran Baptistery. Those floral fantasies also included birds, animals, and harvest scenes, though they were not so densely populated as the mosaic here. Ultimately, the tradition rests on scenes like those from Livia's Villa at Prima Porta.

In Northern Europe medieval buildings were structurally distinctive, but not in Rome. In every period, Roman artists and architects turned back to the classical examples they saw all around them. As early as the fifth century there was a renewal of a classicism that had hardly faded; there was another in the eighth and again in the twelfth century. While classicism in other parts of Europe was mainly secular, in Rome a sense of the classical past included monuments of the Apostolic Age. Coupled with the Roman practice of reusing materials from earlier buildings, these repeated revivals blurred stylistic distinctions which in the rest of Europe dramatically separated Early Christian from Romanesque and Gothic architecture.

In Roman churches, the most obvious signs of medieval interventions are cosmatesque floors, a paschal candlestick, and a ciborium over the main altar. Cosmatesque floors are marble mosaics built up of reused materials carefully combined in geometries of intersecting squares and circles. Similar inlays are found on the many white marble spiraling Easter candlesticks in Roman churches. Work of this kind, which reflects classical examples like the floor of the Pantheon, is confined to Rome and its immediate surroundings. The ciborium is a roof of decorated marble supported on slim columns that shelters the altar. Most ciboria have carved ornamentation; some have sculpted figures on them. These usually reflect what is called the International Gothic style of the thirteenth and fourteenth centuries. The Roman ciboria of Arnolfo di Cambio are the most celebrated.

The fourth-century basilica below San Clemente, which the Normans devastated in 1084, is preserved to the height of its original nave columns. A typical Constantinian structure with nave, two aisles, and an apse, the space is confusing because it is broken up by reinforcing walls beneath the colonnades of the smaller upper church. Frescoes at the rear of the church, which date from the ninth to the eleventh century, narrate the legends of saints Clemente and Alessio. A stairway at the back of the nave leads down to the Roman neighborhood over which the Early Christian church was built. Something of a labyrinth, like all archaeological sites, it sheltered partisans during the Second World War. Ngaio Marsh made it a crime scene in her novel *When in Rome*.

Of the two excavated buildings here, one is a first-century structure of tufa blocks; the other, separated from its neighbor by an alleyway no wider than a tenement hall, is a second-century brick apartment building. In the early third century, a mithraeum was built in the open court of the apartment block. Later in the same century one of the rooms of the adjacent house was converted to a church. The existence of that house-church, probably the titulus Clementi recorded in early texts, inspired the building of the basilica above. Like the rest of the area beneath the basilica, the house-church was leveled and filled in with dirt to form a platform for the much larger structure above.

Inside the cozy mithraeum, which is extremely well preserved, two deep sloping benches line a narrow aisle with a marble statue of the god at its far end; rough-cut pumice blocks form a flattened arch above, like the roof of a cave. Devotees of the god reclined on the benches, as Romans typically did at formal dinners, and ate a ritual meal. Roman Mithraism was a Platonic updating of a much earlier Persian cult. The cult image here and the many that survive from shrines within the city and throughout the Empire commemorate a creation myth. The sun god sends a raven to Mithras, ordering him to sacrifice a bull, from which springs the entire cosmos. Evil, in the form of a serpent and scorpion, are also nourished by the bull's blood, and the central struggle of existence begins. Initiates who progressed through each of the cult's seven ranks triumphed in the struggle and earned immortality. Open only to men, and encouraged by the emperors, Mithraism was especially common among soldiers, though others, including slaves and freedmen, could and did join. After Constantine's turn toward Christianity, the cult lost favor and rapidly died out.

Though greatly built up in the twentieth century, the Celian hill in the neighborhood of the Lateran still recalls Constantine's city. Sections of the Neronian aqueduct run on high brick-faced concrete arches along the Via di Santo Stefano Rotondo. A spur line from the Aqua Claudia, it originally served the Domus Aurea. Domitian extended it to provide water for the imperial household on the Palatine. Hospitals on both sides of the road carry on the charitable work of the papal hostels. The tree-shaded open spaces of their grounds break through the dense urban fabric in much the same way that the horti of wealthy Romans did more than two millennia ago.

The grounds of the church of Santo Stefano Rotondo preserve a sense of agricultural clutter and green abundance. This, despite its informality, is an appropriate setting for an imperial shrine, which in its original form merged inside and outside in a manner reminiscent of much earlier Roman traditions. What remains of the church today, which is currently being restored, is the core of a once larger and more complex structure built in the aftermath of the discovery of the saint's burial place in Jerusalem early in the fifth century. Similar in many ways to the Lateran Baptistery, the center of the church is a broad cylindrical drum on a circular (rather than octagonal) lintel that is carried on twenty-two reused columns. The original dome has been replaced by a roof, and an arcade transects the center space. It may have been added to shore up the building in the wake of Norman damage in the late eleventh century. Important additions were also made in the Renaissance and Baroque periods. Windows in the clerestory, many now blocked (though this condition may change in the current restoration), once flooded this central chamber with light.

A dark ambulatory, its original outer arcade walled up, surrounds this core, again recalling the Lateran Baptistery. Four large chapels opening off this space (of which two remain) suggested a Greek cross. The outer walls of those chapels were connected by a circular wall with entrances all around to the outside. Between the chapels this wall supported a series of porticoes that were concentric with the open ambulatory. The complex plan created four curvilinear gardens that were both inside and outside the building. Clearly based on imperial buildings like Santa Costanza, Santo Stefano Rotondo is a circular variant on the basilica form with the addition of an atrium. A visitor entering the building from any angle would enter a curved portico, pass through a curved atrium into a curved narthex, before finally entering a fully circular nave. What he or she would have found there is quite unclear. Both the dedication of the church and its form suggest a martyrium, but historical confirmation is lacking.

The Via di Santo Stefano Rotondo ends in the larger Via della Navicella. A short walk to the left, a fountain in the form of a small ship (navicella) stands in front of the eighth-century church of Santa Maria in Domnica. Like Santa Prassede, Santa Maria in Domnica is a Carolingian redrafting of the Early Christian basilica. Preceded by a façade long attributed to Raphael but now generally thought to be the work of his contemporary Sansovino, the interior is most noteworthy for its mosaics. Scenes on the top of the triumphal arch show Christ between two angels with the apostles. Moses and Elias are below. The apse vault is dedicated, like that in Santa Maria Maggiore, to the Virgin, who holds the infant Christ in her arms. She is surrounded by angels. Pope Paschal I, who sponsored the construction here as well as that in Santa Prassede, kneels in front of them. His head is surrounded by a square halo to distinguish him from the sainted dead.

At the opening of the picturesque Via San Paolo della Croce a travertine arch has been incorporated in the substructure of the Neronian aqueduct. Called the Arch of Dolabella, it was once a gateway in the Servian wall. It marks the passage from the periphery of the city, where suburban horti shared space with densely settled enclaves, to its fully urbanized core. In contemporary Rome, however, this portion of the Celian hill is virtually uninhabited. A few houses and religious founda-

tions line the narrow street. The vast Villa Celimontana, now a park open
to the public, occupies most of the area on the left side of the street. Its
entrance is in an angled section of the wall diagonally across from the
church.

The Basilica of Santi Giovanni e Paolo dominates a small plaza. In
this quiet part of town, there is little activity unless the church, one of
Rome's most popular wedding churches, is in use. Travertine blocks at
the base of the Romanesque campanile once formed a corner of the vast
Temple of the Deified Claudius, the major imperial monument in this
area. The history of the church is similar to that of San Clemente. At the
end of the fourth century a simple basilica was built above a Christian
house-church dating from a few decades before. Sacked by the Normans
in 1084, it was rebuilt in the early twelfth century; the campanile was
added at that time, and the original narthex became the present porch.
The church was remodeled extensively in the eighteenth century and
again some fifty years ago. The form is still that of the first basilica, but
the earliest decoration has vanished.

Excavations beneath the basilica floor have revealed the tight cluster
of buildings squeezed between the Temple of Claudius and the Clivus
Scauri, the steep Roman street that still flanks the church. Though they
are very hard to sort out, the jumble of buildings testify to the dense set-
tlement in this once very central neighborhood. At least five buildings
that vary in date from the first to the fourth centuries have been identified. Many of the rooms in them still have their original painted or stucco
decoration. Most of the paintings are simply fictive marble panels, but
the nymphaeum and a few other rooms have pictorial scenes. The origi-

52

nal house-church, reputedly the scene of the martyrdom of the saints to whom the church is dedicated, stands under the main altar and is decorated with fourth-century paintings. In one of these scenes, two crouching figures flank a third who stands with outstretched arms, a position associated with prayer in the early church. On the opposite wall three figures traditionally identified as followers of the titular saints are arrested and executed.

The Clivus Scauri, with its original Roman paving still visible, descends the hill overarched by buttresses that shore up the basilica. (52) The brick-outlined arches of two-story imperial buildings can be traced on its side wall. The vast apse of the church surrounded by a beautiful colonnade added in the twelfth century dominates the scene. The travertine façade of the church of St. Gregory the Great rises out of the greenery on the right. Built on the site of the great pope's house, it retains nothing of its origins. "This church was the paternal home of Pope St. Gregory, which in the second year of his pontificate he consecrated to St. Andrew the Apostle. He prayed to Almighty God that whatever person would chose to be buried in it would, if he were a true Christian, be granted eternal life. When he had finished his prayer, an Angel appeared to him and said, 'O Gregory, your prayer has been heard'" (Palladio, *Descritione de le Chiese*).

The Basilica of Santa Sabina on top of the Aventine hill is generally
agreed to be the most beautiful example of its type that survives in Rome
today. Built in the early fifth century and remodeled at various times over
the years, it was repristinated early in the twentieth century. For once,
that heavy-handed process, in which the accretions of centuries are
scoured away to the bare brick of an idealized original, has achieved harmony and beauty. The austere interior represents the familiar grammar of
the basilica: a nave flanked by ranks of matched reused columns with an
arcade and clerestory above; a triumphal arch and terminal apse; and
single side aisles. The restored windows of the clerestory, which are
glazed with translucent alabaster, fill the nave with a diffused light.
Original marble panels survive above the columns, but the rich mosaics
that must once have filled the spaces beneath the clerestory and decorated the triumphal arch and apse vault have all disappeared. A monumental inscription on the back wall flanked by two lively figures gives
some indication of its richness.

The rarest treasures of this extraordinary building are carved wooden
doors of the fifth century which are nearly intact and still in place. Like
stone-carving, woodworking was highly developed among the Romans, but
the ravages of fire and climate have left few examples. Divided by a naturalistic frame into twenty-eight panels, of which ten have been lost, the
doors parallel the lives of Christ and Moses. The top left scene of the
Crucifixion, one of the earliest representations known, shows Christ open-
eyed and without a halo. Next is the scene of the multiplication of the
loaves and fishes, then the wedding in Cana, and the risen Christ re-
proaching the skeptic St. Thomas. Other traditional scenes include the

judgment before Pilate; the angel at the sepulcher; and Moses leading
the Israelites through the desert.

Inside its sheltering walls on the other side of the Tiber, the Basilica
of Santa Cecilia seems aloof, like Sant'Agnese or Santa Croce in Geru-

salemme. That sense of remoteness reflects
the will of the sequestered community of nuns
who now inhabit the basilica, rather than its
neighborhood, Trastevere, which has been
densely populated since antiquity. The church
was built on the site of a large Roman house,
and excavated rooms beneath it can still be
visited. It is approached through a large
walled garden, an expanded version of the
original atrium. The interior of the church,
which dates from the ninth century, was reorganized in the eighteenth century. Pairs of
nave columns were grouped in piers; the

53

clerestory windows were enlarged; and the flat ceiling was recreated as a
shallow vault. Only the apse with its original mosaic of Christ surrounded
by saints remains unchanged. To the left of Christ stand St. Paul, St.
Cecilia, and Pope Paschal I, who holds a model of the church in his
hands. (53)

According to legend, St. Cecilia vowed in childhood to remain a virgin.
When her father insisted that she marry a pagan named Valerius, she per-
suaded Valerius to embrace Christianity and a life of celibacy. Together
with his brother Tiburtius, the three performed acts of charity; like other

early Roman saints, they looked after the burial of Christians. For refusing to sacrifice to Jupiter, the brothers were put to death; Maximus, the
officer charged with their execution, was converted at the scene of their
martyrdom and soon followed them. Cecilia buried all three and was herself sentenced to death. Suffocation in the caldarium of the private bath
complex in her own household was the bizarre method chosen. (That
room, much redecorated, is now a chapel off the left aisle of the church.)
When this attempt was unsuccessful, the saint was to be beheaded;
though struck three times by the executioner's sword, she remained alive.
A painting by Guido Reni above the altar in the chapel represents this
scene.

Surviving this attempted execution for three days, the martyr died and
was buried outside the city walls, but when invaders threatened in the
sixth century, her body, like that of many other saints, was removed to a
site within the walls. At that time her coffin was opened, and the saint's
body was reported to be perfectly preserved. It was opened again in
1599, and her perfect preservation again verified. The sculptor Stefano
Maderno sketched the body and produced the veiled, reclining figure of
the saint which now lies in front of the high altar.

The greatest artistic treasure of Santa Cecilia can be seen only on
a guided visit. The west wall above the doors is enclosed behind a
screened gallery from which the cloistered nuns can hear services in the
church. During restorations in 1900, a magnificent painting of the Last
Judgment by Pietro Cavallini was discovered there. The fresco, which dates
from about 1290, breaks the mold of Byzantine convention. Like Giotto
in Tuscany, Cavallini revolutionized painting by making it more realistic

54

and more emotionally charged. (54) The
iconography of the vividly painted scene is
standard: Christ appears in Judgment
between Mary, John the Baptist, and the
Apostles. Below are angels with brightly
feathered wings who sound the trumpet call
to those below, the blessed and the damned.

Inside its impressive portico, San Crisogono, built in the twelfth century on the site of a fifth-century church, is a familiar interpretation of an
Early Christian basilica. It has a three-aisled interior with an apse at the
far end. It was originally decorated with mosaics, of which only a portion,
representing the Madonna and Child between St. James and St. Crisogono,
survives. Next to the basilica is the small seventeenth-century church of
Sant'Agata. Of no artistic interest, it houses in the third chapel on the
left an image of the Madonna that is very important to the Roman community. Called the Madonna de' Noiantri, she is the patron saint of
Trastevere.

Santa Maria in Trastevere, fronted by its picturesque and busy piazza,
is the physical and spiritual hub of the region. Among the earliest of
Roman churches, it is traditionally linked with the legendary Pope
Callixtus. Like Santa Maria Maggiore, its site also commemorates a miracle. In 38 BC a spontaneous upwelling of oil was reported in a veteran's
hospice. The Romans took note of prodigies of this kind, which they
thought of as potential omens, and preserved an annual record of them.
Long afterward the prodigy came to be linked with Christ and the Virgin
Mary. It ranks as one of a handful of events in Roman history that the

Christian Church accepted as prophetic. The church commemorates this event in its mosaics and in an inscription near its main altar.

The first building on the site dated from the mid-fourth century. That structure was rebuilt in the ninth century and extensively remodeled in the twelfth using building materials scavenged from the Baths of Caracalla. Having undergone only minor modifications in the eighteenth and nineteenth centuries, the present church remains for the most part a twelfth-century interpretation of the Early Christian basilica. Above its

deep porch the facade is decorated with a mosaic of the thirteenth century depicting the Madonna enthroned between two donors and a procession of women. (55)

55

The interior of the church is divided into three aisles by two ranks of reused columns that support an entablature pieced together from ancient fragments. The triumphal arch and the apse are richly decorated with mosaics, some by Pietro Cavallini, whose innovative frescoes decorate the west wall of Santa Cecilia. The arch mosaics represent the prophets Isaiah and Jeremiah; the four symbols of the evangelists; and the seven candles of the Apocalypse. Together these symbols represent the past, present, and future, understood as the age of prophecy, the time of Christ, and the end of the world. In the vault of the apse Christ crowns the Virgin as he does in the nearly contemporary mosaic in Santa Maria Maggiore.

56

Through different symbolic schemes, the two mosaic programs present Mary as the pivotal figure who mediates past and present, historical and spiritual time. The central pair are surrounded by Roman saints and a figure of Pope Innocent II, who presents a model of the Church. (56) Cavallini's mosaic cycle, below, narrates scenes from the life of the Virgin Mary. An eighteenth-century inscription on the front of the raised choir—Fons Olei—marks the traditional site of the miraculous upwelling of oil.

Trastevere's long history as a thickly settled urban enclave is disguised by its mythical image. More than any other part of the city, the region across the Tiber stands in the popular imagination for the essence of Roman distinctiveness. The right way to say "we Romans" in Italian is noi altri romani. In Roman dialect it is noiantri, a buzz-word that summons up a nostalgic localism—a self-conscious, and sometimes self-righteous, parochialism. When Romans want to forget that they are Europeans, citizens of Italy's capital, and dwellers at the spiritual center of Catholicism, they revisit Trastevere.

Rome's most popular religious holiday, La Festa di Noiantri, takes place there every August, the month when real Europeans are away from home. In the Roman imagination, Trastevere is a down-home kind of place—molto folklorico, where old-fashioned trades are followed and traditional virtues honored. The major bridge into Trastevere is overlooked by a life-size sculpture in frock coat and top hat of Gioacchino Belli, a poet who wrote nostalgic sonnets in Roman dialect. In restaurants like La tana di Noiantri (tana means den or lair), with frescoed walls and candlesticks in bottles, patrons find old-fashioned cooking strongly flavored with fatback and lard.

This mythologizing can easily become heavy-handed, and at its worst Trastevere presents itself as a Disneyfied "Little Italy" in the heart of Rome. Fun to visit and to walk through but no more (or less) authentic than the complex international city of which it is a part, Trastevere is as eclectic as the rest of Rome, and always has been. (57) Many of its residents are non-Romans, and a substantial percentage are non-Italians. The population in antiquity included resident aliens from every part of the Roman world. Middle Easterners were especially common, and their shrines dotted the area. While the medieval Roman ghetto was located on the other side of the Tiber, in imperial Rome both banks of the river hosted large Jewish communities, from which the first Christian communities undoubtedly grew.

57

Chapter Five

VATICAN REVIVAL

A Christian tradition well attested by the second century located the martyrdom of the Apostle Peter on the spina, or infield, of Nero's Circus. This shadowy monument stood at the edge of a swamp on the Trastevere side of the river in a region known, for obscure reasons, as the Vatican. One of many Christians who forfeited their lives as the emperor sought a scapegoat cult to punish for the Great Fire, St. Peter was buried a short distance uphill from the scene of his lingering death by crucifixion (according to legend). Sometime in the second century, Christian burials began to cluster near a modest monument and a small sunken plaza on the site. Around this Christian shrine, though on a different axis, wealthy families buried their dead in tombs above ground.

When the emperor Constantine proposed a basilica dedicated to St. Peter for this site, he first had to close this cemetery by imperial edict and buy up the ground on which all these tombs had been built. To create a level platform for the building, laborers cut into the hillside above Peter's tomb and built up the slope beneath. Roman builders typically economized on demolition by shearing off existing structures to the level of the proposed terrace, rather than pulling them down to ground level. The truncated tombs and the paths among them were then filled in with dirt and rubble consolidated by retaining walls parallel to the slope of the hill. Later soundings of the basilica mistook these Constantinian substructures for the walls of Nero's Circus; but to date no remains of that structure have been found.

Unlike the Lateran or Santa Maria Maggiore, Constantine's St. Peter's was a martyrium—some have called it a covered cemetery. Like Sant' Agnese and San Lorenzo, it accommodated celebratory masses for a venerated martyr and sheltered the tombs of those who awaited the Resurrection near his sacred remains. The basilica was built in such a way that the monument traditionally identified as the burial place of Peter protruded through its floor. This unusual arrangement was complemented by a structural plan that differed from that of the other Constantinian basilicas. Between the nave of the five-aisled basilica and its apse an intersecting space was imposed—a transept—where the cult of the martyr was celebrated. The presence of the transept in this pivotal church accounts for its widespread use from the Carolingian period onward.

Constantine's church had been built on a very large scale, but devotion to St. Peter soon outgrew it. The basilica was in constant demand for burial masses, and the number of pilgrims visiting the shrine of the martyr continued to swell. A chapter house was added at one end of the transept to house a permanent clergy. In the late sixth century, Pope St. Gregory the Great redesigned the church to better accommodate its double role. Gregory's builders raised the floor of the apse and the central area of the transept above the level of the martyr's shrine. They placed a newly designed high altar directly above. Beneath the new floor they created a buried shrine called a confessio, a crypt-like substructure that came to be imitated in many other churches. One door to this confessio led to an annular corridor that followed the curve of the apse. At its mid-point an intersecting corridor led directly toward Peter's shrine. After per-forming their devotions at the tomb, pilgrims continued around the corri-dor and exited from the opposite door. A steady stream of devotees could visit the tomb in this way without disturbing the liturgy going on simulta-neously above.

As the appeal of St. Peter's shrine continued to grow, its clergy became increasingly powerful and influential. As a beacon for pilgrims and a symbolic center, the Vatican surpassed the distant Lateran. Foreign dignitaries, especially Germans, settled in its shadow—so many of them by the ninth century that the region became known as the Borgo, a romanization of the German word burg, meaning fortress. The concentra-tion of Rome's own population along the Tiber brought St. Peter's close to the center of civic life. Despite these abundant attractions, the medieval popes maintained their traditional government center in the Lateran Palace on the far edge of the city.

When the popes returned from Avignon in 1377 and the Great Schism finally ended in 1417, conditions were ripe for change. The entrenched papal bureaucracy that had clung to the Lateran Palace had long been displaced. The Curia or papal court could as easily be accommodated in one area as another. The Lateran Palace itself had been sacked after 1305 and would need extensive rebuilding if it were to be used again. By contrast, the Vatican continued to offer its long-held advantages of spiri-tual primacy and proximity to the Roman people.

But there was an additional advantage that an embattled papacy might be expected to value especially, namely, security. The Vatican enclave had been walled in the eighth century. Within its protective circuit the tomb of the emperor Hadrian, fitted out as a fortress and long known as the Castel Sant'Angelo, offered an impregnable sanctuary for the papal court in times of emergency. So while the Lateran remained (and still remains today) the basilica of the bishop of Rome, the papal residence and the papal bureaucracy were established at St. Peter's. In the middle of the fifteenth century, for the first time in its history, the Vatican became the spiritual and governmental center of the Roman Church and the city of Rome.

This new role for the ancient site encouraged a succession of popes to begin increasingly ambitious building projects on three fronts within the Vatican area itself. The simplest and most confined of these was the fortification of the Castel Sant'Angelo and the fitting out of comfortable papal apartments in it. The more ambitious and longer-term projects, begun in roughly the same era and directly reflecting the new centrality of the shrine of Peter, were the construction of a greatly enlarged Vatican Palace and the replacement of Constantine's basilica with a grander building in the Renaissance style.

Architectural surveys of the fifteenth century found the sidewalls of Constantine's basilica more than a meter out of plumb. Rather than shore up the old building, the surveyors recommended its demolition. No one is now in a position to verify their measurements or to judge whether the fate of Old St. Peter's reflected the building's soundness or the Renaissance passion for renewal. Whatever the motivation, Julius II commissioned Donato Bramante to begin a new basilica.

Bramante's task was a curious and difficult one. While destroying Old St. Peter's was certainly risky, replacing it with a successful new structure would confirm that the Renaissance Church and papacy had been radically renewed. The building to be demolished had been the goal of pilgrimage for over a thousand years. Its once-peculiar form—a transept intruding between nave and apse—had become the model for Christian churches everywhere. Bramante's task was further complicated by his own and his era's respect for the authority of classical building types. How was he to justify replacing a genuine antique basilica with a new structure that must inevitably be built in the antique style?

Bramante found the solution to this paradox in the conservative architectural tradition to which Old St. Peter's had adhered. The Constantinian basilica had incorporated neither the sophisticated building techniques nor the classicizing style Roman imperial builders had invented. Surviving examples of these more adventurous styles could be found throughout Renaissance Rome. They included pre-Christian examples like the Pantheon or the Temple of Romulus, as well as Christian adaptations of these forms in shrines like Santo Stefano Rotondo and Santa Costanza. The Basilica of Maxentius and the well-preserved portion of the Baths of Diocletian that Michelangelo later converted into the Basilica of Santa Maria degli Angeli were probably the most significant imperial counterexamples to Old St. Peter's. Because of the conservative choice that Constantine's architects had made, Bramante was free to imagine a new St. Peter's that could be radically different from the old one, yet firmly based on classical ideals.

For reasons that are not entirely clear, however, Bramante and his successors recreated the forms of Roman imperial architecture not in concrete but in cut stone. Although Bramante did use concrete in what he described as the "Roman manner" in the core of his great piers, it was not used elsewhere. Lack of adequate timbers for constructing forms to hold the poured concrete and a poor understanding of the text of Vitruvius are among the reasons cited for this failure to adopt Roman techniques. In the absence of concrete, much of the architectural genius of the successive builders of St. Peter's would go into schemes for locking the stones together and giving them the rigidity of integral concrete structures.

Bramante designed the new basilica, somewhat impractically, as a

58

centrally planned building. Perhaps based on the circular plans favored by late imperial architects, centrally planned domed churches were a passion of many architects in the early sixteenth century. Leonardo's notebooks include sketches of such buildings, and a handful—the work of other architects—were built. Elsewhere in Rome, Bramante himself created an unusual shrine in this style which gives some idea of his conception of St. Peter's. In a cramped cloister next to the church of San Pietro in Montorio, Bramante erected a tiny monument that served as the epitome of High Renaissance aesthetic. (58) Called the Tempietto, it stands on the spot where a secondary medieval tradition located the martyrdom of St. Peter. Circular in form like the martyr shrines Santa Costanza and Santo

Stefano Rotondo, the Tempietto would have
stood in a round courtyard with a loggia, had
Bramante's plan been carried out. (59) The
oppressive square courtyard in which the
temple now stands bears no relation to what
he intended. Despite its cramped setting,
this wonderful building proved to Bramante's
contemporaries that the grammar of Roman
architecture could be used to produce novel
and beautiful results. This is no slavish
recreation of a classical prototype but an entirely new structure in an
ancient idiom. While it is similar to the round temple in the Forum
Boarium, Bramante's structure divides an equivalent vertical space into
two zones. This characteristic of his style improves the proportions of the
colonnade and frames the small cupola, which is raised on a drum,
behind the entablature and balcony in a way that makes it appear higher
than it really is. Stairs at the back of the monument lead down to a crypt
decorated with remarkable stucco work.

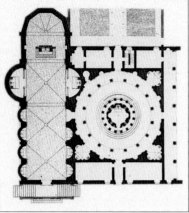

59

Conceived as a massive square six hundred feet on a side, Bramante's
projected St. Peter's would have taken the form of a Greek cross. Four
apsed arms of equal length would meet under an enormous hemispheri-
cal dome. High towers at each corner would fill in the square, and smaller
domes would crown each apse. With this plan accepted, the west end of
Old St. Peter's was demolished and Bramante began work. At the time
of his death in 1514, just one year after that of Julius II, four massive
pillars, the supports for his enormous dome, towered above the partially

demolished Constantinian structure. Then, despite the appointment of a series of architects, including Raphael, Peruzzi, and Sangallo, to succeed Bramante, the project remained as he had left it for almost thirty years. In 1546 Michelangelo, then aged seventy-two, received the papal commission, which he held until his death eight years later.

Though Michelangelo scaled down and modified some of Bramante's ideas, he carried out his general plan. He eliminated the corner towers and connected the apses with a diagonal wall that reflected the scale and profile of Bramante's piers. He substituted a steeper dome raised on a drum and surmounted by a lantern, after the pattern of Brunelleschi's celebrated dome on the cathedral of Florence. (Access to the dome and the lantern is at the north end of the church.) He eliminated three of Bramante's entrances to the basilica in favor of a single doorway on the side of the building facing toward Rome. He retained Bramante's second-

ary cupolas, and under his successors two of them were built.

The transformation of Bramante's and Michelangelo's centrally planned building into the structure that stands today took place during the seventeenth and eighteenth centuries. Carlo Maderno added a nave flanked by chapels to the city end of the building. While its center aisle reflects the separation of Bramante's piers, its side aisles are no wider than the thickness of the massive piers themselves. Maderno completed the work with the addition of a narthex and a façade that bears little resemblance to Michelangelo's design. Under a massive cornice surmounted by an attic that supports monumental sculptures, the two-story façade is separated into bays by pilasters. Its center bay, which shelters the doors and a benediction loggia, mimics a Greek temple front. An extra bay has been added at each side of the façade. Originally designed to support massive towers like those Bramante imagined, they have been somewhat incongruously topped by elaborate clocks. It is traditional to condemn this enormous façade not only for its inelegance but because it screens every part of Michelangelo's church except the dome from a viewer in St. Peter's Square. (60) Critics have called it "vandalism and a crime against architecture."

The final stage in the design of the basilica was the addition of the sweeping travertine portico that stretches out from its flanks and embraces the elliptical "square" in front. This magnificent structure, designed by Gian Lorenzo Bernini, was completed in 1667. Bernini's model was the modest atrium that stood outside the first basilicas. He bent this traditional square into a continuous curve and blew it up to proportions that rival the greatest Roman buildings. (61)

61

Behind Maderno's façade, an imposing narthex introduces the scale of

62

the interior. Two monumental
equestrian statues recall the
imperial heritage of Old St.
Peter's. The statue on the right by
Bernini represents Constantine;
opposite stands an eighteenth-
century statue of Charlemagne,
who was crowned emperor in Old
St. Peter's in the year 800. Five doors, including the Porta Santa, which
is opened only in Jubilee Years, lead to the nave. The center door is
one of the few objects from Old St. Peter's. Cast by Filarete in the mid-
fifteenth century, it represents scenes from the life of Peter and Paul.
The massive interior of St. Peter's with its colossal monuments, its gold
and marble decoration, is calculated to overwhelm. (62) Benchmarks in
the floor record the size of other important churches.

The first chapel on the right, directly inside the Porta Santa, houses
Michelangelo's *Pietà*. Completed by the sculptor when he was twenty-
three years old, it is his only signed work. Borrowing its form from a typical Madonna and Child, here Christ's mother cradles the body of her
adult son in her arms. The chapels along both sides of the basilica
enclose the tombs of cardinals, popes, and other religious figures from
the seventeenth through the nineteenth centuries.

Under a red velvet canopy the final nave pier shelters a celebrated
bronze statue of St. Peter seated on a throne and making a gesture of
benediction. The work was long assumed to date from the fifth century,
but it is now generally dated to the thirteenth century and attributed to
the sculptor Arnolfo di Cambio. The apostle's toe, kissed by generations

of pilgrims, has become as smooth and featureless as a riverworked

stone. (63)

Bernini refashioned Bramante's great piers as chapels dedicated to

the principal relics of the Church, those which are directly related to

Christ. He created niches for monumental statues
in the base of each and added balconies above
from which the relics are displayed. On the pier
of St. Peter's statue, there is a three-times-life-
size statue of St. Longinus by Bernini. After
piercing Christ's side with a lance at the crucifixion, Longinus, a Roman centurion, was suddenly
converted. During the Easter season a relic of the
lance is displayed from the balcony above.

The pier to the right and behind the altar
houses a monumental statue of Constantine's
mother, Helen, who returned a portion of the True

63

Cross to Rome. The pier behind the altar to the left is dedicated to St.

Veronica. During Christ's walk to Calvary, Veronica offered him a cloth to

wipe his face. The cloth—or Veronica—preserved an image of the face.

This miraculous image, which, like the Shroud of Turin, appeared in

Europe in the mid-thirteenth century and may date to that era, is dis-

played during Holy Week from the balcony above her image. The final

pier is dedicated to St. Andrew; the relic preserved here is the apostle's

head.

Despite its massive scale, the soaring nave is focused by a towering

baldacchino, itself framed by Bramante's enormous piers. The work of

Bernini, completed in 1633, the altar canopy, supported on serpentine

64

bronze pillars, is a Baroque version of the ubiquitous ciboria above the medieval altars of Rome. Its scale responds to the gargantuan spaces around it. (64) The spiraling columns recall those which Constantine donated to the basilica. (These much smaller originals have been incorporated in the ornate balconies Bernini fashioned on the inside faces of Bramante's piers.) The gilded bees on Bernini's massive columns symbolize the Barberini family under whose patronage the columns were cast using bronze looted from the porch of the Pantheon. The popular Roman view of this outrage was that "the Barberini did what the barbarians didn't."

In the apse behind the high altar Bernini created a shrine for an object long identified as the throne of St. Peter. Inset with ivory panels that are decorated with floral motifs and scenes from the legend of Hercules, the throne belonged to the French king Charles the Bald. It later served as an episcopal throne. Believing it to be the very throne on which St. Peter sat and from which he exercised papal authority, Pope Alexander VII commissioned this monumental Baroque installation. The monument asserts papal claims, still vexed in seventeenth-century Europe, to represent the legitimate apostolic succession. Statues of four doctors of the Church—St. Augustine, St. Ambrose, St. Athanasius, and

St. John Chrysostom—hold an idealized throne aloft and support the papacy's claim. Angels circle in golden clouds pierced by the sun's rays; an image of the dove of the Holy Spirit in stained glass crowns the scene; together, they acknowledge heavenly recognition of the succession.

Two papal tombs flank the throne shrine. To the right stands Bernini's monument to the Barberini Pope Urban VIII, whose image is supported by personifications of Love and Justice. Justice and Prudence stand beside the monument of Pope Paul III, the pontiff who first commissioned Michelangelo as architect of St. Peter's. The Sacristy of the church includes the Treasury of St. Peter, also known as the Art Historical Museum. Such collections usually feature important relics, but this immensely rich display, as it name implies, includes objects of artistic importance.

Among a number of richly ornamented crosses, copes, and reliquaries, two objects stand out for their austerity as well as their beauty. These are the Monument of Sixtus IV and the Sarcophagus of Junius Bassus. The papal monument by Pollaiuolo, who is also well known as a painter, shows the pontiff lying on top of a tomb covered with allegorical figures. In an era when few sculptors worked in bronze, Pollaiuolo's delicate casting and ethereal portraiture rival the work of Donatello. Junius Bassus was Roman prefect in 359, the year he converted to Christianity. The front of his sarcophagus, which was discovered late in the sixteenth century, is decorated with sculpted scenes from the Old and New Testaments.

The floor of St. Peter's is raised above the level of the Constantinian basilica. A highly ornamented confessio in front of the altar as well as a

65

set of stairs at the base of the pillar of St. Andrew leads down to it. The Holy Grottoes of the Vatican shelter the tombs of innumerable pontiffs and many of the tombs and artworks originally built into Old St. Peter's. Behind Maderno's masking façade it is possible to see Michelangelo's design for the side walls of the church. A sinuous fabric flexed against superimposed pilasters, the wall bends around the cruciform building. Arched windows and blind arcades and massive aedicula pierce it. A complexly inflected entablature forms the attic story above.

The other great project of the fifteenth-century popes newly restored to Rome was the construction of a secure and increasingly opulent residence. A very small medieval palace stood next to Constantine's basilica. Even the beleaguered popes of the post-Avignon Schism found it insufficient for their needs, if not positively uncomfortable. When fifteenth-century popes began to envisage larger, more up-to-date quarters, their builders expanded on this medieval core.

Pope Nicholas V had a clearer vision than his immediate predecessors of the Vatican's role as a symbol of papal power and munificence. While his hopes to remodel St. Peter's remained unfulfilled until the sixteenth century, his projects for the Vatican Palace were carried out in his own lifetime. More importantly, his conception of the role the Vatican should

play as a visible symbol of the strength and character of the papacy influenced many of his successors. In addition to his architectural projects,
Nicholas encouraged painters and scholars. A book collector himself, he
sponsored the creation of the Apostolic Vatican Library.

The architects of Nicholas V designed the first addition to the medieval
palace—a square of buildings surrounding an open courtyard, the Cortile
del Pappagallo. (65) The small rooms of this palace were decorated with
frescoes by two exceptional painters of the early Renaissance, Fra Angelico and Pinturicchio. Construction of the fortified Torrione increased the
palace's security. Pope Sixtus IV added the Sistine Chapel, named in his
honor. The private chapel of the popes, it reflected the traditional proportions of the Temple of Solomon and filled a number of symbolic and practical functions. As a religious symbol, it replaced the Holy of Holies of the
Lateran Palace, but its larger size permitted its use as a meeting place for

the College of Cardinals. Its most surprising feature is the fortress-like superstructure with crenellations—deep notches in the upper wall from
which soldiers could defend the nearby palace
from invasion.

Late in the fifteenth century a new papal building called the Belvedere was begun far uphill from
the palace block. Designed by Pinturicchio, it
was intended to be a casino—an elegant pavilion
where the papal court could relax amid some of
the beautiful plantings of the extensive Vatican
Gardens. (66) Within a few decades of its creation,

66

the Belvedere was converted into a summer residence for the pontiff and his court. At the turn of the sixteenth century, the pace and scale of building in the Vatican suddenly expanded. The Borgia Tower was added to the palace block to complete its inner defenses. A few years later Bramante added a Renaissance façade to the palace that enclosed the Cortile del Pappagallo. Raphael decorated one of its loggias and a series of rooms next to it for Pope Julius II.

The main block of the Renaissance palace houses the most famous suite of papal apartments, those chosen by Julius II for himself and decorated at his insistence by Raphael and his followers. The majestic *Disputa* in the Stanza della Segnatura is the first fresco Raphael painted for Julius II. At the center of the composition is the host, the consecrated wafer of bread which in the daily miracle of transubstantiation becomes the body of Christ. Connecting the host with images of the Holy Spirit, Christ, and the Father—the Three in One mystically present in the consecrated wafer—the fresco spells out visually what transubstantiation implies.

The composition also brings to life a common element of Early Christian architecture. Raphael's perspective changes the flat wall into an arched space that is like an imagined apse. Within a gilded rondel, Christ sits at its center, as he does in so many mosaics in the apse vaults of Roman churches. A U-shaped line of clouds beneath separates the fictive apse vault—its gold background emerges at the top of the composition— from the lower area where the altar stands. The crowd above and the crowd below this crucial boundary are parallel in some ways but distinct in others. Secure in the presence of God, the saints sit above in order and majesty. Through meditation, study, and disputation, theologians on earth struggle to grasp the mystery whose highest expression for them is the enigmatic host.

Raphael places Dante, the theological poet, and himself, apparently as theological painter, among them. The painter and poet belong in this group because each is able to offer a vision of the visible and invisible simultaneously. The perspective lines of the composition, however, converge high above the heads of the crowd in the room, suggesting that the frescoes appeal to an ideal observer above the human scale.

The companion piece to the *Disputa,* and perhaps the most celebrated single painting of the Italian Renaissance, is Raphael's so-called *School of Athens,* though a better title would be *Philosophy,* pure and simple. Natural Philosophy looks down on the scene from the ceiling, just as personified Theology surveys the *Disputa.* The central figures in the fresco are Plato the idealist, who points heavenward, and his one-time student, the more pragmatic Aristotle, whose gesture embraces all things below. Socrates in olive drab ticks off the points of an argument on his fingers; the cynic Diogenes, who defied convention and preached a radical simplicity, sprawls on the steps. Pythagoras bends toward a diagram on a slate; Ptolemy, whose geocentric universe still governed both scientific and religious cosmology, holds a celestial globe. There is no single conversation here; the distinct impulses that Plato and Aristotle represent spawn intense little seminars among separate groups. Only the arched frame of the painting itself and the fictive architecture that echoes its curve encompass and unify the entire group.

That background architecture suggests a majestic if puzzling building. Huge piers decorated with bas-reliefs, their shallow niches filled with sculptures, support coffered vaults. Between the first and second bay there appears to be a dome. The most distant bay appears to be flat-roofed like a triumphal arch. It is probable that this huge structure in Roman imperial style is Raphael's idea of Bramante's planned recon-struction of St. Peter's. It is not a simple model of that structure, or of any real building; its openness to the sky and the apparent inconsisten-cies among its elements mark it as painterly and fictive architecture. By this subtle framing, Raphael has positioned the three related arts of architecture, painting, and sculpture not just as key elements in philoso-phy but as the superstructure of that discipline. Only the arts, he seems to suggest, have the power to harmonize and survey the whole realm of philosophy.

That notion is further emphasized by the incorporation of artists' portraits into his scene. Euclid, who bends to measure a circle with his compass, has Bramante's features; the painter Sodoma is the figure in white behind him; Raphael stands further back—the philo-sophical painter this time. The bearded

67

man in short tunic and turned-down leather boots who stares distractedly at the floor is Raphael's magnificent portrait of Michelangelo. (67) Some have seen a portrait of Leonardo in the figure of Plato.

Three grand allegorical figures on the inner wall represent Fortitude, Prudence, and Temperance. A figure of Justice looks on from the ceiling above. Fortitude strokes a lion's head with one hand and clutches an oak tree with the other. The traditional symbol of perseverance in the face of adversity, the oak is also an emblem of the Della Rovere, the family of Julius II. Prudence has two faces: a young woman who contemplates her image in a mirror and an old man who looks into the past. Temperance holds a bridle in her hands by which passion is to be reined in. The fourth painting, broken into by the room's window, represents Mount Parnassus, a real mountain near Athens that has traditionally been identified as the home of the Muses. Apollo (whose statue peers from a niche in the *School of Athens*) sits at the top of the mountain and at the center of the composition. The nine muses—patron goddesses of all the literary and fine arts—surround him; each carries a symbol of the art she represents.

Laurel trees, sacred to Apollo, stand in the background, and eighteen laurel-crowned poets fill out the rest of the composition. Some are historical; others are portraits of humanists in the papal court. Homer, his hand outstretched, turns his blind eyes toward the sky. Dante stands to his right and Virgil to his left. Raphael—now the poetic painter—is behind him. Boccaccio looks out from among the trees. The Greek poet Sappho, who casts her painted shadow on the real window frame, holds up a scroll with her own name written on it.

The adjacent room, called the Stanza di Eliodoro, was commissioned by Julius II sometime after his 1512 expulsion of French forces from Italy. Though none of its four frescoes depicts this event literally, each symbolizes some aspect of the Pope's triumph. The *Mass at Bolsena* represents a miracle of the thirteenth century. According to tradition, a Bohemian priest, unconvinced that the host actually changed into the body of Christ, was stunned to see real bloodstains in the form of a cross on a cloth where it had rested. Julius II venerated the relic of this miracle on his march against the French, and attributed his victory to its intervention. In Raphael's fresco, the Pope is present as the miracle takes place. The kneeling figures at the foot of the stairs below the pontiff are officers who led the papal forces. They are among the most striking of Raphael's portraits.

In the lunette directly opposite, Raphael has created a parallel composition. Here the scene is dark and the stairs face the viewer. Stricken soldiers replace the triumphant generals. The central altar in the *Mass at Bolsena* has been replaced by an angel whose surrounding aureole echoes the curve of the arch behind it. The scene is the miraculous *Liberation of St. Peter* from prison; symbolically it represents the liberation of Julius, Peter's successor, from the French. The episode is recounted in Acts 12:6–9: "On the very night before Herod had planned to bring him forward, Peter was asleep between two soldiers, secured by two chains, while outside the doors sentries kept guard over the prison. All at once an angel of the Lord stood there, and the cell was ablaze with light. He tapped Peter on the shoulder and woke him. 'Quick! Get up,' he said, and the chains fell away from his wrists . . . He followed him out with no idea that the angel's intervention was real: he thought it was just a vision. But they passed the first guard-post, then the second, and reached the iron gate leading out into the city, which opened for them of its own accord" (Confraternity translation).

The painting from which the room takes its name is based on the third chapter of the apocryphal Second Book of Maccabees. The impious

general Heliodorus was ordered to Jerusalem to seize the treasure of the
Temple. "But at the very moment when he arrived with his bodyguard at
the treasury, the Ruler of spirits and of all powers produced a mighty
apparition, so that all who had the audacity to accompany Heliodorus
were faint with terror, stricken with panic at the power of God. They saw
a horse splendidly caparisoned, with a rider of terrible aspect; it rushed
fiercely at Heliodorus and, rearing up, attacked him with its hooves. The
rider was wearing golden armor. There also appeared to Heliodorus two
young men of surpassing strength and glorious beauty, splendidly
dressed. They stood on either side of him and scourged him raining
ceaseless blows upon him. He fell suddenly to the ground, overwhelmed
by a great darkness" (22–27).

The scene is Solomon's Temple, identified by the menorah to the right
of its central altar. The architecture, which recalls that of the *School of
Athens,* evokes new St. Peter's as well. Julius is once again present at
the scene, carried in from the left. One of his bearers is the artist
Raimondi, whose etchings popularized Raphael's work. Julius's left hand,
with its index finger slightly outstretched, points toward Raphael himself.

The final scene in the room, the *Expulsion of Attila,* was a symbol of
the Pope's driving out of the French forces. Pope Leo III confronted the
leader of the invading Huns outside the city of Ravenna in the fifth century. With the miraculous aid of St. Peter and St. Paul, he repulsed
them. Raphael has reset the scene by placing Roman monuments in the
background. The Colosseum appears beneath Paul's feet; a broken aqueduct is directly in front of the papal crown. Before the fresco could be
completed, Julius II died and was succeeded by Pope Leo X. The new

Pope appears twice in the fresco: first as a cardinal on the extreme left and then as Leo III, a figure who could have been painted only after his accession. The composition pits the calm security of faith against the invader's furor. The Pope and his stolid entourage stand at ease with their eyes toward the viewer in complete indifference to the invaders who rush headlong toward them. The Huns, their wild-eyed horses plunging and rearing, surge in a confused mass toward the Christian defenders. With his white beard streaming and the feathers on his helmet echoing the flames that destroy the countryside behind him, Attila closes on the Pope until all this furious energy is frozen in place by the vision in the air above.

The first of the Raphael stanze on the normal Vatican tour was the last to be completed; Raphael's followers designed and painted it during the reign of Pope Clement VII. Called the Room of Constantine, it is decorated with a series of frescoes that repeat the great secular founding legend of the Catholic Church. These familiar scenes show the miraculous apparition of the cross to Constantine and his subsequent victory over Maxentius at the Milvian Bridge. The emperor's baptism is set in the Lateran Baptistery and the officiant, Pope Sylvester, is represented with the features of Pope Clement VII. The scene in which Constantine presents a golden statue representing the Roman state to the Pope is especially interesting. Renaissance humanism, the guiding spirit of the rest of the Raphael stanze, had shown in the mid-fifteenth century that the donation of Constantine, which this fresco commemorates, was a ninth-century forgery.

The Stanza dell' Incendio was painted in 1517 under the pontificate of Leo X; its earlier vaulted ceiling is by Perugino, from whom Raphael

won the commission for the stanze. Raphael was still alive when the
room was completed according to his designs, but the wall frescoes are
thought to have been painted mainly by his students. The theme of the
room is the celebration of signal events in the pontificate of Popes Leo III
and Leo IV. The image of Pope Leo X is sometimes substituted for that of
his namesakes, and the frescoes also symbolize key events of his
Renaissance pontificate.

In the *Coronation of Charlemagne by Pope Leo III,* for example,
Charlemagne has the distinctive shovel nose of King Francis I of France,
and Leo III is actually Leo X. The fresco celebrates an alliance between
the two rulers that was signed in 1515. The *Naval Victory of Leo IV over
the Saracens at Ostia* celebrates a crucial Roman battle against foreign
invaders in 849, but it also alludes to contemporary plans for a crusade
against the Turks. The scene around the window depicts Leo III's oath in
the face of a false accusation. The contemporary allusion is to the
Lateran Council convoked by Leo X.

The most striking and dramatic scene in the room is the large fresco
of the *Fire [Incendio] in the Borgo,* which has recently been attributed,
though not without controversy, to Raphael himself. According to the
Liber Pontificalis, in 847 a fire broke out in the area around the Vatican,
which Leo IV miraculously extinguished by making the sign of the cross.
The Pope is visible just right of center in the background of the scene
framed by the benediction loggia of Old St. Peter's. Farther back and to
the left the mosaic decoration of the old church is visible. The left side
of the composition is dominated by a nude figure who lowers himself
from a high wall to escape the fire. Perhaps inspired by Michelangelo's

work on the Sistine ceiling, this figure, long attributed to Giulio Romano, is one of the very few nudes in the Raphael rooms. The figure is surprisingly disproportionate, however, and the musculature is both overly articulated and unconvincing. At the edge of the composition, a young man carries his father to safety on his back. A young boy leads the pair and a woman follows. While something like this might have occurred during the

Borgo fire, these figures fit the traditional pattern for the representation of the Roman hero Aeneas as he leads his wife and son and carries his father from burning Troy. (68)

The Borgia Apartment occupies the floor directly below the Raphael stanze. Pinturicchio and his workshop decorated it in the

68

early 1490s for the infamous Pope Alexander VI. Julius II lived here for a time in the early years of his pontificate. The first three rooms have painted ceilings. The fourth room, which served as the Pope's study, is decorated with images of the liberal arts. The fifth, called the Room of the Saints, is Pinturicchio's masterpiece. Its frescoes depict the Visitation; the meeting of St. Paul and St. Anthony in the desert; the legends of St. Barbara and St. Susanna; plus the martyrdom of St. Sebastian. The centerpiece of the room is a legendary confrontation between St. Catherine of Alexandria and pagan philosophers in the presence of the emperor Maximianus. While Raphael imagined a harmony between philosophy and theology in his paintings for Julius, Pinturicchio staged a more traditional confrontation between the two disciplines under the baleful eye of authority. The fresco includes portraits of key figures in the papal court, as well as a self-portrait of the painter. The following room, dedicated to the mysteries of the faith, contains figures of kings and prophets as well as a portrait of the Borgia Pope kneeling in full pontifical regalia.

While the Sistine Chapel is synonymous with the work of Michelangelo, he is not the only Renaissance painter who worked there. The ceiling and the front west wall are his, but the frescoes on the side walls are the work of a variety of earlier Renaissance painters. Raphael's tapestries were also placed here on ceremonial occasions. The wall frescoes parallel events from the lives of Moses and Christ. The story of Moses begins behind the altar on the left wall. The first two panels by Perugino and Pinturicchio represent Moses and his wife Zeporah and the circumcision of their sons. *The Burning Bush* and the three following scenes are by Botticelli. Cosimo Roselli painted the *Crossing of the Red Sea, Moses on Sinai,* and the *Adoration of the Golden Calf. The Punishment of Core, Dathan, and Abiron* by Botticelli is reset in Rome with the arch of Constantine in the background. Luca Signorelli and Bartolomeo della Gatta painted the final scenes of Moses' death and the passing on of his rod to his successors.

On the opposite wall, scenes of the life of Christ unfold in the same direction. They begin with a *Baptism* by Perugino and Pinturicchio; *Curing the Leper* and the *Temptation in the Desert* by Botticelli; *Calling of Peter and Andrew* by Domenico Ghirlandaio; *Sermon on the Mount* and another miraculous cure by Roselli; the *Passing of the Keys to the Kingdom to St. Peter* by Perugino; and the *Last Supper* by Roselli. Scenes on the back wall are late sixteenth-century repaintings of early Renaissance works. The *Resurrection of Christ* is paralleled with the miraculous protection of the body of Moses by the archangel Michael. The spaces above this band of frescoes and between the windows of the chapel are decorated with idealized portraits of twenty-four pontiffs painted by Ghirlandaio and Botticelli, among others.

Just as Raphael's work for Julius II contrasts with the relatively straightforward histories and allegories produced in the palace for earlier popes, so does Michelangelo's work in the Sistine Chapel. As a patron, not only did Julius call for the most adventurous and innovative style of painting, but he also seems to have appreciated the intellectual challenge of difficult and unconventional subjects. Though Michelangelo began the work with many uncertainties, in the end he provided both majestic figures and a transcendent idea.

The contrast between his ceiling and the band of earlier frescoes beneath is marked. In the lower band, parallel narratives unfold in boxed scenes in a pattern that had changed little since the illustrative mosaics in the nave of Santa Maria Maggiore. Instead of a unified composition, each individual scene opens its own deep picture space behind the common wall. Michelangelo, on the other hand, conceived of the vast ceiling as a unit and created a fictional architecture to organize it into distinct but clearly related zones. The real ceiling disappears and with it the multiple and confused fictive spaces of frescoes that anchor themselves in the real walls of the building. In a treatment that paves the way for the magnificent illusions of the Roman Baroque, Michelangelo's figures appear alternately in front of, on, or within a completely imaginary architectural frame. His ceiling is far more complex symbolically than the narratives beneath. His central sequence of scenes and the statuelike figures that surround them fit together in complex and enigmatic ways.

The actual ceiling is a wide and shallow vault intersected by a series of much smaller vaults; a triangular cornice above each window marks the lines of intersection. (The outward thrust of this poorly designed arch has been countered over the centuries by the addition of huge buttresses outside the chapel.) The organizing plan of the vast ceiling is relatively simple. Its anchors are the massive thrones where biblical prophets and classical sibyls sit centered between the triangles above the windows. To Renaissance thinkers, the sibyls—Greek and Roman seers—represented intimations of Christ's birth that were present in classical sources, while the prophets performed the same role in biblical culture. There are five thrones on each long side, with sibyls and prophets alternating. A single enthroned prophet crowns the end walls. Each high-backed throne is topped by a continuous cornice which frames the central picture space of the vault. The cornice juts out at the side of each throne, where it is supported by "marble" putti. Nude men sitting on blocks above hold bands of cloth or swags of greenery from which gilded medallions hang. A "vertical" band springs up behind each throne, crosses the center vault, and connects to the opposite throne. In this way the fictive cornice anchored in the thrones and the ribs or pilasters which spring from it unify all the figures that appear to be in front of the architecture, while they create frames for the paintings "behind" it.

Michelangelo began his work on the chapel at the end farthest from the altar. While majestic and powerful, the Delphic sibyl and the prophet opposite her are smaller than the figures—many of whom seem too massive for the space allotted them—that he painted later. The nudes above these figures are glossier; their skin textures brighter and harder than those of the later figures. The central scenes in this and the two adjacent zones bustle with characters who are too small to be seen clearly. The fictional spaces are so deep that they threaten the delicate illusionism of the massive frames. Evidently it was only after the scaffolding had been dismantled in preparation for the next stage of the work that Michelangelo was able to see how these panels looked from the floor. His approach changed dramatically. These early scenes are seldom reproduced and poorly known; of course, the remaining scenes in the chapel include the most celebrated images in the world.

The symbolism of the chapel is a complex working out of a simple principle. Old Testament history, which unfolds in the center scenes, gains both a secular and a New Testament interpretation through the framing figures. Through the Incarnation, the sibyls and prophets suggest, the events of Genesis become universal spiritual truths. The ancestor figures in the lunettes above the windows and the family scenes in the window triangles carry the Old Testament story forward genealogically to the time of Christ. This double path is similar to that in Santa Maria Maggiore, where both a spiritual and a genealogical tradition pass through the Virgin Mary. Michelangelo's program also responds to the symbolic link between the Sistine Chapel and the Temple of Solomon (hence the appropriateness of Old Testament scenes). It also embraces the iconography of the lower band of frescoes which parallel the lives of Moses and Christ. Michelangelo's message, like that of the lower frescoes, is the transference of the Old Testament or Mosaic legacy through Christ and the conversion of the Roman Empire to all mankind.

The central scenes moving forward from the altar are the heart of the story. As creation unfolds, God separates the light from the darkness; then in a curious double movement, he creates the sun and moon. In Michelangelo's most famous scene, God—whose muscular frame is revealed only in this single fresco—creates Adam manifestly "in His own image." Next he creates Eve from Adam's side. In a striking double scene, Michelangelo juxtaposes the temptation of Adam and Eve by a humanized serpent and the pair's expulsion from the Garden of Eden. The rest of the central panels, which focus on the enigmatic story of Noah, record mankind's gradual recovery from this low point. Noah sacrifices; he follows God's command and preserves the seeds of each earthly species on his ark while the rest of impious mankind is destroyed in a universal flood. The ark is traditionally recognized as a symbol of salvation; but it also represents the distinction between those chosen by God and the gentiles, a distinction that is also represented in the contrast between prophets and sibyls. And just as the fictive architecture of the ceiling links the gentile and biblical traditions, Christ's incarnation erases the once fundamental distinction between the two and gathers all mankind into the ark of the Catholic Church.

Debate about the cycle's symbolism comes to a head in the effort to interpret the last scene on the ceiling, which represents the drunkenness of Noah. In this uncommon scene, Noah, overcome with wine and completely naked, is discovered by his sons. Michelangelo could hardly be suggesting that the majesty of creation comes down to this inglorious

69

figure and his humiliation. (69) St. Augustine argued that the biblical story refers symbolically to the humiliation Christ endured before his crucifixion. A moment of human degradation prophetically anticipates that moment of greatest divine generosity when Christ suffered rejection as a man in order to redeem mankind.

Two decades after completing the ceiling frescoes, Michelangelo returned to the Sistine Chapel to begin work on *The Last Judgment*. The project was conceived by Pope Clement VII shortly before his death as a memorial of the terrible events of 1527, when Spanish and German troops under the Duc de Bourbon besieged and devastated the city. Contemporaries imagined the event as equal to the barbarian invasions of the fifth century; some scholars see it as the end of the Renaissance. Despite these dire associations, Rome recovered quickly from the sack. After Clement's death in 1534, his successor, Paul III, confirmed the commission, and Michelangelo began work on the massive painting, which occupied him for some six years. He treated the end wall of the chapel as a single picture space, just as he had imagined the ceiling, but he abandoned the fictive architecture he had relied on for the earlier composition and treated the vast wall as a single canvas. In the upper corners, where the apocalyptic painting meets the earlier one, he created visible subdivisions like embracing wings, which echo the lines of the framed frescoes above.

While his ceiling fresco was unconventional, the Last Judgment was
a traditional choice for the west walls of churches from the Middle Ages
onward. Cavallini's frescoes behind the enclosed gallery at Santa Cecilia
are fragments of one such scene. In Michelangelo's composition, Christ
descends in terrible majesty in the upper center of the composition and
repulses the damned with an upraised arm. The Virgin Mary and a small
company of saints surround him. St. Bartholomew holds his flayed skin in
his hands; the face is a portrait of Michelangelo himself. Those who are
bound for salvation rise to the right of Christ, while demons attempt in
vain to drag them down. On his left, the damned plummet toward a hell
whose central figures owe a significant debt to Dante's *Inferno*. Charon,
"the demon with eyes of fire," ferries the dead across the River Styx,
where they are judged by a serpent-tailed creature called Minos. "When
the damned soul comes before him, he confesses everything and this
connoisseur of sin knows what place in Hell is his; he wraps his tail
around his body once for each circle he's to be sent down to" (*Inferno* 5).
According to Vasari, Minos' face is a portrait of Biagio da Cesena, Pope
Paul's master of ceremonies, who criticized Michelangelo for placing
nudes among his paintings for the chapel. The squeamish Biagio had his
revenge, however, or at least his spirit did; Pope Paul IV commissioned
Daniele da Volterra to paint clothes on Michelangelo's figures.

The Belvedere, built on a hilltop far distant from the fifteenth-century
core of the Vatican Palace, was designed to offer a delightful view over
the city and the countryside, but it was also meant to be a picturesque
structure in the distance when seen from the main block of the palace.
Designed by a painter, it looked like something that might be found in
the background of a Renaissance landscape. Bramante's most audacious

project for the Vatican Palace was the creation of a monumental link between the papal residence beside the basilica and the distant Belvedere. His plan called for superimposed galleries that decreased from three stories to one as they climbed the hill. Papal carriages moved from one building to the other on a level roadway at its top. Though modified by a succession of architects and revised by additional structures, Bramante's plan forms the core of the enormous Vatican Palace of today.

Bramante's design called for the creation of a monumental element in the classical style that would serve the same picturesque purpose. He designed a huge outdoor apse that was built in the late sixteenth century by Pirro Ligorio. Known as the Nicchione—the big niche—it also reconciled the line of his galleries with the off-angle ground plan of the Belvedere. The long vista Bramante had created was broken into and the sightlines blocked when two intersecting galleries—the Braccio Nuovo and the Vatican Library—cut across it. The extensive Vatican museums were pieced together from rooms in the Belvedere, Bramante's long parallel galleries, and these cross-galleries added to them. Only the Museo Gregoriano Profano, the Vatican Pinacoteca (Picture Gallery), built in the 1920s, and the newly completed entry hall lie entirely outside this plan.

The Vatican collections are very diverse. The museums include a large ethnographic collection that reflects their international missions over the centuries; a sadly undistinguished collection of modern religious painting; Egyptian and Etruscan collections of importance; and a mind-numbing assembly of historic papal carriages. The greatest strengths of the collection, however, are the small but exquisite collection of paintings in the Picture Gallery; the frescoed rooms of the Renaissance palace and Sistine Chapel; and the many collections of Roman antiquities.

It should come as no surprise that the bulk of what the popes have
collected over the last half-millennium and the greatest part of what is on
display is Roman art. There are a few priceless Roman wall paintings;
many more mosaics, which in older installations are reset directly into
the floors or walls; an enormous collection of inscriptions (generally not
open to the public); Early Christian pieces; and a host of Roman sculptures of all sizes and styles from every conceivable period.

Roman sculptures in the Museo Pio Clementino form the core of the
vast and eclectic collections. These objects were first installed in an open
courtyard of the Belvedere Palace at the insistence of Pope Julius II, a
man of extraordinary insight and imagination who employed Bramante
and Raphael to design and decorate his palace and Michelangelo to paint
the Sistine Chapel. The purpose of the collection was of a piece with the
taste that demanded a rebuilding of Old St. Peter's and an extensive
remodeling of the Vatican Palace: to display outstanding examples of
Roman art that could guide the sensibility of artists and patrons as they
began a Renovatio Romae—a renewal of the dignity and grace that characterized the long-vanished imperial capital. The museum itself has
always been a workshop where architects and designers have not only
studied but worked to recreate Roman interior spaces. The goal was
always to achieve a fusion between architecture, decoration, and the art
on display.

This fusion was guided at first by a very limited experience of Roman
interiors from the imperial age, like those rooms of Nero's Golden House
that Renaissance artists explored. More generally the designers of the
Pio-Clementine rooms worked with literary texts that described the riches
of private villas, the imperial fora, the Palatine, and especially the sump-

tuous Roman baths. As this area of the museum grew between the sixteenth and the nineteenth centuries, that goal remained its guiding principle. Unlike modern museum practice, which aims to isolate and objec-
tify pieces either aesthetically or historically against a neutral backdrop,
the Pio-Clementine collection recreates Roman grandeur through the
assembly of historical objects within a series of dramatic architectural
settings. The spirit of renovatio is objectified in the struggle to measure
up to what the Renaissance and succeeding periods saw as the highest
artistic ideal.

To the right of the new main entrance is the Atrio dei Quattro Can-
celli. Beyond it to the left the beautiful Scala Simonetti, named for its
eighteenth-century designer, leads into a magnficent room created by the
same architect. Called the Sala a Croce Greca (Room of the Greek Cross),
its outstanding objects are the porphyry sarcophagus of Constantia, which
originally stood in the church of Santa Costanza, and that of her mother,
Helen. A fourth-century mosaic—with a shield, the bust of the goddess
Minerva, and the phases of the moon—is set into the floor. Sculptures in
the Egyptian taste and Roman portraits complete the ensemble.

The domed Sala Rotonda, also designed by Simonetti, is like a miniature Pantheon restored to its original richness. A large porphyry basin fills
the center of the room; it stands on a Roman mosaic with mythical combat scenes in its center and nymphs, deities, and sea serpents around its
outer edge. Sculptures in the room include the *Jupiter of Otricoli,* a
Roman copy of a fourth-century Greek original, and the colossal *Hercules*
in gilded bronze. Struck by lightning in antiquity—a mark of divine dis-
pleasure—the statue was ceremoniously buried near the Theater of
Pompey.

The room beyond, also designed by Simonetti, features one of the
most celebrated objects of the Vatican collection, the *Belvedere Torso:* a
signed statue of Hercules (or perhaps another mythical giant) seated on
an animal skin. (70) The torso was discovered early in the sixteenth century and greatly influenced Renaissance artists, especially Michelangelo,
who recreated its contours in figures on the Sistine ceiling.

The Gallery of the Animals houses a vivid menagerie of domestic crea-
tures plus exotic predators and their hapless prey. It testifies both to a
Roman taste for sentimental literalism in art and an appetite for the
bloody staged hunts in the Colosseum. Beyond this room stands the
Cortile Ottagona, the original Belvedere courtyard. The earliest installation in the Vatican, it differs from the later ones most remarkably in the
specific Roman ideal it evokes. Bramante designed a peristyle, an open-
air space with fountains and plantings surrounded by a portico that sheltered the sculpture collection. Simonetti imagined the Belvedere as part
of an urban palace; Bramante and his generation saw it as a hortus—a
suburban villa—like that of Maecenas or Livia or the notorious but better
known Domus Aurea. Bramante's grand design linked
inner and outer, domestic architecture and garden
space, in a way that Romans would have appreciated
but later generations repudiated.

Among the celebrated works long associated with
this courtyard, two especially stand out. These are the
Apollo Belvedere and the *Laocoön* group. Though it is a
work of inferior quality, the *Apollo*—naked except for
the cape draped from his arms—projects the aloof calm
that marks Hellenized Roman art. The tensionless,

70

71

uninflected torso, the relaxed stance, and the impersonal face represent an ideal of serenity that may seem forced to modern eyes (71) The American painter Benjamin West, who saw the *Apollo* for the first time in the late eighteenth century, imagined its impassivity in a very different light: "By God," he said, "a Mohawk!" The turbulent *Laocoön* is very different. (72) Twice restored, the group represents a famous scene in Virgil's *Aeneid* when monstrous sea serpents strangle a priest and his two young sons as they sacrifice to Neptune. "First the twin serpents entwine the poor bodies of the two sons binding them and biting their pitiful limbs; with their tails they wrap them in giant spirals; gripping their waists and necks, the serpents curl around their heads. Laocoön meanwhile tries to undo the knots with his hands. His ceremonial bindings drip with black poison, and his horrendous screams reach to the stars" (*Aeneid* 2.215–221). From the Renaissance on, artists studied and drew this work, which was uncovered in 1506 near the Domus Aurea. At the end of the eighteenth century the German critic Lessing used it as the basis for a book on the representation of emotion in art and literature.

Beyond the Cortile a series of rooms—all part of the original Belvedere—continue the display. The second on the right beyond the courtyard offers a glimpse down the remarkable spiral ramp that Bramante added to the villa. Sometimes less crowded than the rest of the museum, these intimate rooms lead into two of the more daunting parts of the col-

lection (the upper floor of this part of the museum houses the extensive
and important Etruscan collection). The Museo Chiaramonti occupies one
of the rare stretches of Bramante's connecting corridors that was completed during his lifetime and according to his design, though windows
now enclose his open arcades. Each sidewall here is divided into some
thirty shallow bays packed with Roman sculpture of all sorts. Neoclassical frescoes in the vaulted ceiling complete the decoration. A room like
this one explains why the word "gallery,"
meaning corridor, designates an exhibition
space for art. Unlike modern galleries which
guide the eye from one distinct object to
another, this gallery offers a variety of expe-
riences. The vista, which is meant to be
overwhelming, shows the entire collection
at a single view. Works in the niches are
grouped in ways that should spark a dia-
logue between artworks. Finally, there is
the chance to be captured by a single
piece. Each of these impressions can vary

72

with the time of day, the weather, the shadow of a cloud that highlights
one work or area and obscures another. Until the mid-nineteenth century,
visitors toured the galleries at night by torchlight, as ghostly visions of
the Roman past came uncertainly into the light and just as suddenly disappeared.

The Braccio Nuovo is one of two transverse arms connecting
Bramante's twin corridors. Added in the early nineteenth century, the

gallery is brightly lit by skylights. Its exhibition style is otherwise similar
to that of the earlier Chiaramonti gallery, with its multitudes of Roman
works arranged in long vistas and smaller subgroups. One of the prizes of
the collection is the *Prima Porta Augustus,* excavated near Livia's Villa at
the same site. Caught in mid-speech, the emperor extends his arm in a
gesture of apparent inclusiveness. The remarkable detail of the breast-
plate and the generally fine state of preservation mark this as an especially important work. In the central hemicycle there is a personification
of the Nile River with a sphinx to identify it as Egyptian and a cornucopia
to symbolize the richness of its floodwaters. Sixteen little figures scram-
ble over the recumbent god, and comic scenes of combat decorate the
back and base. Pygmies battle with crocodiles and hippopotamuses, and
ibises with crocodiles. Exotic stereotypes of this kind are a standard of
Roman popular art.

The Museo Gregoriano Profano was established by Pope Gregory XVI in
the mid-nineteenth century and installed in the Lateran Palace. In 1970
the collection was relocated to the Vatican. This newest of the Vatican
installations reflects the modern style of presenting and highlighting individual objects. The collection is rich especially in Greek sculptures that
are otherwise represented in the collections primarily through Roman
copies. These include a grave stele of the fifth century, some fragments
of sculpture from the Parthenon, and a fine head of Athena. Nearby are
Roman sculptures closely connected with Greek workshops, which
include another Athena and a dramatic Marsyas. The well-preserved figure of the dramatist Sophocles is especially fine. Reliefs from the altar of
the Vicomagistri represent a Roman sacrifice in some detail. The proces-

sion includes three bulls, priests, musicians, and magistrates; assistants carry household gods and an image of the genius of the emperor. The collection also includes a number of high-quality Roman portrait busts. The same building houses the Museo Pio Christiano and the extensive Missionary Ethnological collection.

The building housing the Vatican Pinacoteca or Picture Gallery was opened in 1932. Begun in the seventeenth century and lost in part to France at the end of the eighteenth, the painting collection includes works from the Vatican Palace, the Sacristy of St. Peter's, the papal residence at Castel Gondalfo, and elsewhere. The pictures, which span the thirteenth to the eighteenth centuries, are arranged chronologically. Unlike most great Roman picture collections, which are strongest in works of the Baroque period and later, many of the best paintings in the Pinacoteca come from earlier periods, and the Renaissance is well represented.

Among the earliest objects is a starkly simple image of St. Francis of Assisi by Margaretone of Arezzo. The second room, devoted to Giotto and his followers, highlights the *Stefaneschi Altarpiece,* a polyptich commissioned by a cardinal of the celebrated Roman family and painted by Giotto and his assistants. It stood over the altar of Old St. Peter's. Other significant works include *Christ before Pilate, St. John,* and *St. Peter* by Pietro Lorenzetti; and others by Simone Martini and Taddeo Gaddi. The following room features works by Fra Angelico, Masolino, and Filippo Lippi. Room four contains fragments of two frescoes by Melozzo da Forli painted in the fifteenth century and later removed from their original sites. The more complete of the two depicts the appointment by Pope Sixtus IV of a prominent Renaissance humanist, Bartolomeo Sacchi, as director of the Vatican Library. The following three rooms continue the chronicle of fifteenth-century works.

Room Eight is the largest and most impressive of the collection. Ten tapestries designed in 1515 by Raphael hang here, as well as several of his most significant paintings, including the magnificent *Transfiguration*. Flanked by such celebrated paintings as the *Madonna of Foligno* and the *Incoronation of the Virgin,* the *Transfiguration* complicates the lucent colors of his early works with deep shadows; the stability and symmetry that characterize the most celebrated scenes in the Vatican Palace are displaced here by a wilder swirl of figures and forces. Among the later works in the collection, the *Deposition* by Caravaggio stands out.

The Sala degli Indirizzi features a number of small, precious objects in glass, bronze, and ivory dating from antiquity into the Middle Ages. These include a beaker decorated with marine animals from the fourth century and a glass disk with the earliest known representation of saints Peter and Paul. There are many Late Antiquity and Early Christian ivory panels, some of very high quality, engraved with scenes and figures. A door on the left side of this room opens into the room of the *Aldobrandini Wedding.* This small fresco, discovered in 1605, is one of the most compelling of the few ancient paintings that have survived. It is an enigmatic scene with brooding figures painted in muted though rich colors.

The Museo Sacro, a precious collection of Early Christian objects, leads directly into a long corridor that is broken into a number of smaller rooms and dedicated to the exhibits of the Apostolic Vatican Library. Representative objects from that extraordinary collection and short-term exhibits are displayed in these long galleries. The special exhibits are generally more interesting than the permanent display, which features bibliographic curiosities like the biggest and smallest books, unusual bindings, and especially rich illuminations.

In 1451 Pope Nicholas V gave the Vatican's informal collection of books a librarian and a home. A quarter century later, Pope Sixtus IV formalized the creation of this library with a papal bull. At that time the manuscripts in the library, which was housed in a room overlooking the Cortile del Pappagallo, numbered about 2,500. In 1587 at the instigation of Pope Sixtus V, the architect Domenico Fontana designed a new home for the expanded collection in a wing of the palace that transected Bramante's courtyard. The vast collections of the library, which are open only to scholars, are still housed in this intersecting corridor.

A long brick wall with crenellations at its top sets out from the lower stories of the papal palace to the left of St. Peter's. Masked at first by Bernini's colonnade, it makes its way to the nearest bastion of Castel Sant'Angelo. In 1527, as Spanish and German troops fired from below, Pope Clement VII ran the full length of the passageway behind the crenellations. He reached Castel Sant'Angelo, where for five months he and the luckier members of his court were besieged inside. The emperor Hadrian had designed this massive brick-faced drum which stands across the Tiber from the Campus Martius as a mausoleum. Hadrian and his successors were buried in the new structure, which was originally faced with marble, decorated with friezes and artwork, and probably crowned with a living garden. Closer to the center of Rome, the Mausoleum of Augustus, a similar structure, had by the early second century become completely filled with imperial burials.

In Late Antiquity and the Middle Ages, the vast drum was emptied of its tombs and stripped of its ornaments. When the popes returned to

Rome in the fifteenth century, they fortified the Vatican Palace and reconfigured Castel Sant'Angelo as a combined military bastion, a retreat for the Pope, and a dreaded prison for his enemies. Fortified outworks in the typical Renaissance star patterns were added to protect the building against cannon fire. As late as the nineteenth century, it figured as a symbol of tyrannical oppression in Puccini's opera *Tosca*. (73)

Inside the central drum, a spiraling ramp leads under vaulted ceilings to a central chamber; here a drawbridge above a deep shaft controls access to the space above. The view from the top toward the Vatican and the city is magnificent. Renaissance cannons and piles of iron and cut-stone cannonballs are everywhere. The light and airy papal apartments decorated in the late fifteenth and early sixteenth centuries contrast strongly with the dismal cells of those who met papal disfavor.

73

Chapter Six

RENAISSANCE
IN THE RIVER BEND

The return of the papacy to Rome in 1377 gradually
brought wealth and prominence back to the city. The
overhaul of the papal palace and St. Peter's was paralleled in the smaller projects of each member of the
Roman Curia. Cardinals refurbished churches, built
palaces for their extensive households, and commissioned paintings and
sculpture. A wealthy Church attracted secular men of wealth, who themselves built palaces and cultivated the arts with more license than their clerical counterparts. The trickle-down economy that began with the papal court
and prominent bankers and merchants spread through all levels of Roman
society, from manufacturers and importers of luxury goods to shopkeepers,
market gardeners, and servants. Above all it enriched the builders and made
construction the city's major industry.

The return of political stability brought pilgrims back to the papal city in
unparalleled numbers, boosting the economy still further. Wealth in such
abundance was not always well spent. Vows of celibacy could be difficult to
maintain; pilgrims far from home turned into randy conventioneers. Rome
had always been notorious for prostitution, but by all accounts the number
of prostitutes, and their prominence and influence in Roman society, sky-
rocketed during the Renaissance. The French essayist Michel de Montaigne,

who visited Rome in the winter of 1581, noted in his journal that "he had found no particular beauty in Roman women worthy of that preeminence that reputation gives to this city over all others. And as in Paris, the most singular beauty is to be found in the hands of those who put it up for sale" (*Journal de Voyage*, p. 192).

There were thugs of all descriptions, too. Pimps, thieves, and highway robbers necessitated or at least justified the bodyguards and armed escorts who surrounded the prominent and wealthy. Montaigne wrote that "going out at night is hardly safe and that even the houses are so insecure that men of means are commonly advised to deposit their purses with the city's bankers to avoid being robbed, which has happened to many" (p. 190).

The passion for modernization that led to the replacement of Old St. Peter's and radically changed the Vatican Palace was evident throughout the Borgo. Near its confines another of Rome's great Renaissance architects, Antonio da Sangallo the Younger (1483–1546), designed two important structures for Pope Paul III (1534–1549). One of them, the church of Santo Spirito in Sassia, remained unbuilt until the last decade of the sixteenth century. Using traditional features of Early Renaissance façades—the flat two-story screen with its characteristic scrolls—Sangallo moved beyond his models to create a dynamic, three-dimensional effect. Both stories are articulated by pilasters. The central bay is emphasized by a deep round window above the shallow doorway. Niches in the remaining bays create a further sense of depth in the wall.

Sangallo also designed the incomplete Porta Santo Spirito a short distance away for Paul III. (74) In its adaptive imitation of a Roman tri-

umphal arch, it reflects the classical
ideals of Bramante and the High Renaissance, but its monumental scale and
curved façade pave the way for the
Baroque. Bramante's generation would
probably have divided a wall of this
height into two or three horizontal zones

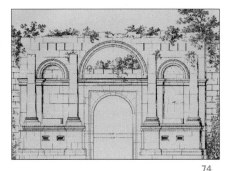

74

on the model of the Colosseum and Theater of Marcellus. Sangallo
instead erected four colossal travertine columns on high pedestals and
used them to frame two monumental niches and an open gateway. Only
the lower two-thirds of the structure was built according to Sangallo's
plan, and so his massive columns remain without capitals and with nothing to support.

The long Via della Lungara links Sangallo's Porta Santo Spirito to the
Porta Settimiana in Trastevere. The street was laid out under Pope
Alexander VI and completed under Julius II in an area outside the city
walls that made the Vatican and Trastevere separate enclaves. For centuries the road was lined by villas with gardens that stretched up the hill
or toward the river. Though urbanized in the nineteenth century and dis-
rupted by the Tiber embankments, some stretches of the street retain this
suburban character today. Just inside Trastevere, the Via della Lungara
provided access to the Ponte Sisto, which linked up with the business
and population center across the Tiber. Through twisting streets in
Trastevere, themselves regularized under subsequent popes, it connected
to the Tiber docks. Both pilgrims and merchandise followed it to St.
Peter's.

Near the southern end of the Via della Lungara, close to the Porta Settimiana and the Ponte Sisto, the papal banker Agostino Chigi built and decorated his sumptuous suburban Villa Farnesina. Its antique model was the hortus, or country house, common in the imperial period and known to Renaissance scholars through written texts. Chigi's architect, Baldassare Peruzzi, designed a simple C-shaped structure with a loggia on its river side and another that faced the garden and was embraced between the building's extended wings. (75) In structure and purpose the building was similar to the Palazzo Belvedere designed by Pinturicchio, though the Farnesina was more strictly classicizing in style.

The two-story brick building is divided into vertical bays by shallow

75

pilasters and zoned horizontally by an entablature between its two stories; a second entablature with an ornamented frieze crowns the façade. Though generally well preserved, the building we see today differs in some important ways from its fifteenth-century appearance. The now austere façade was once richly decorated with stucco work; the loggias, originally open to the weather, are glassed in; the modern entrance has been shifted to the back of the building. Most significantly, the intimate connection between the villa, the river, and the cityscape beyond has been severed by the Tiber embankments. Now tightly enclosed in its degraded grounds, the villa gives no hint of the imperial ideal it was meant to renew. Its purpose was to offer a prospect, both meditative and real, on the city from a green vantage point.

While the façade and the setting have lost much of their quality and appeal, the interior of the villa, with its magnificent frescoed rooms, is an unmatched treasure of High Renaissance art. The jewel of the collection is the extraordinary Loggia of Psyche, with its vast frescoed ceiling designed by Raphael and painted by his assistants. The structure of the loggia roof is very similar to that of the Sistine ceiling, and the subdivision of the painted space into smaller areas reflects this. In place of Michelangelo's fictive architecture, however, which springs from the prophets' and sybils' thrones, the organizing framework here suggests an elaborate trellis or pergola thickly wreathed with leaves, fruits, and vegetables. It is a sophisticated version of a structure that might be built in the fields to celebrate a rich harvest. The large paintings that fill the center of the ceiling are treated as painted tapestries attached at their edges to the harvest frame.

In theme as in presentation, these majestic scenes contrast both with Michelangelo's and with Raphael's own work in the Vatican. Depicting the *Wedding of Cupid and Psyche* and *Psyche's Reception on Mount Olympus,* the scenes are classical rather than biblical in inspiration. While Michelangelo's Sistine ceiling teems with male nudes, the frescoes here include both male and female nudes painted with a more direct sensuality. The fruitful harvest evoked by the fictive trellis extends to the humans and gods, whose sexual ripeness and fecundity is evident. Sensuality is apparent in all the frescoes of the Farnesina, and it is often attributed to the licentiousness of Renaissance Rome.

There are more general reasons, however, for the themes of this loggia and the other apartments. Apuleius inserted the story of Cupid and Psyche in the comic misadventure he called the *Metamorphoses* but

which is more familiar as the *Golden Ass.* The inset episode is not a
mere love story but an allegory of the process by which the soul (psyche
means soul) achieves immortality through love. Plato expressed the same
idea in his *Symposium,* when Socrates says, "There is a certain age when
human nature is desirous of procreation—procreation which must be in
beauty and not in deformity; and this procreation is the union of man
and woman, and is a divine thing; for conception and generation are an
immortal principle in the mortal creature" (*Symposium* 206, Jowett
translation). Neoplatonism, which was extremely important in the
Renaissance, championed the same idea, and it is likely that a
Neoplatonic ideal of philosophical love is the guiding principle in this
fresco and in the villa generally.

    The Loggia of Galatea, which originally opened onto the river, is full of
images of water, water deities, and watery landscapes. In the greatest

single fresco of the villa painted by Raphael, the
nymph Galatea drives a shell-shaped chariot
pulled by dolphins through a sea thick with nere-
ids and their lovers. Three cupids circle above.
(76) In the adjacent panel by Sebastiano del
Piombo, the monstrous Polyphemus (the Cyclops
of the *Odyssey*), who has loved and lost Galatea,
looks off into the distance. The bedroom of
Agostino Chigi on the second floor is decorated
with scenes from the life of Alexander the Great
by Sodoma. *The Marriage of Alexander and
Roxanne* carries on the themes of the loggias

76

below. The Perspective Room, also on the second floor, which was frescoed by the villa's designer, Peruzzi, gives a sense of the builder's inten-
tion. Through fictive porticoes the viewer looks out on the distant city of
Rome, just as Chigi's guests would have done in reality from the rooms
below. The graffiti on the walls of this room, some of them in German,
date from the occupation of Rome in 1527 by imperial troops.

The Palazzo Corsini stands across the Via della Lungara from the
Farnesina. The façade, added in the eighteenth century, linked contemporary structures to a smaller palazzo built in the early sixteenth century
by Cardinal Raffaele Riario. Riario was one of the many relatives of Pope
Sixtus IV, whose improvements to the papal city were overshadowed in
the eyes of his contemporaries by his outrageous devotion to his family. If
not a co-conspirator in a plot to assassinate the Medici rulers of Florence
and replace them with his own nephews, the Pope was certainly suppor-
tive. His foreign policy in general boosted the political ambitions of his
family, and the wealth of the papacy found its way to them. Their osten-
tatious Roman palaces reflected a trend that was common enough in the
Renaissance.

The impressive building, which has been owned by the state since the
late nineteenth century, serves a number of functions. Its grounds are the
city's Botanical Garden, and one of its wings houses an important national
academy. Its most important feature, however, is the Galleria Corsini,
which contains a small but superb group of paintings that have recently
been restored to their original settings. Among the more significant works
in the collection are a *Last Judgment* by Fra Angelico (where Christ's gesture of condemnation prefigures Michelangelo's); *John the Baptist* by

Caravaggio; an *Adoration* by Bassano; and later works by Van Dyck and painters of the Spanish Baroque, including Murillo and Ribera. The collection, which was consolidated in the seventeenth century, includes works acquired by the family somewhat earlier.

The organization and display of the papal collections in the Vatican Palace acted as a spur to the cardinals and to wealthy Roman families. Starting in the seventeenth century, art collections like this one became an important feature of palaces throughout the city. While many of them have been dispersed over the centuries, a surprising number, both privately and publicly held, survive to the present day.

At the end of the tiny Via de' Corsini is the entrance to Rome's Orto Botanico. The city's first botanical garden, dedicated to the propagation of medicinal plants, was founded at the end of the thirteenth century. The present collection follows the plan of gardens that once stretched from the Corsini palace up the slopes of the Janiculum. Though its plantings are eclectic and international rather than historical, they offer a hint of the relationship between a suburban palace and its gardens. This is especially true at the garden's upper limit, where giant plane trees, some three to five hundred years old, overshadow a Baroque stairway with a fountain at its center.

The spacious green villas on the Vatican side of the river looked toward a city that was close, crowded, and disorderly. Confined within a deep bend of the Tiber, the heart of the Renaissance city grew up on the ruins of an area which in the Roman period had been sparsely populated and filled with public monuments. The Campus Martius lay beyond the boundaries of Rome's traditional core, though well within the limits of its

third-century walls. When the aqueducts were cut and the heights could
no longer sustain large populations, Romans scavenged for living space
in this low-lying area of town. The medieval city which flourished here
was swept by periodic flooding and devastated by the removal of the
popes to Avignon in the early fourteenth century. After the reestablish-
ment of papal government in the mid-fifteenth century, the Campus
Martius (now Campo Marzio) became the scene of intense development
and urban renewal.

The amenity and order of imperial Rome had vanished with its fabric.
The Renaissance blossomed in a city that in many ways recalled the earlier Rome of the Republic. The inhabited areas of the city in Trastevere
and the Campo Marzio were crowded with buildings that bent and twisted
the street plan into a maze. The narrow streets were full of garbage and,
in December or January, apt to be buried in mud if the river overflowed.
The new order and decorum that ruled in the Vatican needed to be
extended to the city, but the impediments to orderly development were
precisely those that Julius Caesar and Augustus had faced.

It was impossible to reorganize this chaos wholesale, though the new
palaces, many with piazzas, gave at least a breath of light and air and a
limited focus to the surrounding neighborhoods. Planners also managed
to cut a few straight roads through various parts of the Campo Marzio.
The beauty and efficiency of these direct routes had some residual organizing effect on the streets nearby. Not until the seventeenth century,
when Rome began to expand beyond its medieval confines, could the
planning that had characterized the Roman Empire again be imposed,
but then only on newly reclaimed areas of the city.

Passage from the riverside villas to the crowded Renaissance town was eased by a Roman bridge that was brought back into service late in the fifteenth century. One of eight bridges that had spanned the Tiber in antiquity, the Ponte Sisto was built by Agrippa and extensively remodeled under Antoninus Pius. Remodeled again in the late fourth century, it was damaged by high water in the winter of 589. After the great flood of 792 it became unusable. Pilgrims flocking to the Vatican in the Jubilee year of 1450 were so densely crowded on the Ponte Sant'Angelo—the one serviceable bridge to the Vatican area then remaining—that many lost their lives. As the Jubilee of 1475 approached, Pope Sixtus IV decided to repair Agrippa's bridge and restore it to use. The little-known Baccio Pontelli may have been the architect. A Latin inscription on the city side reads: "Sixtus IV, Pontifex Maximus, at great care and expense repaired this bridge which had with good reason been known as 'the broken bridge' for the use of the Roman people and the multitude of pilgrims who will participate in the Jubilee."

The bridge that increased the flow of pilgrim traffic also sped the movement of freight between the river port in Trastevere and Rome's commercial and population center in the Tiber bend. The bridge was widened in the late nineteenth century by the addition of raised walkways supported on massive sills that masked the Roman structure. These additions were removed in the 1990s and replaced by a uniform roadway with parapets of brick and travertine.

The Campo Marzio within the Tiber bend was so densely settled that no systematic rebuilding or reorganization of the area was possible. With few exceptions, even the most powerful Renaissance patrons, like the oligarchs of the Roman Republic, made only piecemeal incursions into its

tightly woven fabric. (77) Most of what they built were private palaces,

though a few were devoted to public

business; in some cases an open piazza

was cleared in front of the buildings. Two

areas in the Campo Marzio have

remained open since antiquity: Piazza

Navona, the infield of a stadium for

horse racing built by Domitian, and the

large piazza known as Campo de' Fiori,

an open square in front of the Temple of

Venus Victrix in the Roman period,

whose name means "field of flowers."

77

In the Middle Ages, the "field" was the scene of tournaments and

public executions. "On the eleventh of January, 1581, as M. de

Montaigne was leaving his apartment, he discovered that Catena was on

his way to execution. He was a notorious thief and captain of a robber

band, whose terrible crimes had terrified all of Italy. He was especially

notorious for the murder of two Capuchin friars whom he had forced to

renounce God, promising on that condition to spare their lives . . . The

victim is preceded by a large crucifix draped with black and surrounded

by a large company of men in masks. These are said to be gentlemen

and notables of Rome who belong to a confraternity that is pledged to

accompany criminals on their way to execution. Two of them stay with

the criminal in the cart and preach to him, while one of them holds

before his face and has him kiss an image of Our Savior. This is so people will not be able to see his face. At the gallows, which is nothing but a beam between two supports, that image is held continually before his eyes until he is hanged. He made a typical death without speaking or moving; he was a dark man about thirty years old. After his death, they cut him into four pieces. They seldom kill men in any unusual way and exercise their savagery after death . . . As soon as they are dead, one or several Jesuits or others place themselves above the crowd—one here and another there—and exhort them to benefit from this example" (Montaigne, *Journal de Voyage,* p. 187).

A somber monument in the center of the piazza commemorates the most notable of these executions, that of Giordano Bruno, who was burned alive on February 17, 1600. Erected in 1887, the controversial monument was seen as a symbolic indictment by the newly installed national government of a notorious abuse by the papal government they had replaced. Since 1869 the piazza has hosted an enormous outdoor market which had for many centuries before that been held in Piazza Navona. Surrounded by restaurants and specialty shops, the square is completely taken over every morning by a host of vendors who pack up and disappear by mid-afternoon. The west end of the piazza, which gets the morning sun, is dominated by flower stalls. The midsection belongs to the fruit and vegetable sellers. Produce varies with the season. In early spring, there are blood oranges from Sicily, individually wrapped in printed tissue paper, clementines from Spain—the more expensive with stem and leaves attached—pears, apricots, apples, and cactus fruits. Tiny artichokes with stems and leaves, lettuce in every variety and shade of green, broccolini and broccoletti, sheaves of dandelion and peeled stems of puntarelle are grouped and mounded on the vegetable sellers' tables.

Later there are berries, melons, squashes
of every shape, white and yellow peaches,
and plump round Roman watermelons.
(78) All are patiently arranged and re-
arranged throughout the morning for maximum appeal, and shoppers look without
touching. As the day goes on, the careful
arrangements on the stands grow smaller,
while discarded leaves and stems pile up
on the black cobblestones below.

78

The fish sellers crowd together at the cold and shady south end of the
piazza. They offer every size and variety of Mediterranean fish, from
spigola to dorato, sardine to swordfish, plus cockles and winkles and
other curious shellfish, pearly squid, and whole implacable octopus.
Strings of plucked fowls hang over the doors of the butchers' shops at
the edge of the piazza. Each delicatessen window frames a still life of
sausages and cheeses in fifty shapes and shades.

The Cancelleria is an enormous palace that dates from the end of the
fifteenth century; it was built for the powerful Cardinal Raffaele Riario.
Made of travertine blocks robbed from the Colosseum, the vast structure,
once attributed to Bramante, overwhelms and encloses the cardinal's titular Basilica of San Damaso. (79) Since the sixteenth century it has

housed the offices of
the papal secretariat
or chancery. The
façade is divided
into three horizontal

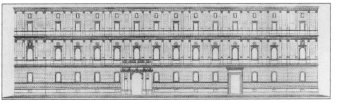

79

zones in a style that recalls the Tabularium, the Colosseum, and the Theater of Marcellus. Bramante used this style repeatedly and with great success, but this building was near completion in 1499 when the Milanese architect first arrived in Rome. Its unknown designer—perhaps Baccio Pontelli—arrived at similar principles through the example of Alberti and the Florentine Palazzo Rucellai.

The ground floor is punctuated by simple arched windows. The two upper stories are divided into bays by slim pilasters above more substantial plinths. The corners of the long sides project outward, bringing the long succession of bays to a definite end. Windows on the second floor are arched and topped by flat cornices. The smaller rectangular windows on the third level have the same cornices; the tiny arched attic windows above them resemble the mezzanine windows of Roman shops. The somewhat irregular rhythm of the windows contrasts with the even beat of the symmetrical bays. While the building is very impressive, judged by the standards of a few decades later its individual parts appear too small and delicate to adequately fill the spaces they occupy, and the design as a whole lacks the clarity, coherence, and dimensionality of Bramante's work. The large inner courtyard features two superimposed travertine arcades supported on antique columns (like the nave arcade of a traditional basilica). Bracket-shaped pillars support the corners. The third story imitates the exterior façade.

Further down the Corso Vittorio Emanuele II stand the remains of the misnamed Palazzetto Farnesina ai Baullari which houses the Museo Barracco. When the street was widened in the nineteenth century, one bay was shaved away and the building was reoriented toward the new monumental avenue. The original façade, now narrowed, faces the Via de' Baullari. The side of the building facing the Corso Vittorio Emanuele II is a reworking of the original design attributed to Sangallo the Younger. The interior of the small palace, which is decorated with eighteenth-century frescoes, houses the sculpture collection assembled by Giovanni Barracco and given to the city at the end of the nineteenth century. The collector's aim was to chronicle the development of sculptural technique through Egyptian, Syrian, Cypriot, Greek, Etruscan, and Roman examples. While the collection does not rival any of the great Roman museums, many individual pieces are very fine; the installation, completed in the 1980s, highlights individual objects.

The design of the Palazzo Vidoni-Cafarelli is often attributed to Raphael, but work on the building did not begin until 1524, four years after his death. Whoever the architect may have been, his original design survives only in one portion of a building that has expand-ed over the centuries. The central seven bays of the long façade that faces the Via del Sudario are original. (They are distinguished from the other ten bays that face this street by the absence of gabled windows in the first floor.) In the heavily rusticated first story, shops with mezzanine windows above them alternate with doorways. In the extremely elegant piano nobile, pairs of attached columns divide high windows with balconies and blind openings above; they support a massive entablature. (80) The con-trast between the rough ground floor and refined and open piano nobile is striking. A simple attic story with elemen-

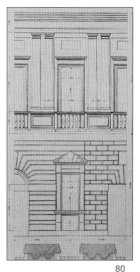

80

tal pilasters completes the structure. Though based on Bramante's princi-

ples, the palazzo seems to leap beyond them.

The Palazzo Farnese stands on its own piazza at the end of the Via

de' Baullari. The piazza sets off the building and offers a view of its

entire façade. (81) The massive palace was designed by Sangallo the

Younger for Cardinal Alessandro Farnese in 1515. Like many Florentine

palaces of the period, the building is a free-standing block with a central

courtyard. Sangallo designed its three

horizontal zones, which are separated

by thin cornices and distinguished by

their window treatments. Near the

end of Farnese's pontificate as Pope

Paul III, Michelangelo took over as

architect. He made slight but signifi-

cant modifications to the plan. He

added bracketed windows to the first

81

story, sometimes called "kneeling windows"; he modified the entryway

and added the large window above, which is surmounted by the Farnese

coat of arms. From it the Pope could greet the crowds in the piazza.

Michelangelo's most significant addition, however, was the enormous cor-

nice beneath the roof, which responds to the scale of the whole façade

rather than just to that of the upper story. (82) This addition transformed

Sangallo's horizontally subdivided wall into a single unit. The building

houses an important sculpture collection and extraordinary frescoed

rooms by Carracci with imagery linked to Raphael's Farnesina.

The Palazzo Massimo alle Colonne was designed by Baldassare

Peruzzi, the architect of the Farnesina. In the twenty tumultuous years that separate the two commissions, both Rome and architecture had experienced great changes. The canon of the High Renaissance was giving way to the more complex and more uncertain standards of Mannerism. The dynamism of the first decades of the century and its great patrons, like Julius II and Agostino Chigi, was choked off by the sack of Rome in 1527. In its gloom and heaviness, Palazzo Massimo alle Colonne, built shortly after the invasion, seems to reflect a period in which Rome's self-confidence had been shaken. The palace façade is curved to match the site, which was originally occupied by the Theater of Domitian. The building

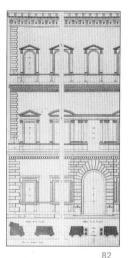

82

itself appears to be upside-down. (83) Its lowest story is divided by Doric pilasters into a series of bays that are broken in the middle by the columned entryway from which the palace takes its name. Above a wide entablature, the upper stories blend together in an area marked only by

83

the outlines of what appear to be squared building stones. In reality the squared blocks are patterned stucco over a brick wall, but the building seems to be rusticated above and set on columns below. Seven windows with linked sills rest on the heavy cornice. Above them two rows of mezzanine windows pierce the netlike wall. A projecting cornice overshadows the topmost row.

The ornate façade of the Palazzo Spada, built in the pontificate of Paul III for Cardinal Girolamo Capodiferro, is at heart a

Renaissance façade in the tradition of Bramante and Peruzzi. Its first story of rusticated stone is topped by three additional stories separated by thin cornices under an overhanging roof. Quoins at the building's corners carry the rustication from the bottom story to the roof. The abundant and very dynamic stucco work, however, creates a Mannerist conflict between real and fictive architectural elements on the façade. The confusion is especially marked in the piano nobile, where shallow niches with gabled pediments alternate with windows topped by flat cornices. The niches display statues of distinguished Romans. Stucco swags hang from the frames of the mezzanine windows above; and fictive round medallions stand between them. Plaster garlands hang from the "real" cornice. Inscriptions in square frames alternate with the rectangular windows in the top story. Conflict between real and fictive elements continues in the courtyard. Decorated by acanthus swags, its bands of bas-reliefs depict battles between centaurs and lapiths, and others between sea gods and harpies. Twelve niches enclose statues of the principal Roman gods.

The most curious and celebrated feature of the palace is the Perspective Gallery set in place a hundred years after the opening of the palace itself. This Baroque curiosity, which can be seen through the wooden grill of a library window, shares the taste for architectural play that animates the Mannerist façade but takes it a step further. Designed by Borromini, the gallery, which is about thirty feet long, appears to be nearly three times that length. The controlled viewpoint, the upward sloping floor, the carefully proportioned columns, and the apparently life-sized statue at the gallery's end painstakingly craft this playful illusion. (84) When an attendant walks into the tiny courtyard, the shrunken gallery and diminu-

tive statue suddenly reveal their true scale.
The collection of paintings exhibited in the
Galleria Spada was assembled in the seventeenth century after the Capodiferro family sold
the palace to Cardinal Bernardino Spada. Like
the Corsini collection, which was organized at
about the same time, it represents the taste of
the highest clerical class and the display of art
to create a sense of wealth and refinement.
Religious subjects, and especially images of
popular saints like Jerome and Mary Magdalene,
predominate; scenes from Roman history and

84

mythology along with a few commissioned portraits fill out the collection.
There are paintings of Cardinal Spada by Guercino and Guido Reni, as
well as religious and historical portraits by both. Titian's *Portrait of a
Violinist* and the *Landscape with Windmill* by Jan Brueghel the Elder are
exceptionally fine. Two magnificent terrestrial globes by the Dutch cartog-
rapher Willem Blaeu show the known world circa 1620. Though these
individual works are wonderful, it is the decorative ensembles of paintings, furniture, and precious objects in four rooms that have remained
largely unchanged since the seventeenth century that dominate.

One of the very few extensive public projects in the Campo Marzio,
the Via Giulia was a long street conceived by Julius II and laid out by
Bramante. The street parallels the Via della Lungara, with which it is
linked by the Ponte Sisto. Its main purpose was to connect the Vatican
physically and perhaps symbolically with the population and commercial

center of Rome, though it also
served other purposes. Traced on
a map of Rome, the Via della
Lungara, Ponte Sisto, and Via
Giulia form a deep and narrow U
that bears a striking resemblance
to the system of long parallel galleries Bramante designed to link
the Vatican Palace with the Bel-

vedere. Through this resemblance, his street plan links the Vatican both
physically and symbolically with the city.

Bramante intended the Via Giulia as more than a symbol, however. It
carried pilgrims and simplified the movement of goods into the heart of
Rome's business district. The new street served this commercial quarter
in other ways. It eased communication among papal institutions already
in the area, such as the Chancery, the mint, and the Apostolic Chamber.
Bramante was also commissioned to design a grand Tribunal on the Via
Giulia, where the notaries and the commercial courts could be housed
together in a single building. In his *Life of Bramante,* Vasari wrote, the
Pope decided that Via Giulia would house all the offices and the business
of Rome in a single place for the convenience that it would afford to merchants in their dealings, which had up to this point been very difficult.

The project was abandoned in mid-century, and the Via Giulia developed in unanticipated ways. While it remained a central axis of the
important Florentine community, no significant construction took place
along much of its length before the eighteenth century. Consequently,

the picturesque street, though sixteenth century in conception, is home to only a few buildings from the period. (85) The back of the Palazzo Farnese, with its triple loggia overlooking the river, is visible through the gates at the end of the garden, and at its corner a covered walkway trailing vines arches over the street. (86) The great palazzo is just the sort of grand residence that Pope Julius II and Bramante imagined for their Via Giulia, but the Farnese dramatically turned its back on the new street. Or it might be more accurate to say that the palace attempted to leap over Bramante's street. The passageway that begins at the corner of the palace garden and spans the street was originally intended to cross the Tiber and link the palace to the Farnesina across the river. Michelangelo conceived of the project for Pope Paul III; it would have connected the Farnese and Farnesina in much the same way that Bramante had connected the Vatican Palace and Belvedere a generation before. The extremely ambitious project was soon abandoned.

The Palazzo Falconieri stands just beyond the archway on the left. Built in the seventeenth century, it reflects the traditions of Renaissance architecture in its rustication, monumental doorway, balconies, and large cornice. The third cross street on the left leads to the short Via di Sant'Eligio, which takes its name from the church of Sant'Eligio, designed by

86

Raphael, perhaps in partnership with Bramante, for the guild of gold- and silversmiths. Following a collapse at the beginning of the seventeenth century, the interior was rebuilt according to the original plan, but the exterior was modernized. The centrally planned domed building is in the form of a Greek cross with short vaulted arms. Beautiful in itself, especially in the contrast of its supporting members against the plain white walls, the building is also interesting as an experiment with the form that Bramante intended to develop in St. Peter's.

Carceri Nuovi, or New Prison, its plain façade pierced by small barred windows, was erected in the late seventeenth century. It is now the headquarters of Italy's National Anti-Mafia Administration. (Rome's active prison, called Regina Coeli—-Queen of Heaven—stands across the Tiber on the Via della Lungara.) Huge rusticated travertine blocks some four or five courses thick are visible here and there along the left side of the street. They are especially prominent at the corner of the Via de' Bresciani, where they also support long travertine benches, which are known as "the sofas of Via Giulia." These substructures are the remains of Bramante's abandoned Tribunal project.

Rome's powerful Florentine community of bankers, artisans, and artists lived at the far end of the Via Giulia. Beside the balcony of number 66, the Palazzo Sachetti, a confusing inscription declares, "Home of Antonio da Sangallo, Architect—1543." The building, designed for Cardinal Ricci of Montepulciano, is often attributed to Sangallo, but it is more likely the work of lesser-known architects. There is no evidence that Sangallo lived there. Divided into three stories by thin cornices, the palace has kneeling windows on its ground floor. The monumental entryway has a balcony above. The piano nobile has modest windows topped

by square mezzanine windows. Above the third floor windows, an elaborate cornice supported on brackets completes the façade.

The Palazzo Medici-Clarelli at number 79 reflects the familiar formula
of Renaissance palazzo design. The so-called House of Raphael across
the street at number 85 was built by Sangallo on a piece of property the
celebrated painter had bought shortly before his death when the Via
Giulia was in its earliest and most optimistic stage of development. Unlike its neighbors up and down the street, this small building defies the
canons of High Renaissance style. The lowest story, with its heavy rustication and shops with their mezzanine windows, is entirely traditional.
The upper two stories, however, where the rustication is lighter and more
shallowly etched, suggests the Mannerist inversions of the Palazzo
Massimo alle Colonne.

The church of San Giovanni dei Fiorentini was intended to be the
centerpiece of Rome's Florentine community. The Medici Pope Leo X
solicited designs for the project from Sangallo, Baldassare Peruzzi, Sansovino, Raphael, and Michelangelo. Though they were never carried out,
these designs, like Bramante's Tempietto, were important formulations of
High Renaissance ideals. Sansovino began the project in 1519 as a centrally planned building like Bramante's and Michelangelo's projects for St.
Peter's. Sangallo, who favored a more traditional basilica shape with an
extended nave and transept, soon stepped in. Giacomo della Porta, who
took over the project after Sangallo's death, added nothing to his design.
Michelangelo was later called in to redesign the dome, which was completed long after his death by Maderno. Borromini—who, like Maderno, is
buried in the church—redesigned the choir chapel.

In all, the project took a century to complete. While changes of design slowed the project, the site, which is very close to the Tiber, also created problems. Enormous amounts of money were spent to stabilize the boggy ground beneath the apse. The importance of the project as a symbol of Florentine architectural achievement probably also interfered. The austere interior, which was enriched in the Baroque period, reflects the subdued tone of the late sixteenth century—after the Council of Trent— rather than the exuberance and confidence of the 1520s.

The area at the end of the Via Giulia has been completely reshaped during the last century by the Tiber embankments, the construction of two new bridges, and the opening of the Corso Vittorio Emanuele II. The piazza has paid enormously for this opening. The sides of buildings have been sheared away, and the area between the church and the Corso Vittorio Emanuele II transformed into a small-scale bus depot. On the far side of this major artery, however, the dense fabric of the Renaissance city closes in again. (87) One of three streets at the end of the Ponte Sant'Angelo, the Via Paola, was opened in 1533 under the sponsorship of the future Pope Paul III. Like the longer Via Giulia, it represented an effort to regularize the area and channel the flow of traffic to and from the Ponte Sant'Angelo.

The first street to the right leads from the Via Paola through the Arco dei Banchi; in the sixteenth century it was known as Cortile de' Chigi. The bank of Agostino Chigi, patron of the Farnesina, was located here. An inscription on a marble panel set into the wall just inside the far end of the grottolike archway records the high water from two Tiber floods. The main inscription in Gothic script shows the flood level from December 1276 and is the earliest record remaining. A smaller inscrip-

tion above records the slightly higher water
level of 1640.

Diagonally across the Via del Banco di
Santo Spirito, the Vicolo del Curato begins;
within a block its name changes to the Via de'
Coronari. Also known as the Via Recta, this
Roman street through the far Campus Martius
had kept its straight course more or less intact
against the encroachments of medieval building. Under Pope Sixtus IV its few kinks were
removed. The coronari or "crown-makers" of

87

its name refer to the manufacturers and vendors of sacred crowns, as
well as rosaries and other religious articles, whose shops lined the street
in the sixteenth century. During the Renaissance, hotels, hostels, and
apartments for pilgrims that were concentrated in this area provided a
resident market for religious goods. "We stayed two days at the Osteria
del Orso and on the second day of December, we moved into rented
rooms in the house of a Spaniard across from Santa Maria della Tinta.
We were well accommodated there with three bedrooms, a living room,
pantry, stable and kitchen for twenty ecus a month, which also included
the cook and wood for the kitchen fire. Apartments here are generally a
little better furnished than in Paris. To the extent in fact that there is
great plenty of gilded leather, which covers the walls of the lodgings. We
could have had one at the same price as ours nearby on Vaso d'Oro furnished with cloth of gold and silk, like the rooms of kings" (Montaigne,
Journal de Voyage, pp. 188–189). The beautiful, and quiet, street with

its abundance of sixteenth- and seventeenth-century houses is a pedestrian walkway closed to through traffic, though not to residents, delivery
vans, and motorinos. Galleries, jewelers, and antique sellers now fill most
of the shops.

At numbers 9–15, Via del Banco di Santo Spirito, directly across from
the Arco dei Banchi, stands another of Raphael's great architectural projects, the Palazzo Alberini. Also known as the Palazzo Alberini-
Cicciaporci, its original façade is on Vicolo del Curato. Designed and partially built in the third decade of the sixteenth century, the innovative
palazzo, like all of Raphael's architectural work, seems decades ahead of
its time. While the lower story is rusticated and pierced by shop fronts
with mezzanine windows above in the traditional fashion, it also incorporates the suggestion of an arcade in its design. A shallow cornice with a
distinctive wave motif on its frieze separates this street-level façade from
the stories above. The shallow detailing of the ground floor is echoed in
travertine pilasters that barely protrude beyond the brick wall. A very
heavy cornice completes the façade; the attic story is a later addition.

The Palazzo del Banco di Santo Spirito (once the papal mint) occupies one side of the Largo Tassoni. Its monumental travertine façade,
which may have been designed by Bramante, was restructured by
Sangallo the Younger in the early 1520s. Like Sangallo's Porta Santo
Spirito, his mint façade downplays the High Renaissance tradition of
division into horizontal bands; and like his gateway, it is also gently
curved. The unifying approach to the façade is especially striking here,
since the palace did indeed have three stories which are expressed very
distinctly on the building's side walls. Sangallo preserved the articulation

of the rusticated lower story, then built an ingenious two-story façade
above using design elements also found on the Porta Santo Spirito. Four
Corinthian pilasters on shallow pediments divide the narrow façade into
three bays of unequal size. The central bay, a blind arch, frames a monumental inscription and a small papal insignia that is linked to two much
larger ones above and below. Round openings in the smaller bays to
either side draw attention away from the actual windows. (88)

The Via dei Banchi Nuovi, which opens to the left, traces the traditional papal route between St. Peter's and the Lateran. Called the Via
Papale, the narrow route, which was pieced together
from existing streets, attracted monumental development from the early Renaissance onward. For part of its
length it formed the starting point for the nineteenth-
century Corso Vittorio Emanuele II. "On the third of
January, 1581, the Pope passed in front of our window.
Some two hundred members of his household in one
uniform or another rode in front of him. Cardinal de
Medici who had invited him to dinner was next to him.

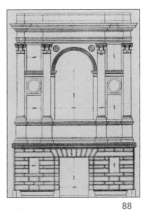

88

The Pope wore a red hat, white robes and a red velvet cape. He was
mounted as usual on a small white horse with red velvet harness, embroi-
dered and fringed with gold. Every fifteen paces or so he gave a benediction. Three cardinals came after him followed by a hundred soldiers in
complete armor except for their helmets and with lances on their shoulders. There was another white horse outfitted in the same way as the
first, a mule, a beautiful white stallion and a litter, all of which followed
the procession along with two pack horses with portmanteaus hanging

from the horns of their saddles" (Montaigne, *Journal de Voyage,* pp. 196–197).

The architect of St. Peter's façade, Carlo Maderno, lived in the early Renaissance palazzo with Cancelleria-style arched windows on the left side of the street (numbers 1–4). Past the Piazza del Orologio, dominated by a huge clock tower designed in the seventeenth century by Borromini, the Via Papale continued in the Via del Governo Vecchio. Numbers 1–3 are the Palazzo di Sangro. (89) The building features a large central portal and shops with mezzanine windows on its first story. There are arched windows with mezzanine windows above them in the second story. The palazzo at numbers 14–17 has a rusticated lower story with shops and mezzanine windows above. The frieze copies the wave motif from the Palazzo Alberini. Its upper stories combine windows and blind openings. Unlike the rest of the buildings on this very upscale street, the Palazzo del Governo Vecchio at number 39 is very run down. Its most distinctive feature is the entryway set off by a diamond-pointed border like the studded collar of a guard dog. Across the street at number 123, the diminu-

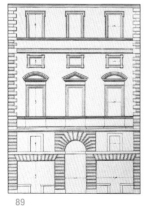

tive palazzo copies decorative patterns from the nearby and slightly earlier Cancelleria.

The church of Santa Maria della Pace, best known for its attached cloister by Bramante, is regarded by some architectural historians as the most interesting early Renaissance structure in Rome. Its curious plan, which resembles a keyhole, combines a large octagonal vestibule with a small nave. (90) In each face of the octagon an arched opening leads to a chapel or entryway. This arcade is repeated on the side walls

89

of the nave in the entrances to its four chapels. The nave, which has no
side aisles, is a bold departure from the traditional form of the Early
Christian basilica. The octagon, which in
effect combines transept, apse, and dome in
a unified structure, is even more striking,
however, both in conception and execution.
Pietro da Cortona replaced the original plain
façade with a Baroque masterpiece in the
late seventeenth century.

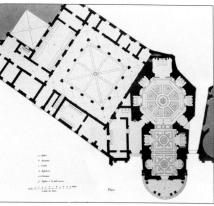

90

In repudiating the traditional Early
Christian model, the architect, perhaps the
mysterious Baccio Pontelli, turned to imperi-
al buildings for inspiration. The Aula Ottagona in the Baths of Diocletian
is one possible source. The coffered dome of the church is a unified
solid, unlike Brunelleschi's famous dome on Santa Maria del Fiore in
Florence or Michelangelo's later dome on St. Peter's. In structure and
appearance both inside and out, this dome recalls that of the Pantheon a
short distance away; and that monument may be the key to the church's
curious design. If the Pantheon's massive porch were walled in, the
resulting structure would be very similar to Santa Maria della Pace.

The innovative church attracted rich patrons, Agostino Chigi among
them. The prominent banker acquired the first chapel to the right of the
nave entrance and hired Raphael to design and decorate it. Peruzzi, who
worked with Raphael for Chigi in the Farnesina, was also involved. On the
nave wall outside the chapel entrance, Raphael painted a group of sibyls
and prophets, evidently in response to Michelangelo's work on the Sistine

ceiling, which was first opened to public view in 1511. Peruzzi's
Presentation of the Virgin, a large painting on canvas, hangs to the right
of the main altar. It was commissioned by Chigi's associate and executor,
Filippo Sergardi.

Bramante's celebrated cloister, completed in 1504, is his first securely
dated work in Rome. (91) Its lower story— an arcade punctuated by Ionic
pilasters on high plinths—echoes the architectural idiom of the Tabularium, Colosseum, and Theater of Marcellus that Bramante would make
completely his own in the Vatican Palace. The cloister's upper story is a
different matter. In defiance of classical tradition as he would come to
understand and as the sixteenth century would canonize it, Bramante
combined two architectural orders in a single story. He also topped pillars
with an entablature (he would later decree that pillars and arcades
belonged together; and only columns should support entablatures). In the
same innovative spirit, he added slim columns between the second-story
pillars directly above the centers of the first-story arches. Placing a support above an empty space was an especially serious breach of decorum.
While the upper story remains controversial, the lower one with its easy
rhythm, evident solidity, and innovative corners was and remains widely
admired. A frieze with a monumental inscription notable for its fine classical lettering separates the two stories.

Like the Palazzo Corsini, the Palazzo Altemps, near the north end of
the Piazza Navona, incorporated earlier medieval buildings into a single
fabric. Its present form owes much to a nephew of Sixtus IV, Girolamo
Riario. It was again remodeled in the sixteenth century when it became
the property of an Austrian collector of antique sculpture, Cardinal Marco

91

Sittico Altemps. The three-story structure is a version of the typical early
Renaissance palazzo, with some interesting innovations. Longhi added the
towerlike gallery with its high arcaded
openings. The ground floor of the
palazzo with its wide doorways and
mezzanine windows echoes the style of
Roman shop fronts like those in the
Markets of Trajan. Roman palazzi often
included ground-floor commercial
spaces like these, which could be used
for family business or rented out. Rental space was sometimes available
on upper floors as well, and such buildings often included tenants of different social classes. Shopkeepers and artisans might live and work on
the first floor, while others of the same class rented apartments above.
The piano nobile, the large elegant second floor of such structures, could
be home to a cardinal or count. As a result, few Roman neighborhoods
had a uniform class composition; there were no distinctly working-class
or upper-class districts until the late nineteenth century.

The Palazzo Altemps now houses a branch of the Museo Nazionale
Romano that is devoted especially to the history of collecting. Despite its
name, the museum retains little from the collection of Cardinal Altemps,
which was already being dispersed by the end of the eighteenth century.
The bulk of the sculpture once belonged to another Roman family, the
Ludovisi, who assembled their large and celebrated collection (some 450

antique sculptures) in the early years of the seventeenth century. They displayed it in the gardens of their magnificent villa on the Quirinal hill. When the villa was razed at the end of the nineteenth century and the gardens carved up for building lots, the Italian state acquired about a quarter of their collection and moved it to the Termini Museum. Recently installed in the Palazzo Altemps, it is meant to stand in for that family's dispersed collection.

Unfortunately, the sculptures and their new setting are not well matched. The vast garden collection of the Ludovisi has been moved indoors, where it is mixed with a handful of other private collections in quarters that are too small. The assembled pieces fill every room of the palazzo, with no space left for furniture or any other trace of domestic life. Though there are patches of fresco in many of the rooms of the piano nobile and beautiful Renaissance beams and ceilings, the installation has transformed the palace into a modern exhibition space. The integration of artwork and palace life, which is preserved in the Palazzo Spada, the Galleria Corsini, and in other Roman collections, is all but absent here. The travertine and stucco courtyard, which may have been designed by Antonio da Sangallo the Elder in collaboration with Peruzzi, is the sole exception. Sculptures are set in its ground-floor arcades as they may have been in the sixteenth century. (92) The open loggia on its second floor is an even more characteristic Renaissance exhibition space. The elaborate fresco painting that depicts a vine-covered garden pergola recalls the decoration of the Loggia of Psyche at the Farnesina.

Most of the collection consists of high-quality Roman reproductions of Greek originals. The statue of a Gaul who commits suicide after killing

his wife is well known, as is the Ludovisi *Ares.*
The massive third-century battle sarcophagus
is striking. The celebrated Ludovisi *Throne,* a
Greek original of the fifth century BC that once
stood in the Hortus of Sallust, depicts the birth
of Aphrodite on its back. The seated pipers on
its sides are especially beautiful. Not all the
objects in the collection passed peacefully into

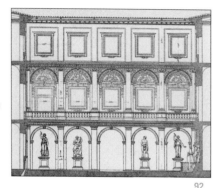

92

the hands of the Italian state. Four famous reliefs, known since the sixteenth century and now on display in the loggia of the palazzo, were confiscated by the Customs Police in 1964 when their owner attempted to
export them illegally.

While in Roman times the center of life in the Campus Martius was
the area enclosed by the Tiber bend, during the Renaissance the quarter
spread eastward to the Corso and south to the foot of the Capitoline hill.
After the Vatican Palace, which it may have been intended to supplant,
the Palazzo Venezia between the Corso and the Capitoline was the first
great palace of the Renaissance in Rome. For modern Italians it is infamous as Mussolini's headquarters. From the balcony above its main entry
he harangued the crowd and reviewed Italian troops as they marched
down the Via del Impero to reclaim the glory of ancient Rome.

Even before Mussolini's era, the palace had felt the inexorable pressure of politics. In the late nineteenth century as plans for the Victor
Emmanuel Monument took shape, the once small Piazza Venezia was
expanded to its present decidedly post-Renaissance scale, and a smaller
palace known as the Piccolo Palazzo Venezia removed from its site and

resituated. The purpose was to make the new monument visible at the end of Rome's nineteenth-century main street, the Via del Corso.

As is the case for many great building projects of the fifteenth century—the Cancelleria, Ponte Sisto, Santa Maria della Pace among them—the architect of the Palazzo Venezia has not been identified with certainty. Whoever he may have been, his design was influenced by the palaces of Florence and the ideas of Leon Battista Alberti. In origin as well as design, the building is similar to the Cancelleria. The core of both buildings was a cardinal's residence; but while Cardinal Riario's grand project overwhelmed and engulfed his titular church, the Palazzo Venezia, though almost as large, remained distinct from the basilica of San Marco. Of the two, the Cancelleria is the more cohesive structure and the one in which the principles of Renaissance classicism predominate. The Palazzo Venezia, on the other hand, blends Renaissance principles with medieval practice. The three horizontal divisions of the façade, which are separated by thin cornices, reflect Renaissance principles of organization, though the zones are not divided into bays and the irregular travertine quoins at the corners are structural and not design elements. The basement story, which fills almost half the vertical space of the façade, is pierced by arched windows. The windows in the two upper stories lack classical ornamentation of any sort, and their rhythm, which reflects the size of the rooms behind, is irregular in the style of medieval palaces. Crenellations and a square defensive tower in one corner, both characteristic of medieval fortifications, finish off the building.

No compromise between medieval and Renaissance principles marks the large and beautiful inner courtyard (though, like many similar spaces throughout contemporary Rome, it is disfigured by the parked cars of the

building's employees). The two-story loggia that overlooks this inner court

is a magnificent version of superimposed arcades based on familiar

Roman models. In strength, proportion, and detail, they are equal to the

work of Bramante. The benediction loggia of the basilica of San Marco,

designed by the same architect, is equally impressive.

The Capitoline hill (Latin: Capitolium; Italian: Campidoglio) was the

religious center of ancient Rome, the governmental center of the

medieval and Renaissance city, and the symbolic goal of the many gener-

ations of patriots who sought to unite and liberate Italy. Every building

on or around it represents some attempt to take possession of the sym-

bolic patrimony of the city, the nation, Rome's ancient empire, or world

Christianity. In the mid-fourteenth century the patriot Cola da Rienzo

used the hill as the base for his short-lived revival of the Roman Repub-

lic. Mussolini's adoption of the Palazzo Venezia as his headquarters was

as much an assault on the nearby Capitoline as it was a staging point for

his appropriation of the Roman imperial fora. The Victor Emmanuel

Monument, which is grafted into the hillside and towers over its other

buildings, made the same attempt.

Like the builders of the Victor Emmanuel Monument, Michelangelo

had a long list of models to address, constituents to satisfy, and symbolic

goals to achieve in his redesign of the Campidoglio. The simplest of

these goals was to consolidate the scattered government buildings that

had stood there since the Middle Ages, to give them a contemporary look,

and to weld them into a harmonious unit. The political task was more

delicate. Michelangelo's patron, Pope Paul III, wanted the project to express the subordination of Rome's civic government to the papacy. The Romans, on the other hand, and Michelangelo himself, who was a strong republican, wanted the monumental center to express the power and dignity of Rome's long secular tradition. At the base of the hill he would redesign stood the Roman Forum, with its Senate house at one end and the Temple of the Deified Julius Caesar at the other. To the left lay the remains of the imperial fora. The towering ruins of the imperial palaces stood across the Roman Forum on the Palatine. To create a symbolic seat of power in sixteenth-century Rome required a response to these powerful if ghostly sites. There was one further rival claimant to the power of the Capitoline. Towering above the rudimentary government center of the era, representing the ascendancy of piety over politics, stood the Franciscan church of the Ara Coeli. While Michelangelo reckoned with this assertive Catholic presence on the hilltop, he was also compelled to respond to the distant but all-powerful Vatican.

Given the reverence for classical culture that was such a strong trait of Michelangelo's era, his response to the Roman fora and Palatine may be surprising. The classical prototype for his Campidoglio complex is an open forum with a Senate building at one end, flanked by structures with loggias like the Basilica Aemilia and Basilica Julia. Yet while echoing this Roman pattern, Michelangelo's Campidoglio turned its back on its models, the historic monuments of Rome's grandeur, and actually blocked them from view. From Michelangelo's Campidoglio it is impossible to catch more than a glimpse of these historic centers. Evidently his aim was not only to evoke these monuments but to replace them. Like Bramante, who tore down an authentic imperial building to replace it with one in the imperial style, Michelangelo blocked Rome's historic center with his own imitation of it.

93

His answer to the challenge of the Franciscan church was similar. The Palazzo Nuovo, which he designed to counterbalance the remodeled Palazzo dei Conservatori, screens the Ara Coeli from view. The response to the Vatican is subtle but real: his complex is oriented in the direction of St. Peter's, and its form recalls the U-shaped Belvedere end of Bramante's Vatican Palace. (93)

Michelangelo's project exceeded his commission, and while the complex was not completed during his lifetime, it has been carried out over the centuries without significant change. The focus of the complex is a gilded bronze equestrian statue of Marcus Aurelius, from the third century AD. The sculpture, thought to represent Constantine, had stood for centuries in front of the Lateran. (The statue in the square today is a copy of the original, which is now installed on the ground floor of the Museo Capitolino.) From this center point an elaborate tracery like a twelve-pointed star spreads out. (94) It is inscribed in an ellipse that rises gently toward the statue like the floor of the Pantheon, or the curve of the earth itself. Though the star was designed by Michelangelo and is shown in early engravings of the piazza, it was not actually put in place until 1940. The ellipse, which had little place in High Renaissance art, is a

94

novelty here; it became a favorite of Baroque architects. Enclosing all these forms is a trapezoidal piazza with its narrow end toward the front. This surprising shape counteracts perspective foreshortening and makes the Palazzo Senatore seem closer and larger than it is. It also causes the flanking buildings to embrace the viewer; they appear to close in behind as one walks forward.

The backstop of the complex is the Palazzo Senatore, which housed Rome's single "senator," the city's chief judicial officer, who was appointed by the Pope. Today it holds the offices of Rome's mayor. The core of the building is the Tabularium, where records of the Roman Senate were kept. In the Middle Ages powerful families had taken over the building and added fortified towers at its ends. Sometime in the twelfth century it became the headquarters of the senator. Corner towers were added by Popes Martin V and Nicholas V. Michelangelo united this complex behind a façade in three horizontal zones with slightly projecting wings at either end to accommodate the medieval towers. The lower story is rusticated; the second and third, which are divided into vertical bays by tall pilasters, are punctuated by square windows. A heavy cornice and balustrade with sculptures above completed the façade.

In front of the building, Michelangelo created a magnificent double stairway that leads directly to the piano nobile of the palazzo. He deco-

rated the base of the stairs with Roman statues of the Nile (resting on a
sphynx) and the Tiber (leaning on a wolf that suckles Romulus and
Remus); both statues had decorated the precinct of the Roman temple of
the Egyptian god Isis. A statue of Pallas Athena sits in the central niche.
He also designed the monumental stairway that leads up to the piazza
and the balustrade decorated with ancient sculptures that fronts it. The
bell tower above was not part of Michelangelo's plan.

The Palazzo dei Conservatori was the administrative center of Renaissance Rome. Parts of the building still house government offices. Wedding
banns are published there, and secular weddings are celebrated in its
chapel. Whatever the power relation between senator and conservators,
the buildings Michelangelo created for them are clearly unequal in rank.
The Palazzo Senatore is the focus of the complex; the Palazzo dei Conservatori, especially after the mirroring Palazzo Nuovo was completed, is
clearly subordinate. Though only two full stories tall—its base is an open
loggia—the conservators' palace harmonizes with the larger palazzo in
several ways. Large pilasters reaching from the ground divide the building
into vertical bays; the heavy cornice, balustrade, and crown of statuary
complete the analogy.

The art collected in the building includes some of Rome's most famous
and most politicized pieces. A handful of Roman sculptures that were
known throughout the Middle Ages and displayed for centuries in and
around the Lateran Church and Palace form the core of the collections.
Like the looted columns that lined the naves of the Early Christian basilicas, these objects were spolia, trophies "captured" from the pagan
enemy, which asserted the superior power of Christian civilization. They
included fragments of a monumental statue of Constantine and the

equestrian statue of Marcus Aurelius (thought to be Constantine) which exemplified the popes' claim to be the emperor's successors. Other objects on display at the Lateran made a more oblique claim to power.

In 1471 Pope Sixtus IV moved these objects to the Capitoline hill, where they formed the core of a secular museum, still heavily freighted with political might. An inscription displayed in the museum records the founder's gift: "In his great benevolence, Pope Sixtus IV, ordered that these singularly important bronze statues, monuments of the excellence and virtue of the ancestors of the Roman people, be consigned and restored to those by whom they were created." Transferring objects that had acquired so much symbolic weight over the centuries from the Lateran to the Capitoline was a political act of great importance. It placed Roman art under the wing of the secular government and restored key symbols of the Roman heritage to the political capital.

The art collection begins in the courtyard of the palazzo, where fragments from colossal images are exhibited along with other works. The head of Constantine along with an arm, part of a leg, a hand, and a foot are all that remains of the statue some forty feet high that stood in the apse of the Basilica of Maxentius. The head of another colossus representing his son, Constantius, is also displayed, along with a gigantic personification of Rome. Large marble reliefs in the stairway came from the triumphal arch of Marcus Aurelius and that of Hadrian. At the top of the stairs is a seated figure of King Charles of Anjou, who served as senator of Rome in the early fourteenth century.

The rooms along the front of the palazzo that overlook the square served as the official suite of the conservators. The first of these is the

Room of the Horatii and Curiati, an enormous hall where the Roman
council met under the watchful gaze of Pope Urban VIII (sculpted by
Bernini and assistants between 1635 and 1639) and Pope Innocent X (by
Algardi, 1645–1650). A gilded bronze Hercules and a bronze head and
hand of Constantine are displayed here. The frescoed walls show scenes
of legendary events from early Roman history. Frescoes in the next room
depict episodes from the early Republic, and its statues are portraits of

so-called captains of the Church, from
which the room takes its name. A few
combine antique bodies with portrait
heads of the Renaissance. The beautiful
Room of the Triumphs enshrines three
celebrated objects from the Lateran that
were donated to the Roman people by
Pope Sixtus IV. These include a portrait

95

of Junius Brutus; a bronze statue of a sacrificial assistant called a camil-
lus; and the bronze figure of a seated boy pulling a thorn from his foot,
the *Spinario*. Not the artistic quality but the political weight of this trio of
objects accounts for their very prominent installation here. Their pedigree
as spolia from the Lateran collection makes them precious: through them
the mantle of Rome's history is passed on to her secular government.

An object in the next room is the most self-evident of these precious
symbols. It is an Etruscan bronze figure of the female wolf—the *Lupa*—
who nourished Rome's founders, Romulus and Remus. (95) Since the sixteenth century this sculpture has served as the symbol of Rome. (The
boys were added in the fifteenth century, perhaps by the Florentine

96

sculptor Pollaiuolo.) The figures in these two rooms are Rome's crown jewels, an artistic patrimony that symbolizes the transfer of power and guarantees legitimacy.

Along with extensive sculpture collections, the palazzo also houses the Pinacoteca Capitolina—the Capitoline Picture Gallery. This is a relatively manageable collection assembled in nine rooms and a long gallery. The works chronicle Italian and European painting from the Middle Ages to the eighteenth century. Highlights include Titian's *Baptism*, Veronese's *Rape of Europa*, and Guido Reni's *St. Sebastian. St. John the Baptist* by Caravaggio is currently in Room VII, which is dominated by Guercino's enormous *Burial of St. Petronilla;* Rubens' *Romulus and Remus* is there also. The panoramic terrace on the third floor looks out over the Theater of Marcellus and the nearby Campo Marzio. It offers a roof-level view over the congested Renaissance quarter. (96)

The Palazzo Nuovo, which houses the Capitoline Museum, was built in the seventeenth century following Michelangelo's design. The building, which completes the symmetrical complex and screens the Ara Coeli, never served any government function. Soon after its opening in 1654, many of the art objects that had been exhibited in the Palazzo dei Conservatori were installed in it. The installations, which have been recently refurbished, reflect the same taste that governs the older collec-

tions of the Vatican Museum. The exhibition spaces are similar as well.
Long galleries subdivided into smaller ensembles open onto individual
rooms of various sizes. The decoration of the rooms is rich and varied,
though the opulence cannot rival that of Simonetti's installations in the
Belvedere.

Some, like the Room of the Emperors or the Room of the Philosophers, are organized thematically. The Room of the *Faun* and The Room
of the *Dying Gaul* are each grouped around a single outstanding work of
art. (97) The Room of the Doves is a prime example of the imaginative
groupings that characterize the collection. It includes multiple portraits,
a child's sarcophagus with scenes from the myth of Prometheus, and
sculptural reliefs with illustrations from the *Iliad;* its walls are covered
with funerary inscriptions. The centerpiece is a delicate mosaic that
depicts four doves drinking from an urn. The objects appear to be united
not by any historical link but by a common
emotional tone: a gentle pathos. Other
highlights of the collection include the
Capitoline Venus, a Roman copy in Parian
marble of a Greek original; the *Laughing
Satyr* sculpted of a blood-colored marble
called rosso antico; and the *Wounded
Amazon.*

97

Chapter Seven

BAROQUE EXPANSION

As the Renaissance city grew, Romans began to imagine a renewal not just of the city's classical beauty and dignity but of her ancient population and territory as well. The frontier lay no further than the Via Lata (Via del Corso). While areas inland of that artery had been densely populated during the Roman Empire, they were too remote from the Tiber to ensure an adequate water supply. Throughout the Middle Ages a scattered population served by wells and the single remaining vestige of the Roman aqueduct system were the only inhabitants among the fields and forests just across the Corso.

The open land beyond was obviously desirable: most of it was higher ground than the Campo Marzio. Past the limits of Tiber erosion, the Pincio and the Quirinal hills began their modest rises. This slight increase in altitude promised disproportionate benefits. It meant breezes and a welcome relief from the summer heat, as well as some protection from the malarial mosquitoes that bred along the river. Altitude also promised security from the devastating floods that submerged the medieval city as often as every fourth winter. But liberation from the Tiber's plagues came at the price of distance from its life-sustaining water.

In the Empire, full-scale development on the slopes beyond the Via Lata had depended on water brought from the distant mountains through the wonderful system of Roman aqueducts. Invading barbarians had cut some of the aqueducts and forced the Romans to block others to prevent their use as viaducts for invasion. By the time of the Renaissance, all but one of the Roman aqueducts had been unused and unmaintained for a thousand years. To reclaim the hills beyond the Via Lata meant repairing or duplicating the Roman aqueduct system.

The task required a high level of technology, but it also required enormous centralized power. Among the Renaissance popes there were some, like Hadrian VI, who resisted imperial power, and others, like Clement VII, who were forced to give it up. The popes who changed Rome, however, were those whose ambition drove them to undertake great projects. Nicholas V and Sixtus IV in the fifteenth century left their marks on the Vatican and the city of Rome. "That terrible old man" Julius II built the Renaissance city and brought a new St. Peter's and Michelangelo's Campidoglio to birth. Two popes at the end of the sixteenth century, Gregory XIII and the much-hated Sixtus V, did even more. Like Nero and his architects after the Great Fire, these adventurous popes and their planners were able to inscribe their visions of renewal on a portion of the Roman map that was virtually without landmarks. They laid out new roads linking the most distant parts of the city; they sponsored the organization of new neighborhoods along these arteries; and, most importantly, they reclaimed the imperial heritage of the control and distribution of water.

In 1572, with water diverted from the Acqua Vergine, the engineers of Pope Gregory XIII created the first public fountain in Rome since

antiquity. Ten days after his elevation to the papacy in 1585, Felice
Peretti (Pope Sixtus V) directed construction of the first aqueduct in
modern Roman history. Like his namesake, Sixtus IV, Peretti was a
Minorite friar, a determined builder, and a fierce advocate for his family
and their fortunes. In his five-year pontificate he limited the size and
constitution of the College of Cardinals, divided the papal Curia into stable subdivisions with fixed tasks, and built, completed, or refurbished
many of the most significant Roman buildings. His enemies charged that
his building projects on the Quirinal hill multiplied the value of land
owned by his family. Whatever his motives, his aqueduct transformed the
development of Rome.

With materials scavenged from the Acqua Claudia, papal engineers
under the direction of Sixtus's architect, Domenico Fontana, built a narrow enclosed channel on top of the still-standing arches of the ancient
Acqua Marcia. By 1587 the eighteen-mile conduit—named the Acqua
Felice—had reached Rome, where it provided water for the heights
beyond the Corso and filled the six fountains of the papal summer villa
on the Quirinal hill.

The arrival of water at the papal palace on the Quirinal set the stage
for another shift in Rome's center of gravity. Gregory XIII had bought and
remodeled a small villa on the hill. Under Sixtus V, Domenico Fontana
enlarged the villa to serve as the Pope's summer palace. In 1592 Sixtus's
successor, Pope Clement VIII, made the Quirinal Palace the year-round
papal residence. The offices of the papal government, and the residences
of cardinals and ambassadors, were soon grouped around this new site.
After a century and a half of intense development, the Vatican Palace

suddenly lost its raison d'être. The compass of Roman power now zeroed on the Quirinal hill, and the once peripheral Via Lata, suddenly centered between the papal palace and the Campo Marzio, became the city's main avenue.

Not far from the midpoint of this central avenue, an undistinguished street called the Via di Muratte turns off to the left. After three uninter-

esting blocks it suddenly widens to reveal the Fontana di Trevi. (98) This surprise appearance magnifies the fountain's emotional effect (surprise was a favorite technique of the Baroque era when architecture and theater were often merged). Inspired by Bernini's Fountain of the Four Rivers in Piazza

98

Navona, the Trevi fountain translates his work in the round into a proscenium-style tableau set against an architectural backdrop that is best appreciated from the front. The seats at the fountain's curved lip are the ideal place to view this spectacle of gods at play. As compelling as these cavorting figures are, they cannot upstage the rushing water itself. That is the fountain's greatest and most significant surprise, the unanticipated gushing forth of water far from the Tiber in the dry heart of the city.

The Roman emperors gave their citizens public theaters and public baths, but above all they gave abundant water as a way to show both their generosity and their power. The popes followed the emperors' lead in this as in so many other things, and the reconnection of the aqueducts and the reintroduction of the various water supplies into Rome was always the occasion for monumental celebration. The water in the Trevi fountain, known to the Romans as the Aqua Virgo and to Italians as the Acqua Vergine, comes from a spring in the Alban hills twelve miles east of the city. Agrippa first brought this water, mainly through underground conduits, into the central Campus Martius in 19 BC. During the Gothic Wars of the sixth century the aqueduct was blocked, but it was restored to at least partial use sometime in the following centuries and continued to bring water to this area throughout the Middle Ages. In 1453 Pope Nicholas V oversaw repairs to Agrippa's aqueduct and built a new fountain to receive its augmented flow. That Renaissance fountain was replaced by the present one, designed by Nicola Salvi, in the early eighteenth century.

A palace façade, divided into a central bay and wings, forms the architectural backdrop of the fountain. The protruding center section, which is itself divided into three bays, suggests both a Roman triumphal arch and the traditional form of a Roman castellum aquae. The Roman architect Vitruvius described the typical form of this symbolic fountain, which both distributes and displays the water of an aqueduct. Papal architects enriched and monumentalized this antique form. In Italian, such a fountain is termed a mostra, which means display, and each of Rome's modern aqueducts has one. The Trevi fountain is the mostra of the Acqua Vergine. Sculptures in the side niches depict the personified

Abundance and Salubrity of the water as well as Agrippa and the young woman who found the spring and in whose honor it is named. The free-standing figure emerging from the center niche represents Ocean with his seahorses. His figure extends the symbolic power that the fountain implies over the whole world.

The fountain's message—underscored by its surprising intrusion into the urban fabric—is the general one of power and beneficence. Its sculptural program defines the nature of the sponsoring power, and its apparently spontaneous welling up in this spot suggests that its source of power is somewhere near. In a Renaissance romance like Ariosto's *Orlando Furioso,* the sudden appearance of a marvel like this fountain would show that a powerful wizard lived close by. The Trevi fountain is a miracle, both a theatrical tour de force and a serious and subtle restaging of Moses' striking of the rock in the desert, and it sets the emotional stage for the papal palace a short distance away. It suggests that the Pope not only dominates in the immediate vicinity of his palace but that his life-giving power extends over the great waters of the world.

As everybody knows, if you throw a coin into the Trevi fountain, you are sure to return to Rome someday, but the magic was different a century ago. Hawthorne wrote, "Tradition goes that a parting drink at the Fountain of Trevi ensures a traveler's return to Rome, whatever obstacles and improbabilities may seem to beset him." Romans, who are connoisseurs of the outpourings of their various aqueducts, rate the Acqua Vergine very highly.

The Via San Vincenzo beyond the fountain leads to the Via della Dataria, which is named for an obscure but once very powerful papal bureaucracy. The datary, headed by a cardinal, was originally responsible for the simple act of dating papal documents. Undated, the documents remained invalid. Over the centuries this minimal power expanded to include control over appointments within the Church. In the Renaissance the office generated considerable revenue by assessing disproportionate fees for its simple but indispensable service. At the end of the Via della Dataria a flight of steps ascends to the Piazza del Quirinale.

The Quirinal hill rises nearly two hundred feet above the level of the Tiber, and its piazza offers a low panorama of Rome's historic center framed against the Janiculum and St. Peter's. From 1592 to 1870 the Pope's official residence was the Palazzo del Quirinale. During that time, the piazza in front of the palace took on some of the functions of the Piazza San Pietro. Crowds gathered here to acclaim a newly elected pope, to show their allegiance and sometimes their dissatisfaction; above all, they gathered to receive the papal benediction.

With the unification of Italy in 1870 and the establishment of Rome as the nation's capital, the Quirinal Palace became the official residence of the king of Italy. In 1945 the monarchy was abolished and Italy became a republic. Since that date the Quirinal Palace has been the official residence of the president of the republic. Because that position is largely honorific and wields little real power, the Quirinal Palace is no longer a focus for political marches, and the piazza in front of it serves no particular purpose. Political power in Rome centers on Palazzo Montecitorio, the meeting place of the Chamber of Deputies, and the nearby Palazzo Madama, where the Senate meets.

The piazza's obelisk, which links it with other Baroque centers, was removed from the Mausoleum of Augustus and transported to this spot in the middle of the eighteenth century. Flanking the obelisk are colossal sculptures of Castor and Pollux (the Dioscuri), twin gods who appeared miraculously when the ancient Romans were in trouble. Their temple was one of the great landmarks of the Roman Forum. These figures, which came from the nearby Baths of Constantine, are among the small number of Roman sculptures that have been above ground and therefore well-known since antiquity. (99) When Sixtus V began plans for the papal summer palace here, the twin horsemen were incorporated into his design. They were moved aside in the eighteenth century to make room for the obelisk. At the same time an antique basin found in the Roman Forum was substituted for the fountain that had been in place since the sixteenth century.

That inconspicuous fountain, if not the most noticeable, was certainly

the most important landmark in the piazza. Flowing with the water of the Acqua Felice, Sixtus V's most important building project, the fountain represented the potential for development in the area. While it is no distance at all from the Trevi fountain, where water from the Acqua Vergine flowed throughout the Middle Ages, the slight difference in ground height created an enormous barrier. The Acqua Vergine enters the city below the level of its uplands; the Acqua Felice was planned from the beginning to provide a high-level water source.

99

Once the water arrived at this small fountain, the modest summer villa of the popes grew into a full-scale palace. The brothers Domenico and Giovanni Fontana, architects of Pope Sixtus V, built seven bays surrounding a monumental portal, then extended their Farnese-style façade toward the city below. Flaminio Ponzio built the perpendicular three-story wing with its higher story standing atop one corner of the Fontana façade like a medieval tower.

To the right of the palace stands the Palazzo della Consulta designed in the early eighteenth century by Ferdinando Fuga. The building served a number of purposes. Its central floors housed the civil and criminal courts of papal Rome; the Secretariat had offices here, and the papal guards were garrisoned on the ground floor and in the attic. The center of the façade, which projects slightly and is more richly ornamented than the two wings, is further distinguished by the massive sculptural groups on its projecting doorway and on the balustrade above. The five-story building with its heavy ornamentation still harmonizes with the more modest two-story façade of the Quirinal Palace.

The Via del Quirinale, originally named the Via Pia, was laid out in the sixteenth century as a direct link between the city's Renaissance limits and the Porta Nomentana in the distant Aurelian wall. At that time the area, which had been heavily populated during the Roman Empire, was thinly settled and completely rural: the Acqua Felice was still some decades in the future. The road was not intended as a corridor of development, a role it began to assume once the aqueduct was completed—the pace accelerated sharply after 1870. Its purpose was to speed travel to the basilica of Sant'Agnese on the ancient Via Nomentana.

Two of Rome's most celebrated and delightful Baroque churches stand near each other on the Via del Quirinale. These are the church of Sant'

100

Andrea al Quirinale designed by Bernini and the rival church of San Carlo alle Quattro Fontane (also called San Carlino because of its diminutive size) designed by Borromini. Sant'Andrea, begun in 1658, uses the ellipse—a favorite of Baroque architects and the guiding form of Bernini's Piazza San Pietro—as its central figure. Low elliptical projections to either side of the façade, like the embracing colonnade at St. Peter's, create a wide concavity that the semicircular porch thrusts into. (100)

The richly decorated interior is in the form of another ellipse, with the altar placed atypically along its width. Pilasters and walls are decorated with matched panels of marble veneer that create extraordinary patterns in the walls. The main apse fronted by four pillars and illuminated by a hidden window recalls the square recesses in the Pantheon. *The Crucifixion of St. Andrew* above the altar is surrounded by angels and sunbursts. The risen figure of the saint riding a cloud passes through a broken pediment on his way to heaven. Above the heavy cornice, the ribbed, coffered ceiling of the elliptical dome throngs with stucco figures of angels; tiny cherubs look down from the lantern. Theatrical figures themselves, these angels seem to be watching the spectacle of human life as it unfolds in the zone below the cornice. This is not an entirely fanciful suggestion, since there is a link between the ellipse and the theater in Roman tradition. Stage theaters were semicircular, but the amphitheater—in effect, two theaters back to back—was elliptical. In medieval and Renaissance tradition the world was often described as a theater on which God looks down in judgment. (The final image in Dante's *Paradiso* evokes the Colosseum and elaborates on that idea.) It may be that the decoration of Bernini's elliptical church is based on this tradition.

Further down the Via del Quirinale, Borromini, once Bernini's collaborator but for most of his career a rival, created San Carlo, one of his most characteristic churches. He also designed the adjacent cloister. While the interior was his first commission, the extraordinary façade was the last work he completed before his death. It bears some resemblance to Bernini's Sant'Andrea, though Borromini's is a more compact version of the interplay between embracing concavity and thrusting semicircular porch. Beneath its heavy curling cornice, the façade is subdivided into two superimposed zones, with aedicula— miniature temple fronts—and blind oval windows beneath sculpted figures in niches. The statue of San Carlo Borromeo above the doorway is framed by two of Borromini's angelic caryatids; each raises a wing over the saint's head to create a pointed arch above him. (101) The two compact stories above the cornice repeat the pattern of the

101

lower zone. Deep empty aedicula to each side stand beneath symbols of the cross and entwined palms.

The central zone above the convex door is filled with a curious cylindrically framed window. Above it, two putti support an oval medallion crowned by a peaked molding that echoes the profile of the angel's wings below. An elliptical drum encloses the dome. The lantern above is similar to the one on Sant'Andrea delle Fratte. Single columns with arched niches in the concavities between them support a deeply etched cornice. There is also a small pagoda-like belfry at the corner.

The interior of San Carlo, like that of Sant'Andrea which it antedates by some twenty years, is elliptical. With its shallow niches and almost completely detached columns, the surrounding wall appears to stretch and contract in rhythm. Heavy ribs springing from the columns at either narrow end divide the drum into coffered recesses. A complexly coffered elliptical vault rises above a second cornice, configured like a laurel wreath and crown, symbols of victory and martyrdom.

The intersection of which San Carlo forms one corner is known as the Quattro Fontane. At this point the road that Domenico Fontana designed to connect the Piazza di Spagna with Santa Maria Maggiore intersected the earlier Via Pia. This crossing formed a node which helped to transform the two roads from arteries connecting distant points on the map to framing pieces for new development on the Quirinal. The four fountains at each corner of the intersection, representing the Tiber and Arno rivers as well as the Roman goddesses Juno and Diana, were among the first to be fed by the Acqua Felice.

The Via del Quirinale passes the long façade of the Ministry of

Defense. When Rome became a kingdom in 1870, the Pope took refuge in the Vatican Palace, and the Quirinal became the seat of a national government. Just as cardinals' palaces and embassies once surrounded the papal center, the departments of the national government now cluster in this area. Unlike the Defense Department, however, most ministries adapted buildings that had housed the papal government and restructured them to suit new purposes.

The Piazza San Bernardo was originally only a wider stretch of the Via Pia. But in the late nineteenth century the Largo Susanna was created, and three intersecting roads funneled through it on their way to the new train station nearby. A century later, these same roads formed the central axis of Rome's postwar commercial district. Despite this transformation, the buildings that defined the piazza in the early seventeenth century remain. These include the church of San Bernardo, built in the 1590s into an outlying structure of the Baths of Diocletian. The round interior pierced by apses is surmounted by a vault, with wonderful coffering. The Roman oculus that originally flooded the building with light is now enclosed by a lantern and diffused by a shade.

The more prominent churches are those that flank the street, Santa Maria della Vittoria and Santa Susanna. The church of Santa Susanna, now the American national church, was constructed sometime before the eighth century on the traditional site of the saint's martyrdom. Built as a three-aisled basilica, it was reduced to a single aisle in the late sixteenth century. The façade, which is a modest extension of Mannerist principles, was added by Maderno in the early seventeenth century.

Maderno also created the nearly identical façade of Santa Maria

102

della Vittoria. That church is best known for Bernini's Cornaro Chapel, which enshrines his *St. Teresa in Ecstasy,* one of the most compelling and controversial monuments of the Baroque. The chapel is conceived as a magic theater. Well-heeled, portly men of the sponsoring family sit in sculpted boxes to right and left of the altar. A Baroque sunburst showers its gilded rays on the figure of St. Teresa, who reclines above the altar, her lips open in ecstasy as a boyish angel bends to pierce her heart with his arrow. (102) These two figures capture the paradoxical blend of the deeply spiritual and the blatantly sensual that St. Teresa herself reports in her writings. Invited to share her mystical union with God, the spectators in their galleries are like personified readers of the saint's confessions. The self-conscious staginess of the scene and its sensual spirituality are hallmarks of the Baroque sensibility.

At the end of the square, perpendicular to the two churches, stands the mostra of the Acqua Felice. Like the architectural background of the Trevi fountain, this freestanding monument combines the form of the triumphal arch with the triple outlets and basins that Vitruvius dictated for the Roman castellum aquae. From top to bottom the monument displays symbols dear to its sponsor, Felice Peretti, Pope Sixtus V. His emblem, the cross above three mountains (which some believe represent those hills of Rome—the Quirinal, Viminal, and Pincio—that he worked so

earnestly to develop) tops the monument. Supported by angels, his shield
stands below, with obelisks to either side. In any other monument they
would pass for simple ornaments; but, given the Pope's use of these symbols to define important intersections in his new grid plan of Rome, their
presence here is certainly deliberate. The monumental inscription in the
attic of the arch describes the source of the water, the length of the
aqueduct, the brief span of time in which it was completed, and its
name. The symbolism of the figures in the three arches below is biblical,
and it relates to Sixtus not in family terms, as the upper areas of the
monument do, but in his role as Pope.

   Though clumsy artwork diminishes their impact, all three scenes
establish biblical precedents of the most exalted kind for this Pope's act
of bringing water to the city. Two of the scenes record episodes in the
long wandering of the Israelites in the desert, from the time of their
escape from Egypt to their triumphal entry into the Holy Land after
Moses' death. In one, Aaron guides the Israelites to water. In the central
scene, Moses strikes the rock with his rod and water pours out. In the
remaining scene, Joshua leads the Israelites across the Jordan. Given the
enormous scale of the Moses and the long association between the leader
of God's chosen people and the office of Pope, it is undoubtedly his miracle that the Pope saw himself repeating. As astounding as this claim
might seem, his effect on Rome and that of his successors who imitated
his achievement were undeniably miraculous.

   The Via Barberini was widened in the late nineteenth century, and the
Via Veneto, Rome's Champs Elysées, opened the former Villa Ludovisi to
commercial development. These new arteries converged in the Piazza

Barberini, where they linked with others that led to the train station. Now isolated and out of tune with its setting, Bernini's celebrated Triton fountain is hardly noticed and never heard above the din. The extraordinary fountain rises from a low basin; Bernini wanted the water surface to be visible. Standing on their heads, four comical dolphins support a marine shell with their tails. A Triton kneels in the shell; his head bent far back, with his powerful arms he holds a shell to his mouth. A jet of water rises from the shell as if it were the sound of the Triton's horn.

The entrance to the Palazzo Barberini, which houses the Galleria Nazionale d' Arte Antica, is around the corner from the piazza on the perpendicular Via delle Quattro Fontane. Built for the nephews of Pope Urban VIII, the palace combined the characteristic features of the Renaissance palazzo and villa in a distinctive way that set the trend for later Baroque palaces throughout Europe. It was designed by Maderno, and at his death in 1629 supervision of its construction passed into the hands of Bernini. Borromini, who created a magnificent oval stairway in one of the wings, worked with both architects.

Peruzzi's design for the Farnesina provided the clearest Roman precedent for the innovative palazzo, which retained the embracing wings and garden loggia of the modest villa in an inverted and

103

expanded form. Maderno tripled the loggia's
height and thrust it forward from the main
façade, to make it a grand entrance rather
than a garden access. In this expansion he
imitated Bramante's three-tiered extension of
the Vatican Palace and so called to mind the
papal connections of the Barberini family. He
enclosed this expanded and monumentalized
façade with embracing wings to create a formal reception court—the cour d'honneur—
which became a staple of European palace
architecture. (103)

104

Borromini's spiraling oval stairway is to the right of the main entryway.
Looking up it from below, the ramps disappear and the balustrade and
columns seem to be free-standing. The balustrade and colonnade spiral
upward for no apparent purpose other than the sheer beauty of the form.
(104) The open loggia of the entryway narrows bay by bay as it enters
deep within the building. At its far end a ramp leads upward to the ruins
of once-magnificent gardens; the little that remains of them is neglected
and overshadowed by inelegant buildings. It is sad testimony to the
unplanned, radical transformation of this suburban area after 1870.

The Galleria Nazionale d' Arte Antica, which includes paintings, furniture, and porcelain, is housed in rooms on the second floor—the piano
nobile of the palace. These rooms retain their original frescoes but have
otherwise lost all connection with the artwork on display or with palace
life of the seventeenth century. The exhibition continues on the floor

above. The collection, however alienated from its surroundings, is extraordinarily strong both in Roman works like Raphael's *Fornarina* and Caravaggio's *Judith and Holofernes* as well as works from other regions of Italy and the rest of Europe. A magnificent portrait of Henry VIII and one of Erasmus by Holbein and Quentin Matsys are among its prized objects.

Pietro da Cortona decorated the ceiling of the grand salon with an enormous allegorical fresco celebrating *The Triumph of Divine Providence*. Personified in the center of the composition, Providence defeats time and orders Immortality to crown the Barberini family crest, which is held aloft by Virtue personified. Behind fictive cornices, the open sky swarms with figures who represent good government and the achievements of the Barberini. On the inner wall, Minerva defeats the Titans, a traditional allegory of the triumph of order over chaos. On the left, Peace is enthroned, as the Temple of Janus, traditionally associated with warfare, is closed and the Furies lie in chains. The theme continues in the remaining scenes in which Hercules, symbol of Justice, triumphs over the Harpies, while Religion and Wisdom triumph over Vice and Lust.

The Palazzo Barberini was a suburban villa remote enough from the city to be pastoral but close enough to be a full-time residence. The Villa Borghese, just beyond the limits of the Aurelian wall, was so remote that it could be used only occasionally. This remoteness was also the villa's salvation during the period of intense development in the late nineteenth century that engulfed the grounds of the Palazzo Barberini and swallowed up all but a very few of the abundant neighboring villas within the walls. Designed in the seventeenth century as a suburban villa among smaller gardens, the park was expanded and reconceived as each subsequent

landscape fashion swept through Italy. Neoclassical structures and picturesque ruins were added in the eighteenth century when the gardens were
reorganized in the English style. The nineteenth century saw the addition
of a Roman arch and an Egyptian colonnade. The villa, which was sold to
the state in 1901, includes Rome's zoo—now a biopark—and a riding
complex. While the newly restored gardens surrounding the Casino
Borghese are beautiful and well maintained, heavy public use and spotty
maintenance have left the rest of the vast park in a degraded condition.

The Casino Borghese dates from the same era as the park itself; it was
intended from the first as a luxurious pavilion for a day's recreation rather
than as a residence. It also served as a showplace for the sculpture collection of the cardinal nephew, Scipio Borghese. While the casino, like
the Palazzo Barberini, owes an obvious debt to the Farnesina—the loggia
framed by wings is clearly based on Peruzzi's design—it incorporates
many other inspirations. The twin towers recall the Villa Medici; the stuccoed façade, decorated with statues, echoes the Palazzo Spada. There
are innovations, too: the loggia is placed on the second floor above a pair
of monumental steps, and it is topped by an open terrace.

Entrance to the museum and gallery are in the basement of the newly
remodeled structure. The bulk of the Borghese collection of Roman
sculptures passed into the hands of the French at the beginning of the
nineteenth century. The first floor houses the remains of that collection,
augmented by pieces gathered from other Borghese properties and from
the gardens of the villa. Its most celebrated objects, however, are the
extraordinary sculptural groups Bernini made for his patron Cardinal
Scipio Borghese early in the seventeenth century. These objects have

105

never left the collection, and the majority of them have never left this building. As a result, the extraordinarily delicate works are in an almost unimaginably fine state of preservation.

The first floor rooms were redone in the 1780s at about the same time that Simonetti redesigned the first suite of rooms in the Vatican Belvedere Palace. In their rich marble panelings, stucco work, and frescoes, as well as their artful juxtaposition of classical and contemporary objects, the rooms reflect a similar neoclassical desire to rival the antique. Given the preponderance of seventeenth-century works in the collection and their central position in the rooms, the Villa Borghese seems to assert the superiority of Bernini to the anonymous antique sculptors whose works surround his.

Unlike Donatello's delicate boy with flowers in his hat or Michelangelo's Goliath-sized shepherd, Bernini's *David* is distinguished not by its scale but by its movement and energy. David's face, which is a self-portrait—Bernini is said to have sketched it while he looked in a mirror held by the cardinal himself—is compressed with effort. His body twists as he prepares to launch a heavy stone from the sling held in his left hand. (105) The sculpture captures a moment of balanced torsion; it is not the portrait of a monumental figure at rest.

Power, especially violent power, and the action of a single instant are the themes of all the works Bernini completed for the cardinal. These dynamic qualities play paradoxically against the stolid medium of sculpture in a way that appealed to the Baroque sensibility. Instants are captured in timeless artworks; the most violent movements are frozen forever in stone; rapacious force, fear, and suffering are transformed into objects of terrible beauty.

The brutal *Rape of Persephone* embodies these paradoxes and raises questions like those posed by Bernini's *St. Teresa.* How can the god Hades' lust and his utter indifference to the terror of his victim be reconciled with his divine nature? The structure of the work suggests that a balance might be struck between terror and beauty. The god's majestic hands that seem to sink into his victim's flesh are miracles of sculptural delicacy; his bent arm grounds all the diagonals of her flailing legs and arms. Still, there is the overriding fact of rape and the terror of winter, that recurrent death of Nature that Persephone's abduction brought about.

The *Apollo and Daphne* group is less menacing. Apollo pursues Daphne, but unlike Persephone, Daphne escapes; she is transformed into a laurel tree, which Apollo makes the poet's symbol. If neither the sculptor nor the poet can turn away from violence, each can transform it into something timeless and beautiful, though never comforting or comfortable. Bernini's transformations do not erase his subjects' suffering. If anything they prolong, monumentalize, and eternalize it—and by the same measure make it art. Michelangelo wanted his works to have what he called terribilità, a quality that Yeats called "terrible beauty." Bernini achieved it in his greatest sculptures.

The second floor houses the picture collection begun by Scipio Borghese. He acquired paintings by Raphael, Titian, Veronese, Caravaggio, and a few others. This core collection was increased by works from the

Aldobrandini, Salviati, and Este family collections that passed to the Borghese through marriage. Among the works in the core collection are Raphael's *Deposition,* Domenichino's *Diana's Hunt,* and several works by the master of Roman Baroque painting, Michelangelo Merisi da Caravaggio, including a portrait of St. Jerome, *Young Man with Fruitbasket, David with the Head of Goliath,* and the celebrated *Madonna de' Palafrenieri.* Titian's magnificent *Sacred and Profane Love, St. Dominic,* and *Flagellation* are especially wonderful.

The influence of the Quirinal Palace extended throughout the newly urbanized area east of the Corso. Its presence is especially strong in the Piazza di Spagna. The area around the Vatican called the Borgo had been a foreign quarter throughout the Middle Ages. Clerics from throughout Europe, either short-term visitors or permanent residents, were concentrated there. After the papal palace moved to the Quirinal, a similar foreign community comprising ecclesiastics of all ranks and diplomats from every Catholic nation clustered nearby. From modest beginnings in the seventeenth century, that community expanded to include secular tourists and artists. Though partly closed to cars and trucks, the Piazza di Spagna is still one of Rome's busiest, in part because of the pedestrian traffic that converges on the Spagna Metro stop.

The piazza takes its name from the Palazzo di Spagna on its southwestern side, which was for centuries the residence of the Spanish ambassador to the Holy See. Early in the seventeenth century, the Spanish government bought an existing palace, which they soon replaced. The identity of the architect is uncertain—documentary evidence points to Antonio del Grande. The façade is divided into three hor-

izontal bays with an especially tall base course fitted with mezzanine windows; the rhythm of the windows accentuates the central bay and the
rusticated entrance.

The papal institution that was most closely associated with the international community was the Collegio di Propaganda Fide or Institute for
the Propagation of the Faith. It is one of the few papal offices that has
remained in this part of Rome after the popes returned to the Vatican
Palace in 1870. The Propaganda Fide is the Church's office for the coor-
dination of missionary work. When it was founded in the seventeenth
century, most of the Church's missions were in the New World, where
Spanish rule predominated, so it made sense to locate
it near the Spanish embassy. Unlike a palazzo of the
High Renaissance that demands to be seen from a distance, the narrow street (which the main façade of the
building dominates) forces an oblique view. (106)

The façade, like those of the High Renaissance, is
divided vertically into three zones: a lower story with
openings for shops and square mezzanine windows
above (those to the left of the main entry are blind); a
piano nobile with monumental window frames and alternating arched and gabled pediments; an attic story,
separated by a heavy cornice from those below, which repeats the

106

rhythms of the main floor on a smaller scale. The vertical bays of the
long façade also reflect the conventions of the High Renaissance. The
massive pilasters that divide the bays, however, are on a scale that suggests the Mannerist innovations of Sangallo or Michelangelo.

The most radical departure from earlier traditions comes in the treatment of the walls. In Mannerist architecture, pilasters, however enormous they may become, clearly stand in front of a solid wall. Borromini's pilasters so dominate the façade that the walls between them appear insubstantial. This effect is increased by the heavy articulation of the windows of the piano nobile. Their aedicula—composed of pilasters, reflexed columns, and pediments—rest on a string course apparently anchored to the pilasters. These exaggerated features make Borromini's building appear to be made of massed columns with a thin and flexible membrane of wall stretched between them. Borromini takes full advantage of this impression of flexibility when he bends the wall fabric to emphasize his monumental entryway. In a Renaissance building seen from across a piazza, Borromini's techniques would be less evident. Walking past the building, as the narrow site demands, makes the subtle articulations of the wall membrane, which some have compared to breathing, very active.

Borromini's work appeals to modern architects not only for its genius but also because he treated walls as skins suspended from structural frames. Despite the omnipresent classical ornamentation in his work, contemporary critics, of whom there were many, thought that he misunderstood the fundamentals of Renaissance classicism. A reaction against Renaissance principles is very evident in Borromini's Capella dei Re Magi (Chapel of the Three Wisemen) inside the Propaganda Fide. Monumental pilasters support a ribbed roof, which despite its neoclassical style reflects motifs of the "flamboyant Gothic," where the supporting piers seem to grow branches that intertwine across the ceiling. Like the façade, the interior wall is divided into three horizontal zones and sectioned into vertical bays by massive pillar-pilasters. The flexible wall suspended from them is bent at the corners of the room, as are the moldings on the pillars near them. Arched windows alternate with elliptical ones; pediments between them support the springing of the ceiling ribs.

The church of the Trinità dei Monti was founded by the French king Charles VIII in 1502, though its façade dates from the late sixteenth century. It is one of the few Roman churches designed with twin towers, a style more familiar to its French founders. Like its neighbor the Villa Medici, this church helped to establish the identity of this part of Rome as the quartiere degli stranieri, the foreign quarter of the city. In front of the church is a small piazza that offers a panoramic view of the city and opens onto the Spanish Steps. The obelisk, which links the piazza symbolically with the Piazza del Popolo, was erected in the eighteenth century. The Via Sistina, which begins here, was projected by Sixtus V and his architect, Domenico Fontana, as a continuation of the link that began in the Via del Babuino between the Piazza del Popolo and the church of Santa Maria Maggiore.

The Spanish Steps should be called the French steps, since it was the French kings and the French monks of the church of Trinità dei Monti who commissioned the architect De Sanctis and funded the project. In celebration of their association with this church, which is dedicated to the Holy Trinity, the steps are an architectural representation of that mysterious entity that is simultaneously one and three. The steps descend in three flights, and each of the three blends single and triple structures. Despite these historical and structural links to the French church at its

107

summit, the steps take their name from the Palazzo di Spagna near their base. However unjustly named, the Spanish Steps are one of the great public spaces in Rome. (107) The lowest flight of the stairs, which are decorated with pots of azaleas in the spring, offer front-row seating for the passing scene in the piazza.

With all the artists in Rome during the nineteenth century, there was a great demand for models, and anyone with an interesting face or an unusual regional costume would find his way to the Spanish Steps. "All day long these steps are flooded with sunshine, in which, stretched at length, or gathered in picturesque groups, models of every age and both sexes bask away the hours when they are free from employment in the studios. Here in a rusty old coat and long white beard and hair, is the Father Eternal, so called from his constantly standing as the First Person of the Trinity in religious pictures. Here is the peasant girl who spends her studio life praying at a shrine with upcast eyes or lifting to the Virgin her little sick child, or carrying a perpetual copper vase to the fountain. Here is the invariable pilgrim, with his scallop shell, who has been journeying to St. Peter's and reposing on the way near aqueducts or broken columns so long that the memory of man runneth not to the contrary" (W. W. Story, *Roba di Roma*).

In the middle of the oddly shaped piazza, at the base of the Spanish Steps, is the fountain called La Barcaccia. Designed by Gian Lorenzo Bernini or possibly his father, the fountain, in the shape of a leaky boat, was meant as a garden ornament. When the fountain was built, the

Spanish Steps were a twisting path up a tree-shaded hillside and the
piazza was a sunny patch of dirt. The rustic fountain looks out of place in
the urban square that has grown up around it. La Barcaccia is supplied
with water from the Acqua Vergine. Where water was available, building
followed; the growth of this part of Rome owes everything to the water
bursting from this odd little fountain. Romans and others step onto the
platforms at the prow and stern of the marble vessel and bend to drink
from the jets.

Around the Piazza di Spagna are other monuments that reflect the
character of this part of Rome. To the right of the Spanish Steps stands
the pink Casina Rossa which De Sanctis designed—along with the identical building on the opposite side—as frames for his stairway. The English
poet John Keats and his friend Joseph Severn rented rooms in the winter
of 1821, and Keats died here. The Keats-Shelley Memorial on the second floor commemorates the pair and other English poets who visited
Rome. John Keats came to Rome in search of a climate that would
improve his health. He lived here in the heart of the foreign community
for six months until his death from tuberculosis at age twenty-five in
1821. He was buried in what is known as the Protestant Cemetery near
the Porta San Paolo.

In his final illness Keats occupied a small corner room with two windows—one that looked onto the piazza and the other directly down onto
the Spanish Steps. At a small fireplace still in the room, Severn sometimes cooked or reheated food that they had sent in from a restaurant
across the piazza. The room has high ceilings with pretty wood coffering,
but it is long and narrow and small; there is hardly room for a bed, let

alone additional furniture, and spending months here with a dying man not much older than the kids who crowd the steps outside the window must have been miserable.

Display cases and a small desk with a visitors' book are the only furniture now in the room. A case on the back wall holds Severn's famous sketch of the poet on his deathbed and a copy of a letter describing the death and its immediate aftermath. The other rooms in the museum are lined floor to ceiling with books on barred shelves. Display cases document the Italian travels of Byron and Shelley. Lord Byron visited Rome in spring 1817 and stayed nearby. Percy Bysshe Shelley was in Italy when Keats died, though he did not visit this house. When Shelley drowned off the Italian coast, his body was brought to Rome and buried not far from Keats.

Flanking the Spanish Steps on the side opposite the Keats-Shelley Memorial House is Babbington's Tea Rooms. What nineteenth-century Britons called "the English part of Rome" has shrunk to these two tiny outposts of British culture. The British presence was more strongly felt, and at least in some cases more welcome, in the early nineteenth century. "I try to go into Rome from time to time but I find it boring. There's no theater; not a breath of music; no literary conversation. Dark, dirty bars with lousy service and no newspapers. Everything is a hundred and fifty years behind the times. The people are lazy, soft, and unwilling to work; Nature provides them with everything, but they can't figure out how to use what they've been given. Oh, if only this beautiful country were populated by Englishmen! What an improvement!" (Hector Berlioz).

Like most of the standing stones in Rome, the Column of the Immaculate Conception nearby is an ancient artifact capped with a Christian

symbol. In this instance the crowning figure is the Virgin Mary, and the
column commemorates the dogma of the Immaculate Conception of the
Virgin first promulgated by Pope Pius IX
in 1854. Like many popes who are
reform-minded early in their pontificates,
Pius grew to be quite conservative, especially after the revolution of 1848. He
made the long-held tradition that the
Virgin was born without sin a formal
dogma. He also promulgated the dogma
of papal infallibility.

Near the Piazza di Spagna is another
singular building by Borromini, the
church of Sant'Andrea delle Fratte, for
which the architect designed an unusual

108

cupola and belfry. (108) The brick cupola, which never received the stucco surface Borromini intended, displays the architect's typical flexing of
walls around stiff columns. The uniform material, however, shows how
completely Borromini's design creates the illusion of a difference between
wall and column, when in fact both are crafted from the same material.
The belfry is a curious composite of a convex base and balcony that recalls Bramante's Tempietto. A deeply notched cornice above is supported
by seraph-caryatids in pairs with convex spaces between them; these are
topped by torches that surround the base of a crowned urn. The combination of classical elements, flexed and reflexed walls, and redesigned
personifications is astonishing.

The movement of the papal palace to the Quirinal hill gave the Via del Corso new prominence and demanded a monumental entrance to the city that would center on that avenue. Developments along the route had begun long before, in the fifteenth century. In that era the opening of the Ponte Sisto and the creation of corridors to the Vatican, such as the Via della Lungara and the Via Giulia, had prompted parallel developments on the city's northern edge. The return of the papacy to Rome in the fifteenth century brought crowds of pilgrims from every part of Catholic Europe. The many who were too poor to afford the costs of passage aboard ship came overland to the Holy City.

Redirected from its ancient route during the Middle Ages, the Roman Via Flaminia received these crowds and channeled them toward the city's northern gate, the Porta del Popolo. There it met the Via Lata, which led to the imperial fora and the Capitoline and by secondary roads to the Lateran. Under Pope Leo X (1513–1521), a new road, named in his honor the Via Leonina (the modern Via di Ripetta and its continuation the Via della Scrofa), linked the northern city gate with the occupied areas in the Tiber bend and through them with the Vatican. For the Jubilee of 1525, Pope Clement VII ordered the creation of a second road—now called the Via del Babuino—also starting at the Piazza del Popolo and designed to improve access to Santa Maria Maggiore and the more distant pilgrimage sites on the eastern edge of the city.

The Roman road that led into the Porta del Popolo, the Via Flaminia, opened to traffic in the consulship of Caius Flaminius in 219 BC. Built to last forever like all Roman public works, the Flaminia drove northeastward to the Italian city of Rimini. Extended in the reign of Constantine, it coasted the Adriatic Sea then continued eastward through the Balkans, eventually reaching Constantinople. By the Middle Ages, trade with the East was cut off, and the truncated Via Flaminia was reconnected by a series of smaller roads to routes coming from northern Europe. Renamed the Ruga Francisci, "the French road," it brought visitors to the Holy City for more than a thousand years.

In the seventeenth century, not long after the papacy's move to the Quirinal, Bernini redesigned the Porta del Popolo. The immediate occasion for the redesign was the celebration of Queen Christina of Sweden, who in 1655 abandoned her country and the Protestant religion to become a permanent resident of Rome. Like a magnified triumphal arch, the triple gateway penetrates the Aurelian wall, the massive defensive perimeter quickly built up in the third century to counter the first threat of alien invasion. Inside the gate, the Piazza del Popolo is Baroque Rome's opening statement, and like the first measures of a great symphony, it expresses power, complexity, and deep harmony. The scale is large but not inhuman, impressive but not intimidating.

Several architects over the centuries had a hand in its composition. A central fountain, opened under Gregory XIII, was marked by an obelisk during the pontificate of his successor, Sixtus V. Rainaldi laid out the piazza as a trapezoid—the same figure Michelangelo imposed on the Campidoglio—with its broad end toward the city. Bernini designed the gate and with Rainaldi planned the twin churches that flank the Corso at the piazza's opposite end. The French architect Valadier reworked the fountains and curved and broadened the piazza on both sides in imitation of Bernini's Piazza San Pietro. He opened it toward the Tiber on the right and created ramps leading up to the Pincian hill. This opening to the green hillside brought dramatic changes. It diminished the impact of the twin churches, thereby secularizing the plaza and redefining the area as a garden district rather than an urban gateway.

On the piazza's city side, Santa Maria dei Miracoli stands to the right and Santa Maria di Montesanto to the left of Via del Corso. (109) These churches are not identical in size or plan; Rainaldi and Bernini designed their domes and façades so that the city side of the piazza would seem symmetrical. The façade of each church is dominated by a monumental porch with gabled roof like that of the Pantheon, which is thrust into the piazza by curved bays that sweep back to either side. Merged with the façades of the buildings behind, the side walls make the churches into ceremonial frontispieces for the great urban wedges that stretch into the distance on either side. (110) Balustrades above the façade support stat-

ues like those on Bernini's colonnade at St. Peter's. The nearly identical domes tower above in a style that suggests St. Peter's itself. Baroque Rome was represented in the piazza of that era as an urban scene

109

dominated by images of the Vatican, the pilgrim's goal. This notion was reinforced by the similarity between the three roads that lead from the plaza and the three roads that diverge on the city side of the Ponte Sant'Angelo a little to the east.

110

The three roads that begin at the piazza's southern rim and border its twin churches are the Via di Ripetta on the right, the Via del Corso in the center, and the Via Babuino on the left. These roads channeled traffic into the three major zones of the Baroque city and still serve its prime commercial and political district, Il Tridente, the trident, which takes its name from their three-branched form. The Via di Ripetta leads toward the Tiber—the heart of the medieval and Renaissance city—then on to the Vatican and Trastevere. The Corso cuts through the center of town and on to the ruins of ancient Rome. The Via Babuino goes to the Piazza di Spagna, the area where embassies and hotels came to be concentrated, then through a series of connecting streets on to Santa Maria Maggiore and the Lateran Church at Rome's southeastern edge.

The Via Babuino, which opened for the Jubilee of 1525, takes its unusual name—babuino means baboon—from a disfigured Roman statue with a gaping simian mouth and flowing mustaches that decorates a fountain halfway down the street. For most of its length the Via Babuino goes past upscale clothing stores, elegant printsellers, and antique shops. The Via Margutta parallels the Via Babuino one block to the left. The street is quieter than the Via Babuino, and the shops are similar, though there is more contemporary art in the galleries and even a few shops where artisans work repairing and restoring antiques.

In the eighteenth and nineteenth centuries, many of Rome's artists had their studios in this quiet neighborhood. These artists produced religious works for churches around the world. Tourists shopped mainly for views of the city and its monuments, but there were portrait and religious painters and copyists producing reproductions on every scale of admired works in Roman museums. The end of the eighteenth century was the great age of Roman views. Artists like Rossini and Piranesi combined archaeological accuracy with capricious fantasy to create a Rome of the imagination where the monuments were triple-scale and the people a collection of carnival grotesques. By the third quarter of the nineteenth century, photographs had driven etchings out of the market. Once people began to travel with their own cameras, professional photographers vanished in turn. The last vestige of the trade in photographic views is the Fototeca Alinari at Via Alibert 16, at the end of the Via Margutta. Founded in the nineteenth century, the Alinari firm specializes in historical photographs of Italian life, monuments, and artworks. Their reproductions of great master drawings are especially fine; and their photographic prints, available individually, in portfolios, or in books of their own publication, are very evocative.

Though built in the twelfth century, the church of Santa Maria del Popolo, which sits just inside the Porta del Popolo, was remodeled significantly in the High Renaissance. Pope Paschal II began the church in

1099. According to legend, the Pope was told in a dream to build a
church on this site to protect the area from the ghost of the emperor
Nero, whose tomb was nearby. The Roman Commune paid for the
church, hence del Popolo—of the people—from which the gate and
piazza also take their names. The church was enlarged in the thirteenth
century and remodeled in the fifteenth and sixteenth centuries in the
Renaissance style. The simple travertine façade, which reflects the ideals
of Alberti, is divided by shallow pilasters into three bays of
unequal size. The side doors, surmounted by gabled pediments and arched openings, bracket a monumental central
door with a circular window and gabled pediment in the
second story above. The scrolls and the curved, broken pediment that link the side and central bays were added in the
seventeenth century. (111)

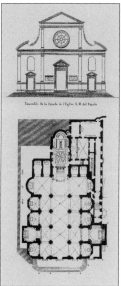

111

The interior was also remodeled in the seventeenth century, but the medieval and Renaissance tombs on the walls
and pavement and much of the earlier ornamentation were
preserved. Aside from the very interesting floor and wall
tombs, there is a wonderful chapel with Renaissance frescoes by Pinturicchio (central chapel, right wall) illustrating
the life of St. Jerome. The second to last chapel on the left side of the
church was designed by Raphael and his assistants for Agostino Chigi,
the banker and art patron for whom Raphael also designed a chapel in
Santa Maria della Pace. Conceived by Raphael as a synthesis of painting,
sculpture, and architecture, it was left incomplete at his death. More
than a century later, Bernini redesigned and completed it for the Chigi

112

pope, Alexander VII. Most of Bernini's work for the Pope manifested the power and legitimacy of the papacy, but this commission celebrated the Pope's own family. While that family was an illustrious one in its own right and long connected with the papacy, as the tombs illustrate, the celebration of family on a ceremonial level here parallels the diversion of papal revenues to Alexander's own relatives, which marred the Chigi papacy, as it had so many earlier ones.

The chapel incorporates fictive tombs in the shape of pyramids—reinterpretations by Bernini of Raphael's design—with outsized medallion portraits of celebrated Chigis, and paintings by Sebastiano del Piombo (not part of the original design) and Francesco Salviati. Mosaics by Luigi de Pace reflect Raphael's plan. Niches in the corners of the chapel contain sculptures commemorating Old Testament figures who foretold the Resurrection: to the right of the altar, *Habbakuk and the Angel* by Bernini; on the left, Jonah vomited up by a diminutive whale—a sculpture designed by Raphael and carved by Lorenzetti. Bernini also made the figure of *Daniel and the Lion*, opposite.

Bramante designed the choir behind the Baroque altar. Its most striking features are the barrel vault with its deep coffers reminiscent of Roman baths and curved, inset windows. The vault of the simple apse is ribbed like a sea shell—another Roman bath motif incorporated here as a symbol of pilgrimage. Two Renaissance tombs of great beauty and importance decorate the walls of the choir. Both by Sansovino, they combine the architecture of a Roman triumphal arch with a tomb sculpture. The reclining figures on the tombs defy medieval tradition: with their torsos slightly elevated, they appear to be sleeping. Two stained glass windows, extremely rare survivals of the Renaissance, are above. All of these works were commissioned by Pope Julius II, who appears as a shepherd in the Adoration scene.

To the left of the high altar is a chapel of amazing impact. On its front wall is an *Assumption of the Virgin* by Annibale Carracci. On either side are two paintings by Caravaggio. They are direct, even aggressive, in the tight space of the chapel and create a claustrophobic sense that contrasts very strongly with the cool tones and remote perfection of Pinturicchio's frescoes. The painting on the left represents the *Conversion of St. Paul;* the one on the right, the *Crucifixion of St. Peter.* Caravaggio's second great public commission, the paintings are extraordinary inventions. Paul lies in the cramped lower third of a canvas that is dominated by the horse from which he was thrown in the moment when God spoke to him. The enormous horse and the brightly lit hand on its elaborate bridle emphasize its traditional role as a symbol of passion and its control. But something beyond human control has happened. The horse's hoof, upraised to spare the fallen rider, suggests the powerful blow Paul has experienced. (112)

113

Like Paul, Peter too is upside-down, overwhelmed by Passion in a different sense. His affliction is caused not by the repudiation but by the imitation of Christ. To avoid comparing himself directly with Christ, Peter asked to be crucified upside-down. His cross, to which he has been brutally nailed, is about to be lifted into place by struggling workmen. The terrified old man, his eyes glazed in pain, stares at his own pierced hand, which clearly recalls that of Christ. (113) Caravaggio's earth tones, his heightened contrast of light and dark, and his fierce psychological intensity mark a revolution in the pictorial and spiritual ideals he inherited from the High Renaissance.

A small set of stairs at the side of Santa Maria del Popolo leads uphill to the Piazzale Napoleone. The overlook there offers a wonderful view of the Piazza del Popolo. Now cleared of the traffic it was designed to channel and control, it looks like an empty municipal swimming pool. Beyond is the jumble of pediments, domes, and bell towers that fill the heart of Rome. Unlike most great cities, the center of Rome has no distinctly modern quarter; skyscrapers are confined by law to the remote perimeter. Consequently, the buildings that stand out are those that represent the city historically, politically, and spiritually: the Pantheon, the Palace of Justice, the Victor Emmanuel Monument, and the dome of St. Peter's. The Tiber is invisible as it loops through the center of town within its embankments, but its course is traced by the columns of plane trees that flank it on both sides. Beyond the river is the tree-covered Janiculum, with its symbolic lighthouse and the enormous statue of Giuseppe Garibaldi.

In its first incarnation, the Villa Medici, like the Vatican Belvedere, was a casino, an elaborate pavilion where Roman nobles of the sixteenth century could spend a day in the country without sacrificing any of the luxuries of palace life. The simple façade with its characteristic towers facing the road is actually the back of the building. A more elaborate façade with enclosing wings and an open loggia faces the formal gardens to the rear. Begun in 1564, the villa predates the opening of the Acqua Felice and the expansive growth of this part of Rome. As running water—exemplified by the goblet-like fountain across from the villa entrance—and the displacement of the papal palace to the Quirinal pushed the Baroque city in its direction, the casino became a villa, a palatial suburban residence.

In 1804 the French government took over the Villa Medici and made it the home of the French Academy in Rome. This institution, founded by Louis XIV in the late seventeenth century, continues to provide fellowships—the Prix de Rome—for French sculptors, architects, and artists to spend three years in Rome at government expense. Artists trained here include Claude Lorraine, Jacques-Louis David, Ingres, and many others. During their residencies, the fellows of the French Academy have traditionally learned the fundamentals of classical art by studying, modeling, and drawing Roman artifacts. Art and architecture were important parts of Louis's plan for transforming France from a series of feuding baronies into a single nation under his absolute control. Official encouragement of the neoclassical style in art and architecture aided his nationalizing and centralizing program by creating a visual uniformity that echoed political solidarity. The program was similar to Augustus' favoring of Hellenistic models in sculpture and architecture.

By the nineteenth century, neoclassicism had acquired two new political constituencies. The French Revolution modeled itself on the recent
example of the revolt in America and on the ancient example of the
Roman Republic. This republican neoclassicism challenged the imperial
neoclassicism of the French monarchy. During the Revolution, the French
Academy changed from a training ground for the establishment to
become the visual arm of the revolt. The new American republic was also
looking for ways to symbolize its character in buildings and monuments,
and like France it turned to Republican Rome as an ideal of liberty.
Neoclassicism in America was represented in sculpture by such nineteenth-century figures as Horatio Greenough, W. W. Story, and Harriet
Hosmer, all of whom studied and worked for long periods in Rome.

Neoclassical architecture gained great popularity in America through
the Greek Revival movement, which owed its vocabulary of "Greek temple" structure and ornamentation as much to Roman as to Greek buildings. As the nineteenth century ended, progressive painters rejected neoclassicism just as it was being revived yet again by architects. Their
interest led to the foundation of the American Academy in Rome in
1895. "It is one of the pleasures of Rome to lounge in the studios of the
best sculptors; and it is at Rome only that sculpture seems to flourish as
in its native soil. Rome is truly the city of the soul, the home of art and
artists. With the divine models of the Vatican ever before their eyes,
these inspiring skies above their heads, and the quarries of marble at a
convenient distance: it is here only they can conceive and execute those
works which are formed from the ideal of beauty" (Anna Jameson, *Diary
of an Ennuyée*).

Directly across from the Spanish Steps, one of Rome's most famous streets, the Via Condotti, begins. If malls had souls, this is what they would pray to become: a beautifully proportioned pedestrian street with the Spanish Steps as its anchor, and elegant, internationally celebrated shops with wonderful things to sell. (114) Halfway down the first block is the Caffe Greco. Founded in 1760 when chocolate and coffee were novelty drinks and the beautiful people powdered their hair and wore fake moles, the list of famous visitors here included

114

Goethe, Gogol, Schopenhauer, Mendelsohn, Berlioz, Stendahl, Baudelaire, Wagner, and Liszt. In the nineteenth century it was a hangout for the many artists who lived and worked in the area. "The Caffe Greco is where artists meet and discuss subjects of art, pictures, and statues, read the French newspapers and fill the air of the crowded little rooms with tobacco smoke. There you may see every night representatives of art from all parts of the world in all kinds of hats from the conical black felt with its velvet ribbon to the stiff French stovepipe; and in every variety of coat from the Polish and German nondescript, all befrogged and tagged, to the shabby American dress-coat with crumpled tails; and with every cut of hair and beard from that of Peter the Hermit, unkempt and uncut, to the moustache and pointed beard of Anthony Vandyck. Peeping in there, one is sometimes tempted to consider philosophically what innate connection there is between genius for art and long uncombed hair and untidy beards" (W. W. Story, *Roba di Roma*). The modern café is still popular, though quite expensive and fairly subdued.

A few blocks north of the Via Condotti is the more vibrant Via della Croce. Much less elegant than the Via Condotti, it combines great charm with the workaday shops that keep the center of Rome alive. Rome's historic neighborhoods are not just for tourists and nine-to-fivers. It's not only the beauty of Rome that keeps Romans from looking for houses in the suburbs. Great care has been taken to maintain community and the services that make it viable. Commercial life here seldom reaches higher than the first floor; above are apartments. To keep life going in a neighborhood like this, the shoe-repair shop, the video rental store, the cheese, pasta, and sausage shops have to be in easy reach. Especially important is the small fruit and vegetable market that appears each morning at the angle of a small side street and offers the variety, though not the abundance, of fresh produce on sale in the Campo de' Fiori. In addition to these necessaries, Via della Croce has a small bookshop that specializes in Roman history, architecture, and archaeology, an art supply store, and two excellent though anonymous restaurants.

Once the frontier of medieval Rome, the Via del Corso became the main street of the Baroque city. Sadly, it has not managed to keep its historic identity intact into this century. The site of parades, religious processionals, candlelight marches, horse races, and the Roman Mardi Gras, so celebrated was the scene on the street that the buildings along the way were constantly being remodeled to provide more seats for the spectacle. (115) "There are verandahs and balconies of all shapes and sizes to almost every house—not on one story alone, but often to one room or another on every story—put there in general with so little order or regularity that if, year after year, season after season, it had rained balconies, hailed balconies, snowed balconies, blown balconies, they could scarcely have come into existence in a more disorderly manner" (Charles Dickens, *Pictures from Italy*). A few of these balconies remain above a street that was widened in the decades following national unification. The broad avenue is now typically choked with traffic; and commerce, which once dominated only at ground level, has completely overwhelmed it. No longer an urban theater, the street has become a degraded commercial corridor.

The Via del Tritone intersects the Corso at the small Largo Chigi. A modest street in the Baroque city, the Tritone was widened in 1881 as the new national capital expanded. Plans for linking it to areas across the Corso led to partial demolition and reshaping of the Palazzo Chigi and the razing of the Baroque Palazzo Piombino. When this project, which would have gutted Rome's medieval and Renaissance quarter, was abandoned, two empty building lots were left. Rome's only neoclassical iron-framed building, now the Rinascente department store, was built on one of them.

Completed in 1887, it was also the first in Rome to follow the Parisian trend of devoting entire buildings to commercial use. Though the construction technique was completely up-to-date, the building's style recalls Renais-

115

sance and Mannerist models. Divided into two horizontal bays by a thin cornice, its arched windows, pilasters, and square mezzanine windows mimic the vocabulary of sixteenth-century models. The enormous arched openings of the lower level, however, were far beyond the structural limitations of Renaissance materials; only the building's steel frame makes them possible.

Chapter Eight

THE SURVIVAL OF HISTORY

The center of power established in the last decade of the sixteenth century remained fixed until 1870. In that year Italy achieved political union under a king who chose the Quirinal Palace as the seat of national government. Before the capture of Rome by nationalist forces, the reigning pope, Pius IX, moved into the Vatican Palace, where he and his successors remained under self-imposed house arrest until 1929. The decades following 1870 saw dramatic changes in all parts of Rome, but especially in the hilltop regions surrounding the Quirinal. Government departments foraged for space in the new capital. Population increased dramatically, spurring the breakup of the largest estates into small building sites. The old through-routes were widened and new arteries were knit together from existing streets. With the arrival of the railroad and the construction of the first train station near the Baths of Diocletian in 1867, traffic increased enormously.

It is fortunate and surprising that so much of Rome's Baroque fabric and the bulk of its significant monuments were able to survive this period of intense development. Their survival is the result of many decisions made in the years following national unification. The gathering of the Italian states into a single nation had been a gradual process. It began in the northern territories of the House of Savoy, the eventual ruling house of the unified peninsula. It spread slowly southward beyond Rome, then turned back to the papal city, which was triumphantly entered through the Porta Pia on September 20, 1870. Pope Pius IX protested the city's occupation from the Vatican. Deprived of sovereignty and refusing to recognize the legitimacy of the Italian state, Pope Pius and his successors remained in self-described exile. The standoff lasted until 1929 when a treaty was signed that recognized the state of Italy as the legitimate possessor of former papal territory and the Vatican as an independent nation.

Long before its conquest, Rome had been picked as the new national capital, but there was no plan in place for transforming the papal city. Two completely different notions competed for approval. One group of planners projected an entirely new government center to be built either beyond the Aurelian walls or in the still undeveloped areas of the Pincio, Viminal, and Quirinal. The alternate view was more conservative and more pragmatic; it called for altering the papal fabric to serve the needs of the new state. In the end, time and money rather than ideals fixed the choice on this less ambitious plan. A new government center built from scratch on empty land would have been enormously expensive and taken years to complete. Negotiations with the papal bureaucracy for the purchase of buildings would probably have taken even longer and in the end might have cost even more, but a key feature of Italian law made such negotiations unnecessary.

It had been the policy of the emerging national government to extend its legal structure to each new area of the country it controlled. A crucial statute called for the expropriation of certain kinds of ecclesiastical prop-

erty. Under this law, Church property that did not serve the lay community directly through ministry, education, health care, or relief would
be expropriated. Churches, orphanages, hospitals, schools, and hostels
were exempt but the property of clerical orders with no public mission
and that of the Church administration were not. With the conquest in
1870, that law was extended to Rome. Under its terms, buildings that
had housed the papal administration were pressed into immediate service. A new government fitted itself into old structures that had in many
cases been designed for very different purposes. By this entirely pragmatic
decision, however, the Italian state preserved the historical fabric of
Renaissance, Baroque, and Neoclassical Rome.

   The nation's first city needed more than government buildings. In
striking contrast to Paris and London, Europe's greatest metropolitan capitals, Rome's population in the year of national unity was slightly less
than a quarter million. That figure doubled within thirty years, and then
doubled again to a million before 1920. Housing for these new and generally affluent citizens, many of whom were employed in government ministries, became a pressing need. Because ancient Rome had been as
large or larger, there was room inside the city walls to accommodate this
enormous expansion. Still, the pace of development was very quick in the
last decades of the nineteenth century. And though the city was nomi-
nally governed by a series of master plans, much of this growth was
unregulated. Private estates were subdivided, and expropriated properties
were sold at public auction. New communities swallowed up open land at
a voracious rate. The area around the Baths of Diocletian, close to the
Quirinal Palace and the new railroad station, was one of the first to be

developed. The Ludovisi estate between the Piazza Barberini and the Aurelian walls was unexpectedly sold and quickly urbanized. The Villa Montalto, once owned by Sixtus V, disappeared in the same way. Prati, the area between St. Peter's and the Tiber, went from farmland to city in a single generation.

Ironically, national unity divided Rome. With its secular government centered in the Quirinal Palace and its religious center beyond the Tiber, Rome became bipolar. The train station, where the bulk of tourists now arrived in Rome, was close to the Quirinal, but the pilgrims' and tourists' goal for the most part was St. Peter's on the opposite side of town. What the city needed was a second broad avenue perpendicular to the Corso that would link its two divided centers. The first step was taken with the laying out of the Via Nazionale from the train station toward the Corso. The earliest plans called for this new route to cut sharply right toward the Quirinal Palace, then left past the Trevi Fountain. Of obvious symbolic importance, this twisting path would have been expensive, destructive, and inefficient. In the end, a straighter course that joined the Corso at its end in the Piazza Venezia was chosen instead.

Beyond the Piazza Venezia, crosstown traffic had to negotiate the twisting streets of the Campo Marzio. Dominated by Renaissance structures, this part of town was not untouched by the Baroque and Neoclassical periods. Important buildings of these periods had been inserted into the Renaissance fabric. In general this had been done with some ingenuity and with considerable care to preserve the historical character of the setting into which new designs were introduced. Most of these Baroque projects clustered near the Via Papale. Like the Via Triumphalis of the Roman Republic, this occasional route had attracted monumental development. In laying out the new street, to be named the Corso Vittorio Emanuele II, Roman engineers of the late nineteenth century continued the Via Nazionale into the Tiber bend by following the route of the Via Papale wherever possible and taking advantage of its Baroque structures to create a passage through the Campo Marzio that was both efficient and impressive.

In the late nineteenth century these building projects combined with other forces to make Piazza Venezia Rome's most significant crossroads. The prominence of the Corso, the demand for improved communication between the city's two power centers, and the selection of the Capitoline as the site for the monument to King Victor Emmanuel II gave the piazza enormous importance. These projects also demanded significant changes to a space that in 1870 was no longer than the main façade of Palazzo Venezia, which bordered it on the west, and only half as wide. The piazza's eastern flank was then closed by the Palazzo Torlonia, and the Piccolo Palazzo Venezia closed it in on the south. The Torlonia was razed and replaced by a much smaller palazzo in Renaissance style which is now the headquarters of an insurance company. The Piccolo Palazzo Venezia was dismantled and moved to a new site. Beyond the expanded piazza a vast arc of closely packed houses that ran from the base of the Capitoline to the Forum of Trajan was cleared of inhabitants—their numbers may have mounted to the thousands—and all buildings there were razed. Most of this open space was then filled in by the massive Victor Emmanuel monument. The rest, with the exception of three green islands between the end of the Corso and the monument, was paved over to form the enormous piazza.

Mussolini chose the Palazzo Venezia as his headquarters and expanded the program of demolition and monumentalization. His two great urban roadways, the Via del Mare (now the Via di Teatro di Marcello/Via Petroselli) and the Via del Impero (now Via de' Fori Imperiali), began in Piazza Venezia. To carry out these projects, thousands more were evicted and hundreds of houses leveled.

Rome's most vilified structure, the snow-white Vittoriano, or Victor Emmanuel Monument, glares down on a city where soft shades of ochre, brown, and ivory predominate. (116) The design reflects a type of Hellenistic monument called a "theater temple" of which there are a few

116

ancient examples in Italy, though none in Rome itself. The temple part of the monument is represented by the columned portico at the top; the theater is formed by the cascading stairs, like the steeply pitched rows of seats in the Colosseum or Theater of Marcellus. Halfway up this avalanche, two diminutive figures in uniform guard the Altar of the Fatherland and Tomb of the Unknown Soldier. At the top of the stairs the open colonnade is crowned by triumphal chariots symbolizing Victory.

Closed for decades, the monument was reopened for the Jubilee in 2000. From the sheltered portico atop its 250 steps, the monument offers wonderful views in nearly every direction. (Ironically, both the Roman Forum and Campidoglio are masked by other buildings.) The overview of the imperial fora and Colosseum from the eastern end is especially fine. The Museo Centrale del Risorgimento, which commemorates the short-lived Roman Republic of 1849 and the followers of Garibaldi who finally unified Italy in 1870, is located inside. Completed in 1906, it was first opened in 1970 on Italy's hundredth anniversary, and then closed again in 1979.

Facing Palazzo Venezia to the north, the enormous Palazzo Doria Pamphili, with its extraordinary galleries of painting and sculpture, is Rome's largest and most conspicuous palace. The core of the building, like its neighbor, dates from the fifteenth century. The building passed from the hands of one papal family to another: from the Della Rovere to the Aldobrandini and finally to the Pamphili. The nephew of Innocent X, for whom Borromini built the Palazzo Pamphili on Piazza Navona, inherited it in the mid-seventeenth century. Work on the palace continued for the next eighty years. The façade on the Corso, designed by Valvassori, was completed last.

The block-long building is divided into a central area and two secondary ones. A central doorway and two side doors protrude from the façade and are accented by a curved balustrade above. The ornate windows of the piano nobile are similar to Borromini's windows in the Propaganda Fide. They are surrounded by aedicula and surmounted by curved pediments that reach almost to the balustrade of the third story. That story is richly ornamented; the windows are bracketed by pilasters and crowned with pediments. The frames of the mezzanine windows, which break into a floral frieze, are delicately curved.

The Galleria Doria Pamphili is one of Rome's most celebrated household museums. Salons on the piazza side of the palace give way to smaller receiving areas and a throne room with windows opening onto the courtyard. Gold and velvet predominate, and big paintings are arranged from eye-level up to the fourteen-foot ceilings. There are many interesting works among them, especially the early landscape paintings in the first room. Beyond a small private chapel on the left, a series of galleries surround a second courtyard. With their narrow passageways, painted vaults, and ample—in some cases, excessive—lighting from multiple windows, these galleries (miniature versions of the long corridors in the Vatican) were designed specifically for displaying art. At the end of the first gallery a small space with a frescoed ceiling houses one of the great paintings of the collection, Velázquez' *Portrait of Pope Innocent X*. The pontiff, who was painted in 1650, has more jaw than he needs; but the strength of the face is evident in the merciless eyes and the take-no-prisoners mouth. Bernini's bust of Innocent nearby is a more benign and less compelling portrait.

The second gallery offers a long and appealing vista past ranks of classical sculptures. The outer wall here faces the Corso, and some of the windows open onto balconies that once offered a privileged view of parades and processions. At the end of this gallery is a succession of rooms with paintings arranged and labeled chronologically. In the second of them is a brooding, fantastic landscape by the Neapolitan painter Salvatore Rosa and an early Caravaggio portrait of St. Mary Magdalen that completely lacks the dramatic shadows of the late works. With her long red hair and bright yellow dress, this Magdalene has an almost Pre-Raphaelite clarity and sweetness.

The next room steps back in time and features a small Brueghel winter scene. Coming across such a cozy, even-tempered painting in a collection like this one, where the scale of the canvases and the pitch of
emotion is generally so much grander, is a little like meeting Grandma
Moses at a Kandinsky exhibition. The picture to the right of the
Brueghel—a portrait of Machiavelli—brings reality back. Diagonally
across the room is a double portrait by Raphael, and beside it a painting
of the biblical seductress Salome by Titian. Next to the Titian is a painting by Sophonisba Anguissola, one of a handful of women who were professional artists in the Renaissance. This image of a husband and wife
shows both the quality of her work and the modest commissions she was
often limited to. The rest of the collection reflects the highly dramatic
tastes of the seventeenth century and the increasing Spanish influence
on the Italian nobility.

The Piazza del Collegio Romano, like many others in Rome's historic
center, has been gobbled up by the city's insatiable appetite for parking
spaces. The thickly packed ranks of cars are overlooked by the long
façade of the Collegio Romano, the Jesuit school that was founded in
1582 by Pope Gregory XIII. Secularized in the nineteenth century, the
school continues in use today. Gregory XIII, one of the great reforming
popes of the sixteenth century, worked to institutionalize the policies of
the Council of Trent, themselves reactions to the Protestant revolution of
the early sixteenth century. In addition to reforming the clergy and the
papal administration, Gregory supported the foundation of schools and
colleges throughout Catholic areas of Europe. His aim was to educate
men for the priesthood who would both carry out the reformation of the

Catholic Church and combat the Protestant enemy through preaching and teaching. He recognized in the Jesuits an organization ideally suited to these twin goals.

Severe and unadorned, the façade of the Collegio Romano reflects the austere spirit of St. Ignatius, who lobbied for its establishment, and the purgative zeal of the Counter-Reformation. Divided into three blocks with the central one projecting and crowned by an additional story, the plain plaster façade defies the conventional vocabulary of ornament. (117) The first and second stories, divided by a thin string course, are of a piece with their identical window frames and square mezzanine windows; there is no piano nobile to be distinguished by its richer ornament and larger windows. The division into bays is rudimentary, with flat projections from the plaster wall serving in place of pilasters.

Piazza Santissimi Apostoli on the far side of the Corso is completely surrounded by the palaces of prominent Roman noble families: the Colonna, Odescalchi, Ruffo, and Salviati. While most European cities have an abundance of squares like this in districts where the nobility created enclaves for themselves, Rome does not. Roman palaces tend to

blend in and become part of the complex and socially diverse fabric of the city, and so it is a little quieter and chillier in this aristocratic ghetto than elsewhere.

The Galleria Colonna offers a view of the life of rich and powerful Romans in the eighteenth and nineteenth cen-

117

turies—a way of life that in this palace continues into the present day. The star of the show here is the Grand Salon, with its ensemble of paintings, sculpture, frescoes, and fine furniture. This huge room is an intact and highly polished piece of the good life. What makes it so captivating is not the quality of distinct objects but the symphonic impression they make in combination, and above all the condition of everything. The Doria Pamphili, the Galleria Spada, and the Palazzo Corsini all have better art, but the rooms in those palaces look run down. In the Colonna Palace everything is polished, and that glow gives the room vitality and energy. An unplanned highlight of the Grand Salon is the iron cannonball half buried in one of the marble steps leading into this room. The ball was fired from a French cannon during the siege of 1849 which ended the Roman Republic and gave Pope Pius IX twenty more years of control over the city.

The Corso Vittorio Emanuele II was the most ambitious and most disruptive project of the new national government in Rome. It served two purposes that were somewhat at odds. It was meant to create a wide artery for traffic linking the Vatican and Campo Marzio to the Via del Corso and Via Nazionale at Piazza Venezia. Its second purpose was to serve as a great ceremonial avenue. Its route was designed to collect and display the most significant monuments of the region to the best advantage. Historic preservation in the modern sense was not, however, one of its goals. There was no interest in saving buildings that did not rank as monuments, and there was no attention given to the integrity of historic communities. Buildings of secondary interest were razed. The roadway, some sixty feet wide, divided a historically unified community down the

118

center. As much as it eased traffic through the area, it created an enormous barrier to traffic *within* it. (118)

Not far from the Piazza Venezia the first leg of the new roadway, called the Via del Plebiscito, passes the Piazza del Gesù. The church of the Santissimo Nome di Gesù (The Most Sacred Name of Jesus), known simply as Il Gesù, is Rome's center for the most powerful Counter-Reformation religious order, the Society of Jesus. St. Ignatius Loyola, the founder of the order, and his small band of followers lived nearby from 1538 until the saint's death in 1556. Plans for the church were already under way within a decade of the society's official recognition in 1540, but financial problems and the difficulty of piecing together an adequate building lot in Rome's crowded center slowed the project. With the sponsorship of Cardinal Alexander Farnese and the substitution of his architect, Vignola, for the order's own architect, the project began to take shape in the last third of the six-teenth century. Vignola's plan for the church combined the central plan of Bramante's and Michelangelo's St. Peter's with the more traditional long nave of the Roman basilica. The hybrid he created not only became the norm for Jesuit churches throughout Europe and the New World but also influenced Maderno's remodeling of St. Peter's itself. Vignola's pro-jected façade for the new church did not suit Cardinal Farnese, however, and a design by Giacomo della Porta replaced it.

A hybrid, too, like the church's interior, Della Porta's façade blends

traditional features of the Alberti-style Renaissance church, like Santa
Maria del Popolo, with Mannerist elements to create a new synthesis.
(119) The two-story façade with its scroll work and pediment reflect
Renaissance traditions, but both the scale of the building and its ornamentation are new. Although they do not unite the two stories, as Sangallo might have done, the magnified travertine columns and pilasters
suggest a Mannerist sensibility. This is especially true in the central bay,
where two small temple fronts, or aedicula, which have been compressed
into the façade, expand the doorway so far beyond its normal proportions
that it thrusts through the cornice separating the two stories. Architectural historians point to this weighting of the center, which is supported
by the modest decoration of the two adjacent bays, as a step toward
Baroque centralizing.

The fabric of the church's interior remains faithful to Vignola's plan,
but its opulent decoration most emphatically
does not. The wide and relatively short nave is
flanked by three pairs of side chapels. The
pilasters supporting the vaulted roof have been
absorbed by the walls that separate the nave
from these chapels, and so the dominant center
space appears open and unobstructed. The focus
of attention is the high altar, which is set directly
beneath the dome and flooded with light.

This plan would have been even more evident
in the seventeenth century, when the building
was completed. In that period of austerity and

119

purification in the Catholic Church, the interior was almost entirely white and gray. Gray travertine capitals and bases set off the columns; their shafts and the vault above were white plaster. The more opulent side chapels had little effect on the overall impression of clarity and simplicity. By the end of the seventeenth century, however, the spiritual temper had changed, and the Jesuits had come to believe that the order's message demanded the overpowering rhetoric of abundance. The church was embellished in every conceivable way. Today it remains a massive treasure vault teeming with colored marbles, gilded ornament, sculptures in

120

stucco and marble, and some of the most acrobatic painting in Rome. While its gaudy decoration threatens to overwhelm the eye, in isolated areas a masterful sense of harmony and proportion manages to gather this cloying array into an ensemble. (120)

The vault of the nave, which combines gilded stucco, ornamental stucco, and illusionistic painting, is a singular example of such a harmony. Painted by Baciccia between 1676 and 1690, with stucco work by Antonio Raggi, the subject is the *Triumph of the Name of Jesus*. The ensemble combines scenes that appear to be in the sky above with figures perched on clouds inside the building or tumbling toward its floor. Indebted, like all such creations, to Michelangelo's Sistine Chapel, the ceiling does away with the divisions that compart-

mentalize his fictive space. Whether embossed, painted, or sculpted, the
entire vault is treated as a single vista. The gilded architecture with its
familiar arched window openings and ribbing may seem to provide a real
anchor against which the painted figures can be measured, but the architecture itself is a fiction. Effulgent light bursts from the depth of sky
above and resolves into a circle of dancing cherubs. The light strikes figures further down the sky and more differentiated; some float just above
the lozenge-shaped opening in the ceiling, while others drift along below
it. The clouds these figures sit on are dark beneath, and they cast long
shadows on the gilded coffers and rosettes. At the end nearest the
altar—so near the prize—a writhing cluster of the damned turn from the
light which wounds their eyes and hurtle in gathering darkness toward
the floor.

Intensely dramatic in the best tradition of Baroque art, a finely tuned
and carefully managed illusion, the ceiling is supreme spiritual theater.
It achieves what religious artists since the beginning of the Renaissance
had aimed for: to make the invisible and imperceptible real and concretely present. The harmony of this superb fiction, which derives from a
single idea just as its composition grows from a single point of light, is
more than the rest of the interior can live up to. The end chapel of the
right crossing is dedicated to St. Ignatius Loyola, whose body is entombed
in its altar. Intended to display a harmony of precious materials and the
decorative arts, the chapel represents the Baroque as a spectacle of
blunt excess without wit or imagination. Golden columns with lapus lazuli
fluting surround a niche where a silver statue of the founder spreads his
arms while attendant angels dance around it. Gilded bronze panels below

display scenes from his life. A broken pediment of jade-green bronze embraces the Trinity above. Stuccoed saints look on from every side, while the good aspire to grace and the wicked are driven into darkness.

The Palazzo Cenci Bolognetti closes the piazza. It was built in the mid-eighteenth century for a family of successful doctors and legal experts. Its prestigious site along the former papal procession route and the prominence of the building both suggest that Roman society was open to important but non-noble families. The palazzo's rusticated lower story with monumental entryway is divided by the pedestals of pilasters that extend through the two upper stories, which they subdivide into five bays. In each of the three central bays there is a single window on each story; in the side bays they are paired. Above their ornate capitals, a frieze disguising mezzanine windows supports a cornice and balustrade. Since 1946 the building has been the headquarters of Italy's most prominent postwar political party, the Christian Democrats. Repeatedly targeted by the Red Brigades of the 1970s, the party was devastated when Aldo Moro, its leader and a former prime minister, was kidnapped. His body was later dropped in the nearby Via delle Botteghe Oscure.

The church of Sant'Andrea della Valle, designed and redesigned by a number of architects over nearly a century, is better known as a setting for *Tosca* than for its daily life as a major Roman church. Sponsored by the Theatine religious order to gain visibility on the Via Papale and to rival Il Gesù, its slow completion, which reflected repeated financial crises in the less popular organization, made it something of an anachronism. Completed in the age of Bernini and Borromini, it reflects the taste of the late sixteenth century. The façade was designed by Maderno and carried out with some modifications by Rainaldi. Alberti-style scrolls link its upper and lower stories, which are separated by a heavy cornice; pilasters in both zones create vertical continuity, as do the blind niches and the pediments of the door, central window, and gable above.

In 1883 selective demolition for the Corso Vittorio Emanuele II began between the Piazza del Gesù and Sant'Andrea della Valle. The second phase of building a year later again followed the ceremonial route of the Via Papale from Sant'Andrea toward the Chiesa Nuova. In addition to the demolition of buildings deemed insignificant, monuments along this stretch of the road were themselves modified. Part of the Cancelleria was taken down; the Palazzo Farnesina ai Baullari, home of the Museo Barracco, was reduced in size and given a new façade. Buildings near the new street were demolished to open vistas toward nearby monuments.

The Via Papale originally passed behind the Chiesa Nuova, but nineteenth-century planners preferred the façade. They removed buildings near the church and enlarged the square in front. From there the road continued to its intersection with the Via Paolo. At first, traffic to the Vatican crossed the Ponte Sant'Angelo. The final link was added in 1926 with the completion of the Victor Emmanuel Bridge.

Like the Gesù and Sant'Andrea della Valle, Santa Maria in Vallicella, better known as the Chiesa Nuova, was designed as the showpiece of a new clerical order. The Oratorians were approved by Pope Gregory XIII in 1575, and they immediately began work on a church close to the Via Papale. The façade, with its massive flattened entryway that breaks through the heavy cornice between its two stories, echoes Il Gesù. The subordination of side bays to center bay follows the same model and

121

introduces an interior originally designed without side
aisles. Before the building
was completed, however,
the walls separating the
side chapels from one
another were cut through;
but despite this change,
the interior is still an
essentially open plan dominated by its nave.

The Oratorian Society was founded by a Florentine priest, later canonized as St. Filippo Neri. A contemporary of the fierce and austere St.
Ignatius Loyola, who lived and died a few blocks away, Neri was a fun-
loving populist devoted to the service of his near neighbors. His order
built Rome's first public library and encouraged popular education. Next
to their mother church, the Oratorians owned a series of buildings in
which they lived and carried out their special missions. These buildings
were redesigned as a single structure by Borromini. Its flexed façade and
reduced scale make it seem to step back from the church. (121) While
Borromini refused to rival the church in scale, he seems to have com-
mented on if not parodied its design. In his façade, complexity, subtlety,
and sly understatement replace monumental assertiveness. Where the
center bay of the church thrust forward and its porch bulged through the
entablature, Borromini's entry on Casa de' Filippini's façade is confined
to the lower story, where it emerges as a slight convexity in a generally

concave surface. In the zone above, the massive window of the church façade is replaced by a small doorway above a semicircular balcony set into a shallow apse with a fictive coffered vault above. The pediment of the church is replaced by a whimsical arched opening—the outline of his famous cherub wings—set above a curved entablature.

The order developed a new kind of sacred music, the oratorio, which incorporated operatic singing and dramas based on sacred themes. Pergolesi wrote the first piece in this form. In the following centuries it became a standard of Baroque music. Borromini designed a special hall inside the Casa de' Filippini, the Oratorio dei Filippini, for presenting the society's performances. Similar in structure to the Chapel of the Re Magi, it is larger and somewhat more subdued. Pilasters break the wall into bays and round off its corners. Along the outer wall, deep frameless mezzanine windows alternate with arched niches beneath a shallow cornice; flat panels fill the bays above. The opposite wall is nearly featureless. A heavy entablature is supported on the pilaster's very unusual capitals. Complexly framed arched windows spring from it; between them the pilasters are crowned by small pedestals from which the flat ribs of the ceiling emerge. They end in an elliptical frame at the center of the shallow vault. The three bays of the end wall are pierced by three entrances: a monumental arched opening in the center and two smaller arches with mezzanine openings above. The cornice continues from the side walls above a balustrade; and a triple gallery, somewhat like a benediction loggia, replaces the sidewall windows. This entry is a variant on several themes. Its three unequal openings recall a Roman triumphal arch; it is also similar to the combination of portal and benediction loggia found at

San Marco and at San Giovanni in Laterano. Its most distinctive features, however, are the extraordinary cornices with which Borromini framed each of the openings.

Borromini also played a part in the creation of Rome's most popular Baroque monument. If the Campo de' Fiori is the city's kitchen, the Piazza Navona is its living room. (122) The vast, elongated piazza stands near the Corso Vittorio Emanuele II on the site of the Stadium of Domitian, a race course donated by the emperor to the Roman people, which opened in 86 AD. Throughout the Middle Ages the infield remained open while houses were built into the grandstands at its edge. In the Renaissance, these modest structures gave way to grander ones. In 1477 the piazza was paved and a public market that had long been held on the Campidoglio moved to it. (The market moved to the Campo de' Fiori in 1867.) On holidays the piazza was the scene of elaborate processions, pageants, and games.

The three fountains that punctuate the piazza were conceived during

the seventeenth century in an effort to harmonize the many independent structures that enclosed the vast space. The southernmost of the three, which is supplied like the rest with water from the Acqua Vergine, was designed by Bernini and built by his

122

assistants. Its central figure is an Ethiopian battling a dolphin. The foun-

tain at the far end of the piazza was designed late in the sixteenth century

but only completed in the nineteenth. The

central fountain is the unquestioned master-

piece of the three. (123)

123

Designed by Bernini and executed by sev-

eral sculptors, the Fountain of the Four

Rivers is a complex monument combining

figural and environmental sculpture with the

crafted flow of water. Though volcanic in ori-

gin, the travertine from which its naturalistic

features are carved looks like a pitted marine

limestone, and the massed ensemble rises

from the center of its wide basin like a wave-

eroded island. Allegorical representations of

the great rivers of the world sit uneasily on projections of the rock: the

Nile (with its head veiled because its source remained undiscovered); the

Danube (124); the Ganges; and the Rio de la Plata. (125) Symbolizing the

Christian inheritance of antique culture, an obelisk like those in the cen-

ter of Piazza San Pietro and Piazza del Popolo towers above.

Like the Trevi fountain, this monument celebrates the triumphant

spread of the life-giving waters of Christian baptism throughout the

world. And like that magnificent fountain or the less successful mostra

of the Acqua Felice, the Four Rivers fountain commemorates a papal gift

of water. The patron of the fountain, Pope Innocent X, whose arms are

prominently displayed beneath the obelisk, commissioned an extension of

124

the ancient Acqua Vergine—the same water celebrated in the Trevi fountain—that emerged here in
the center of Piazza Navona and almost directly in
front of the palazzo of his family, the Pamphili.
The global themes of the Trevi fountain linked to
the nearby papal residence on the Quirinal hill
are displayed in more personal terms here.

Popular tradition interprets Bernini's fountain
as a mocking reply to the façade of Borromini's
Sant'Agnese in Agone directly behind it.

According to legend, Bernini's figures turn away from the façade in hor-
ror, or protect themselves from its fall, or veil their heads to avoid seeing
it. While this view of the fountain is certainly fanciful, the animosity it
reflects was evidently quite real. In his earliest work in Rome—the

Palazzo Barberini—Borromini collabo-
rated with Bernini; but according to the
art historian Paolo Portoghesi, the two
fell out over St. Peter's and competed
for commissions during the rest of their
careers. Bernini, the more traditional of
the two, was far more successful.

Borromini's designs for the church
of Sant'Agnese in Agone were even
more ambitious than the church that
was built. (126) The door and window

125

frames correspond to Borromini's design, but the rounded columns, the
pedimented gable, the modest cornice and attic are formulaic substitu-

tions for his more innovative ideas. In
their defense, however, it should be
noted that these stereotyped features
harmonize with other neoclassical buildings in the piazza. (127) Even with these
equivocations, the church is a striking
and successful building that anchors
Navona and complements Bernini's
fountain.

127

   Borromini's greatest achievement was
in the shaping of the façade. Three of
the church's five vertical bays step back
to form a wide but shallow concavity. His characteristic undulation creates a dynamic rhythm across the façade, but more importantly it opens
the view of the dome. If the center bays were even with the side towers
or, still worse, jutted in front of them, the dome would seem small and
distant. Instead, the blocking wall gives way, and the unimpeded up-
thrust of the dome is freed to echo and extend the vertical axis of the
central fountain.

   Borromini also designed the symmetrical house façades that frame
the church on either side. To the south of the church he built the Palazzo

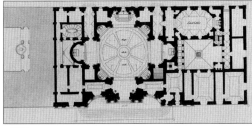

126

Pamphili for Pope
Innocent X. It now
houses the Brazilian
embassy. Despite the
importance of Borromi-
ni's patron, the palace

blends in with the surrounding buildings and carefully avoids rivalry with the church. As a result, its façade is considerably more conventional. This clear subordination of the palace to the church is just the reverse of what was done in the Cancelleria, where the church of San Damaso was absorbed in the cardinal's palace. It suggests not only a different approach to the relation between palace and church but a sense of decorum that harmonizes the entire piazza by a rigorous subordination of all the structures in it to a single focal point. To take up the living room analogy again, it is as if all the furniture were carefully chosen to harmonize with a single prize piece.

The density of building in the Tiber bend meant that many Baroque monuments had to be built into or onto earlier structures. There is no better example of this than the Palazzo della Sapienza, until 1935 the seat of Rome's university. (Since 1935 it has housed the city's archives.) Work on the building began late in the fifteenth century and continued into the seventeenth. The inner courtyard, with its superimposed arcaded porticoes, reflects the style of Bramante, though it was completed a hundred years after his death. The most striking fea-

128

ture of the courtyard, however, is Borromini's University Chapel, Sant'Ivo alla Sapienza. (128)

Borromini made every effort to accommodate his innovative chapel to its conservative setting. The blind arches and inset windows in the gently curved façade replicate the two-story arcade of the courtyard. The corners are crowned with the traditional star and mountains, emblem of the Chigi family. Above the level of the arcade, Borromini began to show both more of his own style and to represent more forthrightly the complex interior space that opens behind the curve of his modest wall. The multiple pilasters that anchor the drum, which are carried up from the stories below, seem hardly able to restrain the bulging mass of its wall. Its convexity contrasts with the gently concave wall beneath, a tension that is carried on inside the chapel. Enormous brackets crowned with abstract finials spring from these pilasters and divide the stepped roof of the dome into sections. The base of the elaborate lantern that crowns the chapel is similar to that of Sant'Andrea delle Fratte: six pairs of columns jut out from concave inner

129

walls. (129) Its deeply notched cornice supports fictive torches and an intriguing helical spire that holds a crown and flame aloft. Above, an openwork cross surmounts a sphere. While interpretations differ, many architectural historians believe the spire replicates an ancient lighthouse. The Light of Knowledge and the Cross of Faith shine from its summit.

In the chapel's interior, concave and convex forms play against one

another in a complex hexagonal plan. Three semicircular recesses alternate with three others whose squared-off sides create the apexes of an
equilateral triangle. Convex walls with deep apses jut from its corners.
Because of the building's radial symmetry (which links it to Bramante's
Tempietto), the interior walls of the chapel pulse in and out in more fas-
cinating and complex ways than those in the oratory. The structure
appears to work in the same way, however; the wall flexes against its
moorings in giant pilasters that bear up an enormous cornice. In the drum
above, the pilasters reappear as ribs that divide the steeply soaring dome
into sections. Ornaments abound in this upper zone; they include the
stars and mountains of the Chigi family and Borromini's beloved seraphs.

The church of San Luigi de' Francesi, the national church of France,
is more celebrated for the paintings in one of its chapels than for any
other characteristic. The façade, designed by Domenico Fontana and others, is undistinguished. The Contarelli Chapel to the left of the main
altar, however, contains three magnificent paintings by Caravaggio. These
include *The Calling of St. Matthew, The Saint and Angel,* and *The
Martyrdom.* Less constricted than the chapel in Santa Maria del Popolo
that is dedicated to Peter and Paul, the paintings here, despite the violence of the saint's struggles, are more meditative. The most serene and
the most conventional of the three is the portrait above the altar; it
replaced an earlier rejected version. The saint writes his Gospel while his
angelic inspiration, hovering in the air above, ticks off the points of the
narration on his fingers. The vocation scene, in which a group of gor-
geously dressed young Romans cluster around a table, is more dramatic.
Jesus enters the room from the same direction as the band of light that

illuminates the figures and extends his arm in a gesture that recalls Michelangelo's hand of God in the Sistine ceiling. He points to Matthew, the moneychanger, who echoes the gesture as if to be certain that he is the one. In the manner of allegorical paintings familiar from the Middle Ages on, the group in the small room is divided in its response. The two younger figures turn toward Christ as if choosing him with their eyes and their gestures. Two other figures remain focused on the heap of gold coins on the counting table.

While Caravaggio has completely domesticated this scene of spiritual choice, *The Martyrdom of St. Matthew* takes place in a symbolic space where violence and salvation contend. The fallen saint, already stabbed by the howling figure above, lies at the brink of a deep abyss. He reaches for the palm branch an angel offers him, while his persecutor tries to force him into the pit. The vortex of surrounding figures recalls the stunned apostles in Raphael's *Transfiguration.*

The church of Sant'Agostino stands at the top of a monumental flight of stairs. Designed in the early Renaissance, the travertine façade features a curious cornice, vast Alberti-style scrolls, and a jumble of incised, space-filling circles and rectangles. The church was a favorite of Renaissance artists: Raphael painted a magnificent image of the Prophet Isaac on the third pillar of the nave; Sansovino sculpted the figure known as the *Madonna del Parto* (Our Lady of Birth) near the main entrance. The most celebrated object in the church, however, is Caravaggio's *Madonna dei Pellegrini* (Our Lady of the Pilgrims; also known as *Madonna di Loreto*). According to medieval legend, the Virgin's Galilean house was miraculously transported to Loreto in central Italy, where it became a popular pilgrimage center. In Caravaggio's painting, the Virgin stands on the threshold of that house, with a very robust infant Jesus cradled in her arms. Two pilgrims kneel in adoration at her feet. The nude infant, the barefoot Madonna, and especially the pilgrims, who belong to the lowest peasant caste, caused considerable scandal in the seventeenth century. The kneeling man's dirty feet were especially offensive. Such figures had no place in the fanciful Nazareth of High Church art.

The Palazzo Montecitorio is home to the lower house of the Italian Parliament, the Chamber of Deputies. Bernini designed the massive structure for the Ludovisi family; in the late seventeenth century, the still incomplete palace was redesigned to house the papal law courts. At the top of sloping Piazza Montecitorio, the curved façade is impressive but not overpowering. Its three stories, separated by narrow cornices, are broken into five vertical sections that are marked off by massive pilasters. The central section, which juts out, was given further emphasis in the remodeling by the addition of a triple arched gateway and a gabled belfry. The pilasters on the end sections are supported by massive rusticated blocks, as if the finished building emerged from rough stone. While the Italian Parliament debated plans for a new government center, it gradually came to feel at home here in its temporary quarters. A large and ungainly addition at the back of the palazzo faces the Piazza del Parlamento. The obelisk at the lower limit of the piazza once served as the gnomon of the vast sundial Augustus erected in the Campus Martius.

The Piazza Colonna opens from the crowded Corso on the side toward the Campo Marzio. With no restaurants or bars around it and closed to traffic, it seems lifeless. Briefly targeted in the late nineteenth century and again by Mussolini as a gateway to the area—both projects were abandoned—the piazza remains much as it was in the eighteenth century. The Column of Marcus Aurelius stands in its center. Erected in the late third century AD, the column commemorates victories of an emperor better known for his Stoic *Meditations* than for his military campaigns. In a continuous frieze that circles twenty times as it rises to the capital ninety feet above, the column tells the story of two military campaigns. The lower half records Roman victories against the Germans; the upper half celebrates victories in the Balkans. These victories did little to stem the threat of Germanic invasion or to calm the fears of the Romans; the Aurelian wall, which was built at the same time, was designed to protect the city against the very German tribes whose "conquest" the column celebrates. When Dante came to Rome in 1300, he was very impressed with the scenes on the column. The ascending multitudes reminded him of crowds of souls slowly scaling the mountain of purgatory while they cleanse themselves of sin. The base of the column and the figure of the Roman emperor at its summit were replaced in 1588. The figure on top is now St. Paul.

The Palazzo Aldobrandini-Chigi dominates the north side of the piazza and continues around the corner onto the Corso. Begun in the late sixteenth century, the palace with its three-tiered façade (the fourth attic story was added much later) is a modest reworking of the Palazzo Farnese ideal. The backstop of the Piazza Colonna is the Palazzo Wedekind, which was built in the early nineteenth century to house the Papal Post Office. It is a confused blend of revived building types that in the Renaissance served distinct purposes. Its portico of reused antique columns supports a terrace of the kind that might be found on a suburban villa. Behind is a façade loosely based on the Palazzo Farnese, with an anomalous clock above.

Designed by the Neapolitan architect Filippo Raguzzini in the early eighteenth century, Piazza di Sant'Ignazio arranges simple spare buildings in very imaginative ways to create an extraordinary space. Raguzzini's main task was to design an urban complement to the dominating façade of the church of St. Ignazio. Using simple materials, which lowered rental cost and speeded construction, he created five modest four-story blocks with commercial space at ground level and apartments for rent in the upper three. The charm of the piazza comes from the intricate fitting together of the side palazzi with their curved fronts and pilaster-like corners. These flank a wedge-shaped building with curved façade and a jutting central bay behind which two of the many streets that enter the piazza converge. The piazza, which is relatively free of traffic, is a charming rococo parlor in the heart of the city.

The church of Sant'Ignazio, designed in 1626 by Orazio Grassi, the architect of the Jesuit Order, imitates Il Gesù. Though somewhat higher, the façade is both similar and less innovative. Its doubled pilasters and soaring porch are toned-down versions of the earlier church. And unlike Il Gesù, its side bays have doors with blind windows above that diminish the centralizing force of the original. The open interior, with its wide nave, three chapels per side, a crossing and deep apse, reflect Vignola's plan. Grassi's design called for a dome which the taller structure could not support. A trompe l'oeil painting on canvas by Andrea Pozzo was substituted.

With fewer windows in the nave and without the light from the dome, the interior of the church is gloomy. In the vault of the nave is a subdued version, also by Pozzo, of Baciccia's extravagant *Triumph.* Here there is no gold or ornamental stucco work; the spatial illusion is created entirely by paint. The real architecture of the church below appears to extend up into a clouded sky. Christ, the source of light in the composition, floats at its apex veiled in mist. Slightly below, surrounded by angels, St. Ignatius stands on a cloud. Jesuit priests in black robes are scattered through the composition, which depicts the missionary work of the order and its spread to all the regions of the world. Allegorical figures between windows are labeled with the names of continents.

There are two stones on the floor for viewing the perspective correctly, one for each end of the nave. In Pozzo's treatise on drawing the classical orders of architecture in perspective, he showed how he had drawn and then transcribed the design for the ceiling onto the vault. He also reported that he loved the experience of walking around the nave and looking at the architecture obliquely before crossing to one of the focal points and having the ceiling snap into correct perspective. It made him feel that the roof had suddenly given way and that the architecture had established a link between earth and heaven.

The fate of Rome, which once rested in the hands of popes and emperors, has for the last century and more relied on the will of national and municipal governments. Those governments have a spotty history of maintaining the city's enormous patrimony of monuments and keeping them open to the public. Throughout the past century, most monuments were open four or five mornings a week at most. Makeshift barriers within them all too often proclaimed wings and galleries in restauro, closed for restoration. In the 1970s and 1980s, organized terror, first by the Red Brigades, then by the Mafia, forced the closure of additional monuments for reasons of security.

As the millennium approached, the city and the nation reversed these long-term trends. (130) Major collections like the vast sculpture holdings of the Museo Nazionale Romano were moved; renewed excavations in the

Forum and on the Palatine began the opening of a vast archaeological park in the center of town. Monuments like the Tabularium, the Vittoriano, and the Domus Aurea, some closed for decades, were opened again to

130

the public. Museum hours were extended, and admission prices—especially for citizens of countries outside the European Union—grew to levels adequate to fund maintenance and restoration. (131) Much of this effort focused on the Jubilee Year, 2000. As the memory of that event fades, however, the question remains: will the national and city governments be able to continue what they have started? Having assumed control over so much, will they have the energy and resources to maintain, restore, and staff it all, or will the in restauro signs of the bad old days return?

The evidence is unclear. The projected archaeological park at the center of town requires the closing of a major artery, the Via dei Fori Imperiali. Plans were long ago made for the road's demolition, but beyond a
regular Sunday closing of the avenue to traffic, nothing has been done.
Pedestrian-only areas color much of the map of Rome's historic center,
but these areas do not exclude delivery vans and the ubiquitous buzzing,
swooping motorinos. Taxis and the increasingly common multi-passenger
vans of tour companies also have free access to them. Its apparent clarity
notwithstanding, "Pedestrians only" is a murky condition. Each year,
despite inflated gasoline prices and a system of efficient buses, trams,
and subways, Rome has more and bigger cars. Automobile access to the
historic center is by permit only, and parking downtown is diminishing,
but the pressure increases. The transformation of the Piazza del Parlamento into an upscale carpark suggests that many of those addicted
to the Saabs, Audis, and Mercedes that plow the
streets are the very ones who write the laws restrict-
ing their use.

Rome has always had graffitti, though in the
past it has been dogmatically political. Tagging of
the New York and LA variety has hit the Metro system hard, and many public buildings are now
scrawled with blubbery initials. Scratching bus
windows is another current fad. Litter is ubiquitous, far beyond the energies of the isolated spaz-
zini in green and white coveralls who patiently
sweep it up with witches' brooms.

131

Broader trends threaten, too. Rome's historic center is being internationalized at an unprecedented pace. Her local industries, especially the ring of small farms that provide fresh produce year round, may well be threatened by the increasing economic integration of Europe. Ten years from now, one hundred years from now, a thousand years from now, what will Rome be like? The enormous swath of time through which the city has already lived forces planners and politicians to think on that almost geological scale.

INFORMATION

While this book stands on its own as a portrait of the city, its format and organization also make *Rome from the Ground Up* a useful guide for travelers. Because of its central idea—that Rome is a series of contiguous rather than concentric and overlapping cities—the book is able to present the city in a way that coheres in space and time. Generally speaking, each period in Rome's long history is represented by a different part of the city and by a separate chapter of the book. Within each historically ordered chapter, monuments follow a sequence that is chronological, but not rigidly so, in order that monuments can be grouped by location. Monuments that have not survived in some fashion have, for the most part, been left out of the book. As a result, the book presents the city both historically and in a series of coherent physical links that are easily followed on the ground. Each chapter is, in effect, an itinerary that a visitor can follow with the aid of a map.

The itinerary begins at Tiber Island, circles the adjacent neighborhood—the site of Rome's ancient port—and ends at the Vico Jugario, which leads to the Roman Forum. Chapter 2 describes the monuments of the Senate end of the Roman Forum, beginning with the Basilica Aemilia near the main entrance. It makes a counter-clockwise circuit of the monuments on the fringes of the Forum, then continues up the Sacra Via past the Regia, the Vestal complex, and the Basilica of Maxentius, to end at the Arch of Titus. Chapter 3 begins just beyond the Arch of Titus at the entrance to the Palatine. It circles the hill, exploring the remains of Augustus' house and the ruins of Domitian's palace. Leaving the Palatine, it explores the Golden House of Nero, the Colosseum, the Market of Trajan, and the imperial fora that augmented the traditional government center. Ranging further afield, it considers the Pantheon and the collections of Roman antiquities once housed in the Baths of Diocletian.

Chapter 4 on Early Christian churches begins in the majestic basilica of Santa Maria Maggiore, not far from the Baths of Diocletian. It describes two other churches in that immediate area, then begins a broad clockwise sweep that embraces the great imperial basilicas on the fringes of the ancient city. This circuit takes in San Giovanni in Laterano and other churches on the Celian hill, then moves to the Aventine before crossing the Tiber to the great churches of Trastevere. Chapter 5 begins a short distance upriver from Trastevere in Vatican City. It looks at St. Peter's, the Vatican Palace, and the Vatican museums.

At the beginning of Chapter 6, the itinerary backtracks a bit in the direction of Trastevere but veers left, crossing the Ponte Sisto and entering Rome's Renaissance quarter, the Campo Marzio, where it examines the urban planning and the great palaces of that era. Chapter 7 chronicles the development of inland territories away from the Tiber. The itinerary begins at the Trevi fountain, climbs the Quirinal hill, then leaves the ancient circuit of the city walls to visit the Borghese gardens and museum. It returns to the city at the Piazza del Popolo and traces the three great

streets that defined and oriented Rome from the Baroque through the
nineteenth century as well as the Spanish Steps. The final chapter focuses
on the very center of Rome from Piazza Venezia along the line of the
Corso Vittorio Emanuele II, then through a circuit of Baroque monuments
back to the Corso. In following its historic course, the book ends very
near where it began at no great distance from Tiber Island.

Energy, interest, weather, and accessibility are all, of course, quite
variable. What one visitor finds absorbing, another finds uninteresting or
unbearable; what should be open may be closed, or hidden under scaffolding; heat, cold, rain, and the inevitable strikes make every day a little
uncertain. With the exception of the itinerary described in the first chapter, which is relatively short and includes fewer monuments than most, it
is probably safe to say that a chapter represents about the maximum that
can be seen in a day. While the book assumes that most of the itineraries
will be followed on foot, Rome's public transportation is very reliable,
comfortable, and wide-ranging. There is every reason to use it to reach
those monuments on the fringes of the city or those like Sant'Agnese and
Santa Costanza that are outside the ancient circuit of walls.

A major difference between this book and guidebooks to Rome is the
absence of practical aids. There is nothing about ordering a cappuccino,
choosing a hotel, or changing money. In the age of Starbucks, the Internet, and the euro, however, these are not serious deficiencies. Nor is
there any of the information that guidebooks typically offer about museum
openings and closings, current exhibitions, admission charges, and reservations. Information on these matters is ephemeral and changes quickly;
hours and charges detailed in a guide only a few years old will not be

reliable. Typically publishers keep up by issuing revised guides every few years. But of course Rome's monuments and museums do not change, even if their hours and special exhibits do. Reissuing guidebooks to keep up with such changes is no longer the most effective approach, since information of this kind is readily available online.

During the telephone age, Italy was a Third World country. But today, cell phones, faxes, and especially the Internet have enabled the nation, like many others that were held back by intractable infrastructures, to vault ahead. Italy—especially Rome, the national capital—is now as well represented on the World Wide Web as New York or Los Angeles. A large and ever-increasing roster of Italian websites—many featuring English translation—keeps tabs on the archaeology, art, and museology of the city. These nicely designed and well-maintained sites stay up-to-date, and so they are especially useful for travelers who need accurate information about what is on display; what hours museums and sites are open; and whether reservations or advance tickets are required. The website of the Commune di Roma—accessible in English—is the best general source of information on museums and monuments.

In Rome itself, the Office of Tourism staffs eleven information kiosks open seven days a week from 9:30 a.m. to 7:30 p.m. Two are located at the central train station (one inside at Track 4; the other outside on Piazza dei Cinquecento). Another is a short distance away on Via Nazionale near the Palazzo delle Esposizioni. About the same distance away in the opposite direction, another kiosk is located near the basilica of Santa Maria Maggiore. Other locations include Castel Sant'Angelo near the Vatican and Piazza Sonino in Trastevere. There is one in Piazza delle

Cinque Lune just outside Piazza Navona, one near the Mausoleum of
Augustus, and another centrally located on Via Minghetti near the Trevi
fountain. The remaining kiosks are found near the imperial fora (Piazza
del Tempio della Pace) and at San Giovanni in Laterano. Questions in
English are graciously answered by the people who staff the kiosks. The
weekly guide called *Romac'é* (pronounced Roma-Chay) is sold at news-
stands for about a dollar. Its listings in Italian are exhaustive; its closing
pages offer current information in English.

FURTHER READING

Ackerman, James S. *The Architecture of Michelangelo*. Baltimore: Penguin
    Books, 1971.

Aicher, Peter J. *Rome Alive: A Source Guide to the Ancient City*, 2 vols.
    Wauconda, IL: Bolchazy-Carducci, 2004.

Argan, Giulio Carlo. *The Renaissance City*, trans. Susan E. Bassnett. New
    York: G. Braziller, 1970.

Benoist, Philippe. *Grandezza di Roma*. Rome: Nuova editrice romana, 1988.

Blunt, Anthony. *Guide to Baroque Rome*. New York: Harper and Row, 1982.

Brentano, Robert. *Rome before Avignon*. Berkeley: University of California
    Press, 1991.

Coarelli, Filippo. *Roma*. Guide archeologiche Mondadori, 3rd ed. Milan:
    Mondadori, 1997.

Grundmann, Stefan. *The Architecture of Rome*. Stuttgart: Axel Menges, 1998.

Hibbard, Howard. *Bernini*. Baltimore: Penguin, 1966.

———. *Caravaggio*. New York: Harper and Row, 1983.

Hopkins, Keith, and Mary Beard. *The Colosseum*. Cambridge: Harvard
    University Press, 2005.

Insolera, Italo, and Francesco Perego. *Archeologia e Città*. Rome: Laterza,
    1983.

Kleiner, Diana E. E. *Cleopatra and Rome*. Cambridge: Harvard University
    Press, 2005.

Kostof, Spiro. *The Third Rome, 1870–1950: Traffic and Glory*. Berkeley:
    University of California Art Museum, 1973.

Krautheimer, Richard. *Rome: Profile of a City, 312–1308.* Princeton: Princeton University Press, 1980.

Letarouilly, Paul Marie. *Édifices de Rome moderne; ou, Recueil des palais, maisons, églises, couvents et autres monuments publics et particuliers les plus remarquables de la ville de Rome.* 3 vols. in 1. Princeton: Princeton Architectural Press, 1982.

McDonald, William L. *The Pantheon: Design, Meaning and Progeny.* Cambridge: Harvard University Press, 2002.

———. *Architecture of the Roman Empire,* 2 vols. New Haven: Yale University Press, 1982–1986.

McGregor, James H. S. *Venice from the Ground Up.* Cambridge: Harvard University Press, 2006.

Platner, Samuel B., and Thomas Ashby. *A Topographical Dictionary of Ancient Rome.* Oxford: Oxford University Press, 2002.

Portoghesi, Paolo. *Rome of the Renaissance,* trans. Pearl Sanders. London: Phaidon, 1972.

———. *The Rome of Borromini: Architecture as Language,* trans. Barbara Luigi La Penta. New York: Braziller, 1968.

———. *Roma Barocca: The History of an Architectonic Culture,* trans. Barbara Luigia La Penta. Cambridge: MIT Press, 1970.

Rowland, Ingrid D. *The Culture of the High Renaissance.* Cambridge: Cambridge University Press, 1998.

Story, William Wetmore. *Roba di Roma.* Boston: Houghton Mifflin, 1894.

ACKNOWLEDGMENTS

My wife, Sallie Spence, who knows Roma backwards and forwards, has been this book's unfailing advocate through many identities. Our son, Ned, was a wonderful partner as I revisited the monuments described in it; my son Raphael—whose name tells so much of the story—has been a constant supporter. Many friends and colleagues have shared their thoughts and insights as the work developed over the years, starting with those at the American Academy in Rome who planted the seed. Joel M. Babb set me straight on Pozzo; Allan Forsyth and Skip Burck were always solicitous and enthusiastic; and my colleague Betty Jean Craige, Director of the Center for Humanities and Arts, helped with the illustrations. I would also like to express my thanks to Susan Sills and Spruill Harder of the Fine Arts Library at Harvard, to Jennifer Hughes of the Harvard University Art Museums, and to David Cobb of the Harvard Map Collection for their assistance. Anonymous readers of the manuscript contributed valuable corrections and suggestions. Joe Beck offered essential advice and a priceless introduction. And Wendy Strothman steered me through unsettled and unfamiliar waters. At Harvard University Press, I thank Lindsay Waters and Thomas Wheatland for their faith in the book, Jill Breitbarth and David Foss for their design and production expertise, and Ian Stevenson and Phoebe Kosman for editorial assistance. I am especially indebted to Susan Wallace Boehmer for the imagination and energy which remade the book from the ground up and gave it wings.

ILLUSTRATION CREDITS

Clifford Boehmer / Harvard University Press: 3, 5, 7, 9, 10, 11, 13, 14, 15, 16, 17, 18, 19, 20, 21, 22, 23, 24, 25, 26, 28, 31, 32, 33, 34, 35, 36, 40, 41, 42, 45, 49, 51, 52, 53, 54, 55, 56, 57, 58, 60, 61, 63, 64, 65, 66, 67, 68, 70, 71, 72, 73, 77, 78, 83, 85, 86, 87, 91, 94, 95, 96, 97, 98, 99, 100, 101, 102, 103, 104, 106, 108, 109, 114, 116, 119, 120, 121, 123, 124, 125, 127, 128, 129, 130, 131; pp. iii, 1, 315

Édifices de Rome Moderne (1840–1857, Paul Marie Letarouilly): 27, 38, 39, 43, 46, 48, 50, 59, 74, 75, 79, 80, 81, 82, 88, 89, 90, 92, 93, 111, 117, 126

Erich Lessing / Art Resource: 69

Fine Arts Library, Harvard University (etchings by Giovanni Battista Piranesi): 4 *(Ponte Fabricio),* 8 *(Plan of the Temple of Fortuna Virilis),* 12 *(Arcade of the First Order of the Theater of Marcellus)*

Guido Alberto Rossi / TIPS Image: 110, 118

Harvard Map Collection, Harvard College Library: 47 (1551, Leonardo Bufalini); pp. 344–345 (mid-eighteenth-century engraving by Giambattista Nolli of Bufalini's 1551 map); pp. 5, 33, 61, 107, 151, 193, 237 (details from Nolli / Bufalini map)

Isabelle Lewis: Maps 1, 2, 3, 4, 5, 6, 7, 8

Katya Kallsen / Fogg Art Museum, Harvard University Art Museums: 6 (Giovanni Battista Piranesi, *Mouth of the Cloaca Maxima into the*

Tiber, Gift of Mrs. Henry Osborne Taylor in Memory of her father,
William Bradley Isham), 29 (Rossini, *Temple of Mars and Wall of the
Forum of Augustus,* Gift of Belinda L. Randall from the collection of
John Witt Randall), 30 (Piranesi, *View of the Colosseum, interior,
Bird's-eye View,* Gift of William Gray from the collection of Francis
Calley Gray), 37 (Piranesi, *View of the Interior of S. Maria degli Angeli
in the Baths of Diocletian,* Gift of William Gray from the collection of
Francis Calley Gray), 44 (Piranesi, *Interior of S. Costanza,* Gift of
Belinda L. Randall from the collection of John Witt Randall), 62
(Piranesi, *View of the Interior of the Basilica of Saint Peter at the
Vatican,* Loan from the Fine Arts Library, Harvard University), 122
(Piranesi, *View of Piazza Navona above the Ruins of the Circo Agonale,*
Loan from the Fine Arts Library, Harvard University)

Rome dans sa Grandeur: Vues, Monuments Anciens et Moderne (1870,
Philippe Benoist and Felix Benoist,): 2, 107, 115; pp. 346–347
(1867 map); p. 281 (detail from 1867 map)

Scala / Art Resource: 76, 84, 105, 112, 113

TerraServer.com: 1

INDEX

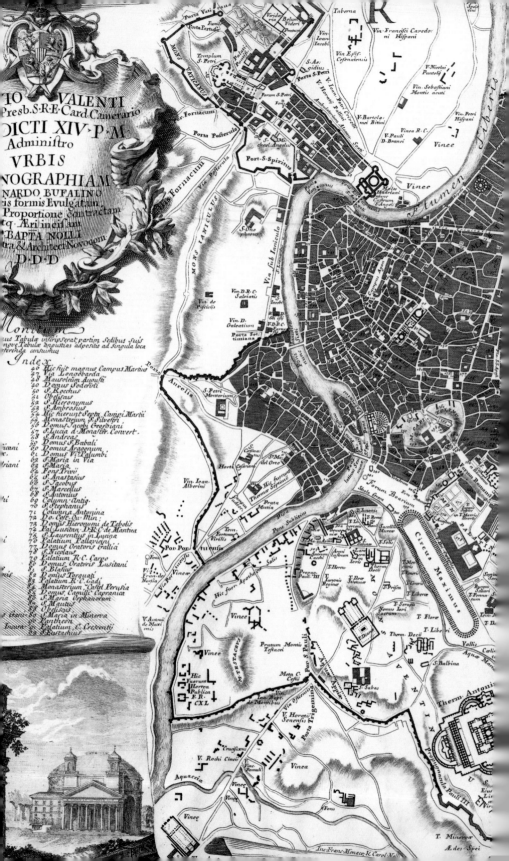

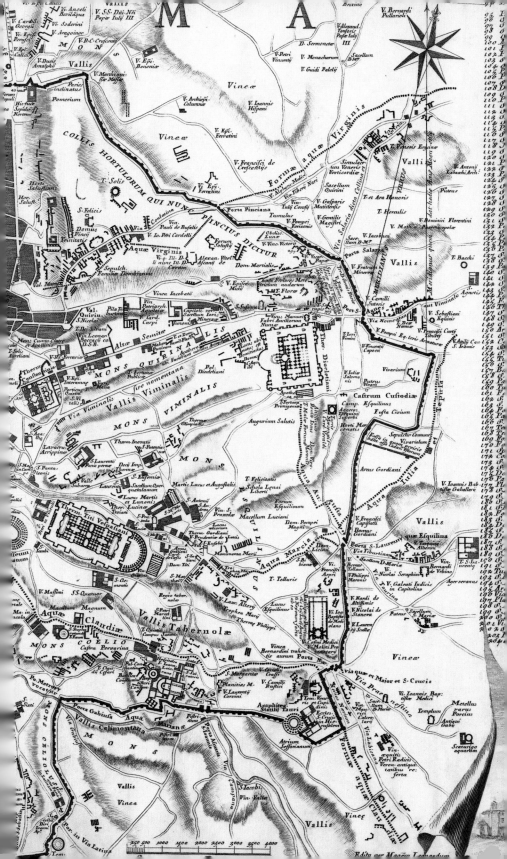

QUARTIERS de ROME
ou RIONI.

I de' Monti
II di Trevi
III di Colonna
IV di Campo Marzo
V di Ponte
VI di Parione

PLAN
de
ROME
MDCCCLXIX.

PINCIO ou Buoncompagni

Villa Ludovisi

Camp Pretorien

Caserne

MONT QUIRINAL

MONT VIMINAL

GARE DU CHEM DE FER

Thermes

Ste Marie Majeure

MONT ESQUILIN

MONT PALATIN

Thermes de Titus
Les 7 Salles

MONT CŒLIUS

Ancien reservoir d'Eau

St Jean Palais Pont de Latran

St Croix de

Thermes de Caracalla

XII

VII   della Regola
VIII   di S. Eustachio
IX   della Pigna
X   di S. Angelo
XI   di Campitelli
XII   di Ripa
XIII   di Trastevere
XIV   di Borgo

ENCEINTES
successives
de
ROME.

Sous Romulus +++++++
Enceinte de 3,000...

En l'an 270
Enceinte de 4,000 de Servius Tullius

Enceinte d'Aurélien..........
en 271 18,000...

Mt Vatican

Mt Janicule

Mt Pincius

Mt Quirinal

Mt Viminal

Mt Esquilin

Mt Capitolin

Mt Cœlius

Mt Palatin

Mt Aventin

Mt Testaccio

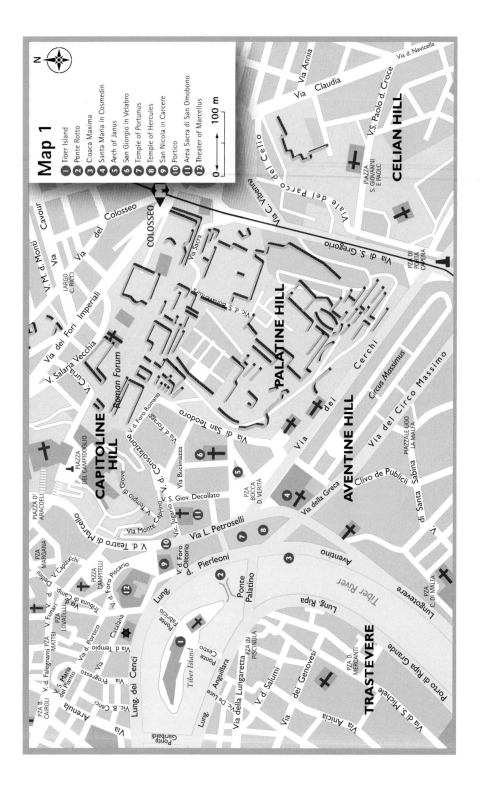

N

Map 1

1 Tiber Island
2 Ponte Rotto
3 Cloaca Maxima
4 Santa Maria in Cosmedin
5 Arch of Janus
6 San Giorgio in Velabro
7 Temple of Portunus
8 Temple of Hercules
9 San Nicola in Carcere
10 Portico
11 Area Sacra di San Omobono
12 Theater of Marcellus

0   100 m

CELIAN HILL

Via d. Navicella

Via Annia

Via Claudia

V. S. Paolo d. Croce

PIAZZA
S. GIOVANNI
E PAOLC

Viale del Parco del Celio

Via C. Vibenna

Via di S. Gregorio

PZA DI
PORTA
CAPENA

Cavour

Via d. Colosseo

COLOSSEO

Via Sacra

V. M. d. Monti

Via

Via

LARGO
C. RICCI

Via dei Fori Imperiali

V. Salaria Vecchia

V. Curia Vecchia

Roman Forum

PALATINE HILL

Cerchi

Circus Massimus

Via del Circo Massimo

PIAZZALE UGO
LA MALFA

AVENTINE HILL

di Santa Sabina

Clivo de Publicii

CAPITOLINE
HILL

PIAZZA
DEL CAMPIDOGLIO

PIAZZA D'
ARACOELI

V. d. Foro Romano

V. d. Foraggi

Via d. Consolazione

V. Tempio di Giove

V. S. Giov. Decollato

Via di San Teodoro

Via Bucimazza

Via dei

Via della Greca

9 6

5

PZA
BOCCA
D. VERITÀ

4

PZA
C. DI MALTA

V.

Vic. Jugaro

11

Via Monte Caprino

Via L. Petroselli

10

7 8

Via d. Teatro di Marcello

PZA
MARGANA

PZA
MATTEI

PZA
LOVATELLI

Via d. Delfini

V. Funari

V. Capizucchi

Tribuna di Campi

PIAZZA
CAMPITELLI

V. d. Foro Piscario

12

d. Foro
d. Olitorio

9

Pierleoni

2

Ponte
Palatino

3

Aventino

Lungotevere

PZA
C. DI MALTA

PZA B.
CAROLI

V. d. Falegnami

PZA
MAITEI

V. S. Maria
del Pianto

Via d. Portico

Catalana

Lung. dei Cenci

Lung.

Ponte
Fabricio

Tiber Island

1

Ponte
Cesto

PZA IN
PISCINULA

Tiber River

Lung. Ripa

TRASTEVERE

Via di S. Michele

Porto di Ripa Grande

PZA D.
MERCANTI

Via dei Genovesi

V. d. Salumi

Via Anicia

Via della Lungaretta

Lung. Anguillara

Vic. De Luce

Ponte
Garibaldi

Via

Vic. B. Cenci

V. Progresso

Arenula

Via d. Tempio

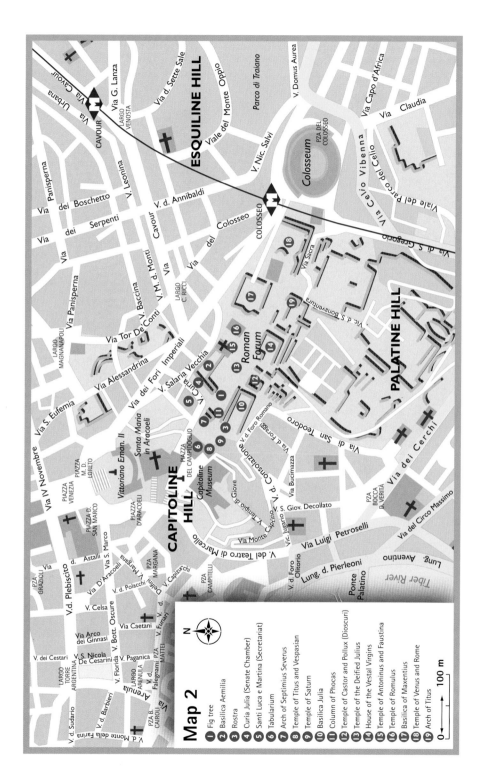

Map 2

- ❶ Fig tree
- ❷ Basilica Aemilia
- ❸ Rostra
- ❹ Curia Julia (Senate Chamber)
- ❺ Santi Luca e Martina (Secretariat)
- ❻ Tabularium
- ❼ Arch of Septimius Severus
- ❽ Temple of Titus and Vespasian
- ❾ Temple of Saturn
- ❿ Basilica Julia
- ⓫ Column of Phocas
- ⓬ Temple of Castor and Pollux (Dioscuri)
- ⓭ Temple of the Deified Julius
- ⓮ House of the Vestal Virgins
- ⓯ Temple of Antoninus and Faustina
- ⓰ Temple of Romulus
- ⓱ Basilica of Maxentius
- ⓲ Temple of Venus and Rome
- ⓳ Arch of Titus

0 ⊢———— 100 m

N

ESQUILINE HILL

Colosseum

PZA DEL COLOSSEO

PALATINE HILL

Roman Forum

CAPITOLINE HILL

Capitoline Museum

Santa Maria in Aracoeli

Vittoriano Eman. II

Tiber River

Parco di Traiano

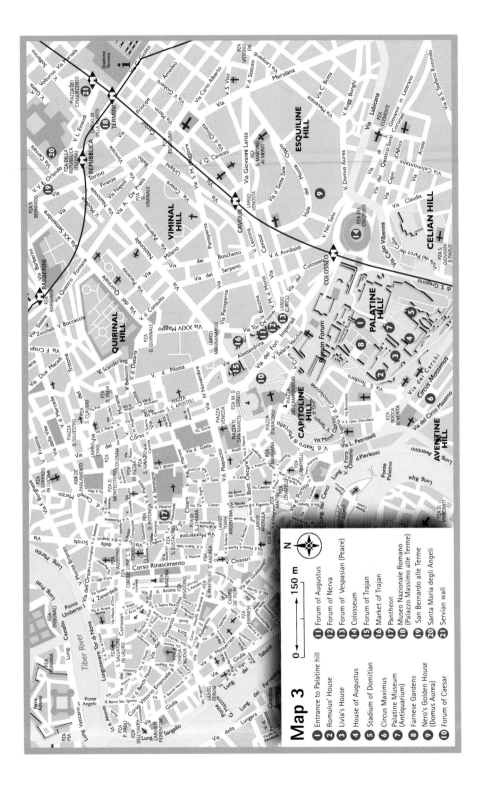

Map 3

0 ——→ 150 m

N

❶ Entrance to Palatine hill
❷ Romulus' House
❸ Livia's House
❹ House of Augustus
❺ Stadium of Domitian
❻ Palatine Museum (Antiquarium)
❼ Farnese Gardens
❽ Nero's Golden House (Domus Aurea)
❾ Forum of Caesar

❿ Forum of Augustus
⓫ Forum of Nerva
⓬ Forum of Vespasian (Peace)
⓭ Colosseum
⓮ Forum of Trajan
⓯ Market of Trajan
⓰ Pantheon
⓱ Museo Nazionale Romano (Palazzo Massimo alle Terme)
⓲ San Bernardo alle Terme
⓳ Santa Maria degli Angeli
⓴ Servian wall

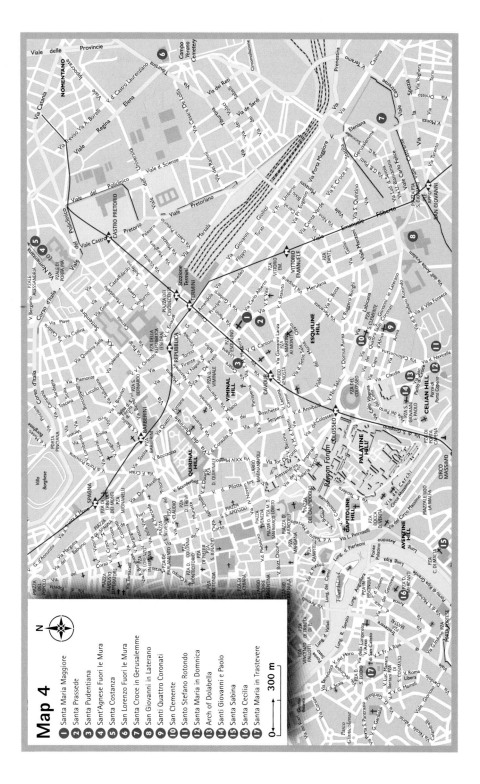

Map 4

1. Santa Maria Maggiore
2. Santa Prassede
3. Santa Pudentiana
4. Sant'Agnese Fuori le Mura
5. Santa Costanza
6. San Lorenzo Fuori le Mura
7. Santa Croce in Gerusalemme
8. San Giovanni in Laterano
9. Santi Quattro Coronati
10. San Clemente
11. Santo Stefano Rotondo
12. Santa Maria in Domnica
13. Arch of Dolabella
14. Santi Giovanni e Paolo
15. Santa Sabina
16. Santa Cecilia
17. Santa Maria in Trastevere

0 ————— 300 m

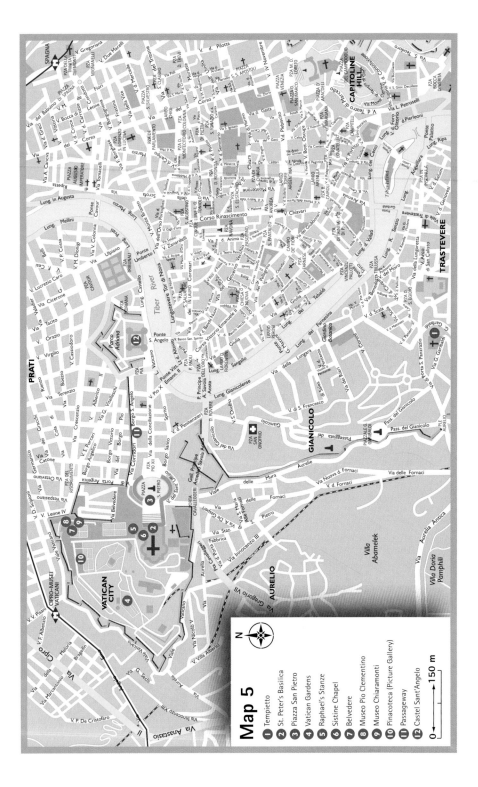

Map 5

1. Tempietto
2. St. Peter's Basilica
3. Piazza San Pietro
4. Vatican Gardens
5. Raphael's Stanze
6. Sistine Chapel
7. Belvedere
8. Museo Pio Clementino
9. Museo Chiaramonti
10. Pinacoteca (Picture Gallery)
11. Passageway
12. Castel Sant'Angelo

0 —————> 150 m

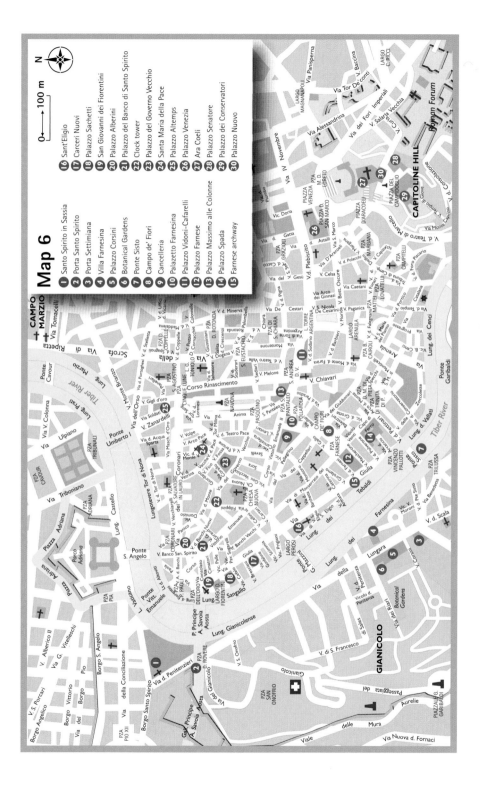

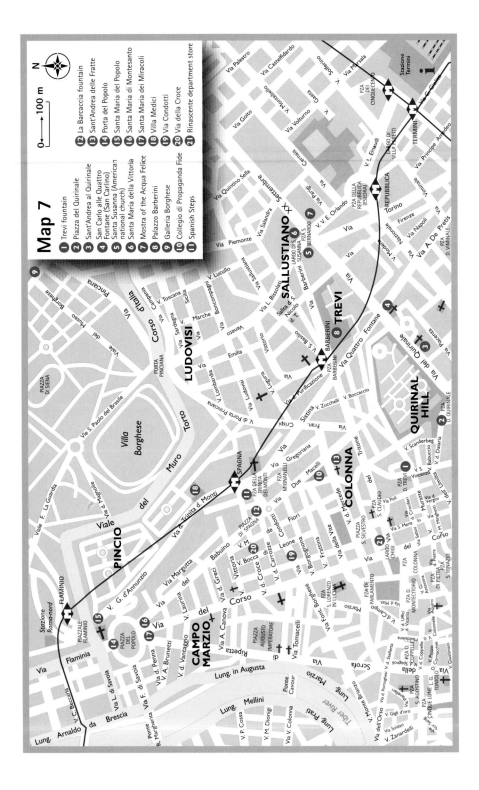

Map 7

1 Trevi fountain
2 Piazza del Quirinale
3 Sant'Andrea al Quirinale
4 San Carlo alle Quattro Fontane (San Carlino)
5 Santa Susanna (American national church)
6 Santa Maria della Vittoria
7 Santa Maria della Vittoria
8 Palazzo Barberini
9 Galleria Borghese
10 Collegio di Propaganda Fide
11 Spanish Steps
12 La Barcaccia fountain
13 Sant'Andrea delle Fratte
14 Porta del Popolo
15 Santa Maria del Popolo
16 Santa Maria di Montesanto
17 Santa Maria dei Miracoli
18 Villa Medici
19 Via Condotti
20 Via della Croce
21 Rinascente department store

0 ⟶ 100 m

N

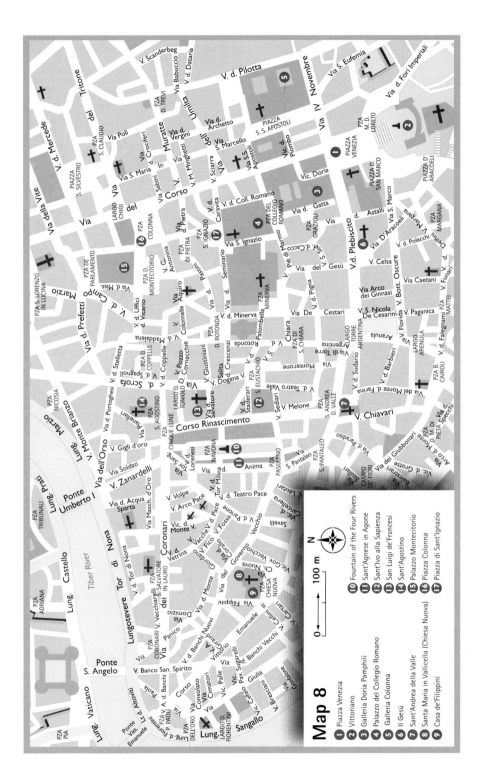

Map 8

1 Piazza Venezia
2 Vittoriano
3 Galleria Doria Pamphili
4 Palazzo del Collegio Romano
5 Galleria Colonna
6 Il Gesù
7 Sant'Andrea della Valle
8 Santa Maria in Vallicella (Chiesa Nuova)
9 Casa de'Filippini

10 Fountain of the Four Rivers
11 Sant'Agnese in Agone
12 Sant'Ivo alla Sapienza
13 San Luigi de'Francesi
14 Sant'Agostino
15 Palazzo Montecitorio
16 Piazza Colonna
17 Piazza di Sant'Ignazio

N

0 ——— 100 m